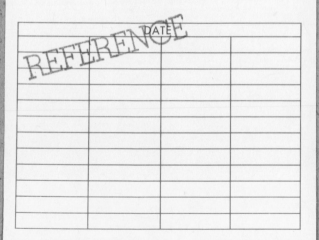

America's Greatest Golfing Resorts

by

DICK MILLER

Foreword by

ARNOLD PALMER

THE BOBBS-MERRILL COMPANY, INC.
Indianapolis / New York

Copyright © 1977 by Dick Miller

All rights reserved, including the right of reproduction
in whole or in part in any form
Published by the Bobbs-Merrill Company, Inc.
Indianapolis   New York

Designed by Jacques Chazaud
Manufactured in the United States of America

First printing

Library of Congress Cataloging in Publication Data

Miller, Dick, 1936–
    America's greatest golfing resorts.

    Bibliography: p.
    Includes index.
    1.   Golf courses—United States—Guide-books.
I. Title.
GV975.M5   917.3′04′926   77–76882
ISBN 0–672–52133–4

To
F.L.H.
with respect and gratitude

Contents

INLAND RESORTS

DESERT RESORTS

GUIDE TO RESORTS

Foreword

Any golfer who ever has hit a five iron with any serious intent, or who warms to such names as Pebble Beach, Pinehurst, or The Broadmoor, will enjoy this book immensely. Though it is a book about golfing resorts, their courses, character, and facilities, it is much more than that.

It is a book about golf—why we play, how we can play certain courses better—and even answers that often murky question: Why does the game keep calling us back? It has been said that golf is the most human of games, and I believe it is. During a round we experience almost all of life's emotions and, too, come to realize that on the golf course—as in life—rarely will anything be as magnificent or as horrible or we anticipate. Every golf hole we play is a judgment of our unity with the forces of nature.

Though many excellent books have been written about the story of golf, its great players, courses, and individual holes, this book particularly, even personally, interests me. Firstly, it is a definitive selection—twenty resorts the author considers to be America's greatest. Once I tried to single out what I thought were eighteen of the best golf holes, and again, fifty-four holes. The first was for a television series and more recently for a book on what I consider the best fifty-four holes in golf. Both times the selection was a long process—constantly mulling over a particular course's or hole's playing value, adding to the list here, deleting there. Though each choice was a labor of love, it was a difficult task.

The resorts selected for this book are evidence that the author has taken great pains and care, knowing that the selection was only as strong as the weakest entry. I have played twelve of the major courses included in this book, and from what I have read about the others, I look forward to playing those. I must admit I would be hard pressed to make more than one or two changes in the author's selection. Of course, as he states, any definitive selection is open for debate.

Secondly, I am pleased that a resort I own—Bay Hill—is included. Naturally, I believe it is a great golfing resort, and continue to tell my fellow touring pros and golfing friends how great it is. The course, as you may or may not know, was not designed by me, but by Dick Wilson. I wish I had designed it. Fortunately, Bay Hill does contain all the criteria to be included in this book.

Outside of those who are directly involved in tournament golf as a livelihood, I know few people who are more qualified than the author to prepare and write this book. He not only is a keen student of golf, but possesses a great feeling for the game and its history. Most importantly, for this project, he has visited 225 resorts in the Americas, and that would be a lot even for a touring pro. The author's knowledge of each resort in this book is both intimate and thorough. He tells us not only about the golfing and social character of each, the resort's history and its founders, which in itself makes fascinating reading, but how it feels to stay at each—the feeling you keenly sense while walking through the lobby of The Homestead, or what it feels like just before you hit your second shot to that slot of a green on the 8th hole at Pebble Beach.

Of course, I cannot write for all the managers and owners of these resorts, but I can about myself at Bay Hill. The author asked what seemed to be hundreds of questions: "Does that bunker usually come into play off the regular tee?" "Are the greens usually this fast?" "Do they hold well?" "What's the chef's or bartender's specialty?" Fortunately, I was able to answer all the questions.

Now I am delighted to read what an excellent job the author did with the answers. I consider this book an important contribution to the game, and a major contribution to golf's literature for those to whom golf is a passion.

Latrobe, Pennsylvania
1977

Preface

Having had the good fortune of growing up in a family that golfed and took golfing vacations, I was exposed to the game and resorts at an early age. The first resort I remember with any clarity was one we visited when I was eight, in the mid-1940s. The resort was in Vermont, and had only a nine-hole course that was singularly undistinguished except for one hole, a short par 3 of 100 yards. It was called the Sugar Bowl. You hit from the edge of a hill down over small evergreens and underbrush to a green that, indeed, looked no larger than the bottom of a sugar bowl. I used a driver.

Less than a decade later, I took up golf in earnest and vacationed at many of the resorts included in this book. I suppose my search for the greatest golfing resorts in the Americas began then. The list of resorts expanded greatly from 1967 to 1971, when I served as associate and travel editor for *Golf Magazine* and was sent around the world to write about golf courses, resorts, and the famous people who played them. In the ensuing years, I have had the good fortune to be assigned golfing articles that have taken me from courses hugging the North Sea in Scotland to those running along beaches by the Pacific Ocean in Hawaii. In all, I have visited either as a journalist or a vacationer some 225 resorts in the Americas. My only regret is that my golf swing is not as sound as my digestion. When I get to play a lot of golf, my handicap varies between a seven and nine. Others times it rockets to a wobbly fourteen.

While preparing this book, I again visited many of the resorts where I had vacationed, and visited those I had not but which were to be included in this book. I played each major course included in this book at least once, some a dozen times, and as many others connected with each resort as was humanly possible.

Although one of the underlying criteria for the inclusion of a resort is that I would visit each again, this selection is not of my favorite resorts. If it were, the book would have a different form and tone. The governing criterion for each resort is the golf course; it has to have a championship course or a first-rate one. Sometimes there is a fine line between the two, but usually the difference is obvious: Pebble Beach compared to Dorado Beach's West Course, for example. The second criterion is the service to the golfer—a well-stocked pro shop, as well as an amiable starter and/or caddie master. The third criterion is the golfing ambience of a resort. This is an ineffable criterion to those for whom golf never has been a passion. A resort course may be historic and even privileged. You can stand on the same tee or green where Bobby Jones drove or putted, where Walter Hagen, Gene Sarazen, Byron Nelson, Ben Hogan, Arnold Palmer, Jack Nicklaus, and Johnny Miller have left their cleat marks. But some of these resorts never have been and may never be played by the game's greats. Yet each resort, in its distinct way, exudes a universal spirit of the game that is keenly felt by golfers who warm to the crack of a well-hit drive or the sound of cleats on a locker-room floor.

Lastly, I can tell you I regret that some of my favorite resorts have not been included in this book, and also that many of yours have not been either. Any definitive selection, of course, is open to debate. Besides bringing to you the greatest of America's golfing resorts, I have tried not only to achieve a geographical balance, but to provide you with a variety of golfing vacations. Many of these resorts are ideal for long weekends, others for a week, while still others deserve at least two weeks. To illuminate further the social and golfing character of each resort, I searched through 25,000 photographs. I hope those that have been selected will add to your golfing pleasure.

New York City
1977

Dick Miller

Acknowledgments

The task of planning and researching this book was made easier and more pleasant by the unending assistance of not only the resort managers and their public relations staffs, but of secretaries and caddie masters as well. To name all would take a chapter. So collectively, my first thanks is to them. And while it is the practice of resorts to extend gratis hospitality to visiting journalists writing about their resorts, for the obvious reason of publicity, I considered myself no more compromised in accepting such treatment than I would in accepting a gimme putt.

Anyone who writes thoroughly about any aspect of golf in the United States would find it almost too laborious to do without the aid and the facilities of the United States Golf Association, and so, to its Executive Director, B. J. Boatwright, and his entire staff, a deep thanks. A special thanks must be added to Golf House's librarian and curator, Janet Seagle, not only for a long and rewarding friendship, but also because her devotion to golf and her knowledge of the game has made this and many of my other writing projects more enjoyable and enriching.

Golf, of course, is a game with a rich literature. Three books were extremely valuable as reference material while I was writing this book: *Sports Illustrated's The Best 18 Golf Holes in America* by Dan Jenkins; *The Story of American Golf* by Herbert Warren Wind; and *The World of Golf* by Charles Price. They are all part of the great timber of golfing literature.

I am particularly grateful to Arnold Palmer for a gracious and generous introduction. He is, in my view, the most important golfer of the modern era.

In dealing with the social character of many of the resorts in this book, I was aided by *Town & Country's* Editor-in-Chief, Frank Zachary, and his entire staff; I am deeply appreciative to all, particularly their former Travel Director, Elizabeth Adams, who was invaluable to anyone writing about travel and other subjects for the magazine.

Other support and guidance was supplied by Stephen Birnbaum, Dan Jenkins, and Robert Trent Jones.

Mostly, I am indebted to Ross Goodner, for not just a long and rich friendship, but because, from the time I began writing this book, he offered continual, unsolicited encouragement and advice. As an editor he commands a very talented blue pencil, but he also is one of golf's leading historians, and thus the burden of checking many of the historical golfing incidents that appear in this book fell on his shoulders. He did not stoop an inch. If by now there are any historical inaccuracies, they are my responsibility.

Many more people are responsible for this book. Over the years of listening to them and questioning them, I have heard things I never would have known about golf, resorts, and the people who visit them. They are Marguerite Allen, Red Allen, Dick Aultman, Al Barkow, Harry Baron, Art Bell, Deane Beman, Ken Bowden, Martin Carmichael, Geoffrey Cornish, Bruce Crampton, Johnny Dawson, Joe Dey, Pete and Alice Dye, Joe Finger, Dow Finsterwald, Nancy Gardiner, Al Geiberger, Doc Giffin, Vinny Giles, Will Grimsley, Claude Harmon, Cynthia Hill, Red Hoffman, Ben Hogan, Tommy Jacobs, Rees Jones, Robert Trent Jones, Jr., Dick Kagan, Kathy Livingston, Carol Mann, Dave Marr, Jack Nicklaus, Vince Pastena, Abby Rand, Johnny Revolta, David Rosen, Doug Sanders, Joe Schwendeman, Garrett Sutherland, Frank Tatum, Dick Taylor, Des Tolhurst, Bob Toski, Ernie Vossler, Tom Watson, and Herb Wind.

SEASIDE RESORTS

THE CLOISTER
Sea Island, Georgia

One of the best golf courses in the world on which to watch a golf tournament is the Augusta National Golf Club, and one of the best places on the course to watch the Masters is at the 11th, 12th, and 13th holes, where Rae's Creek and a spur of it curl menacingly amongst the greens. "Hell's Corner," Gene Sarazen once called it. Amen Corner is what today's players call it, for if they leave the 13th green having parred the three holes, they sigh, "Amen." They know at Amen Corner so many prayers have gone unanswered it is usually where the Masters is lost and won.

In 1958 Arnold Palmer, then with no more than a battalion of an army, came into Amen Corner on the verge of winning his first Masters. He parred the 12th, then hit a long drive around the bend of the dogleg par-5 13th, lashed a heroic three-wood shot to the almost island green, 18 feet from the pin, then rolled in the putt for an eagle. That did it.

A long-time member of Augusta, looking on in utter awe at Palmer's feat, turned to a friend and said, "Arnie is the greatest. He's the greatest human being that ever lived." His friend, thinking this a bit too much devotion, asked, "What about Jesus Christ?"

The perfect follow-through of Louise Suggs winning the 1954 Sea Island Ladies' Invitational.

(*Left*) Excellence at the top. Bobby Jones demonstrates his near-flawless swing during an exhibition at the Sea Island Golf Club in April 1930.

"Palmer is greater than Christ."

"Could Palmer have walked on water, then?"

"No need, Arnie could have carried the water."

Of all the shots in golf where prayers seem to fall on deaf ears, the worst are those that are shot over water. Even ministers of the faith have not always been divinely blessed. A fine golfing priest once stood on the tee of a par 3 facing a rather uncertain midiron shot over a pond. His caddie suggested a five iron.

"Well, son," said the priest, "I think I'll use a six iron and pray." He caught the ball slightly fat, and it sailed into the pond. "I guess I didn't pray hard enough," said the priest.

"Well, Father," quipped the caddie, "where I pray, we keep our heads down."

Such devilish tricks of golf probably emanate from aspects of the game's origin. For golf (as we know it today) was developed by the Scots around the middle of the fifteenth century. They were, by all accounts, a God-fearing lot who indeed believed man was born in original sin and must suffer for his redemption; thus they invented this game of golf. Along the way, they also invented their own whiskey, for when life's burdens became too weighty, man could have a wee nip of the good stuff —appropriately, usually one shot over water.

On America's best seaside resort courses, the golfer faces oceans of water, calling for a variety of shots, from full three woods to punch wedges. There is the Pacific slashing against the seawall on the 18th hole at Pebble Beach; there are the rocks below the headlands on Pebble's holes six through ten. There is the usually blue and calm Caribbean that must be played over seven times on Costasur's Cajuiles course in the Do-

minican Republic. On the Harbour Town Golf Links on Hilton Head Island, Calibogue Sound must be played around on the 17th and 18th holes.

Not surprisingly, in 1972, when the Georgian sportswriters were polled to pick the best golf hole in the state, they selected the 7th on the Seaside Nine at the Sea Island Golf Club, part and parcel of The Cloister. Of the 36 holes that comprise the Seaside, Plantation Retreat and Marshside Nines, the 7th is the best. It is a 435-yard (425 yards from the regular tee and 315 from the ladies' tee) par 4 and incorporates those great twin agents that are a part of every great golf hole—greed and fear.

The 7th tee is surrounded by magnolias and tall pampas grass. The golfer sees all that awaits his drive or drives—a marshy channel to drive across to reach the fairway, a yawning fairway bunker, and far away, appearing like a green saucer, is the green, protected by a steep-walled bunker. But it is the marshy channel flowing in front of the tee and down the left side of the fairway that gives the hole its character and imbues the golfer with a feeling of either fear or greed.

The fearful golfer can drive 80 yards straight across the neck of the marsh, play safely away from the marsh with his second shot, and hit a short iron to the green. A cinch bogey. The greedy golfer can gamble all he wants. He can cut across as much of the marsh as he dares, leaving an open shot to the green. Feeling so inclined, or just feeling fearless, he can drive completely over the section of the marsh that bellies into the fairway, and end up with an easy midiron shot to the green, but he must drive the ball 255 yards and fade it.

If you think that is the way Jack Nicklaus might play the hole, you are right. Playing the Seaside Nine in two casual

The familiar finish of Jack Nicklaus after hitting a drive completely over the leftside marsh on the 435-yard par-4 7th hole, the hardest of the thirty-six at the Sea Island Golf Club.

rounds, he drove over the marsh. But such heroic drives yielded him only two pars. Bobby Jones never birdied the hole the half-dozen times he played it. The best Georgian amateur men fared worse in 1967, when the Seaside and Retreat Nines were used as a sectional qualifying site for the U.S. Amateur. The 7th played to 56 over par in 61 rounds, or a degree of difficulty of 4.9 strokes.

The 7th also has been the scene of several of golf's more bizarre moments. A two-handicap golfer arrived at the tee a neat two under par, and after hooking several balls into the marsh, finally reached the fairway, dubbed his next shot, and landing on the green, three-putted for a fourteen. When he arrived back at the clubhouse someone asked him about his round. "Hell," replied the angry golfer, "if I could ever get rid of those two perfect shots I hit

every round, I'd give up this damn game." And proof that golf is one of the most hypnotic of games was provided by a golfer who drove three balls into the marsh fronting the 7th tee and, having emptied his pockets of Titleists, decided to drop a ball on the other side of the marsh. As he crossed the wooden bridge, he asked his caddie (they are still available) for a pack of three new balls. He carefully opened the package, emptied the three balls into his palm, pocketed the package, and simply dropped the new balls into the marsh. No one dared ask him what he took on the hole.

The man responsible for the Seaside Nine was H. S. Colt, who had designed the Sunningdale Golf Course in England and was one of the many architects who assisted George Crump in designing Pine Valley. At Sea Island, he was assisted by C. H. Alison. As The Cloister began to expand its Sea

The 7th hole's sibling rival, the 382-yard par-4 4th hole, where if the marsh doesn't claim your ball, the bunkers will. A perfect drive will leave a short-iron shot to a small green.

Island Golf Club in 1928, the two were hired to redesign the existing Plantation Nine and design a harder nine with the character of a British links course, a flattish layout at sea level, where the natural elements and terrain would serve as the best hazards and where the emphasis would be on tee-to-green play, not putting—thus the smallish greens.

They wove the Seaside Nine among the marshes, bringing them into play on five holes. They fall on the right of the fairway on the 1st hole, a medium-length par 4, and the 9th, a shortish par 5. On the par-3 3rd hole and the par-4 4th, a shorter variation of the 7th, the marsh is on the left. The nine was to be as durable as that long-staple Sea Island cotton. It has been.

One of the first great golfers to play it after its completion in 1929 was Bobby Jones. He said little about the course, but

left his usual indelible mark by setting a course record that would stand for twenty-nine years, and it indeed proved to be a portent of what would become the sport's most unbeatable feat. Jones played the course in April 1930, just two months before he would go over to the Old Course at St. Andrews to capture the first crown of golf's Grand Slam. He played the easier Plantation Nine in 32 shots, four under par, but could only manage a one under 35 on Seaside, making no birdies, one bogey, and an eagle.

The other nines, Plantation, Retreat, and the newer Marshside, have neither the rustic, windblown look of Seaside nor its playing value. The Plantation, its broad fairways lined with azaleas and live oaks, sweeps gently over old plantation grounds and remains the easiest. Here an errant shot is not a shot irrevocably lost. On

20

Marshside it is. Seven holes wind circuitously around White Heron Lake. When the Georgian golf professionals come to Sea Island every January to play the Georgian PGA Championship, they refer to the Marshside as a three-wood course, since on most of the par 4s and par 5s they have to use three woods off the tees to avoid driving through a fairway into a water hazard.

They prefer Retreat, designed by the late Dick Wilson in 1960. It is a big course, the kind today's pros and long-hitting, low-handicap golfers enjoy. From the championship tees, it can be stretched to over 3,500 yards. Its strength, as with so many modern courses, lies in its long par 4s and bunkering. Fifty bunkers creep strategically into the fairways and form necklaces of sand around the greens. But unlike Seaside, Retreat does not constantly offer the golfer the opportunity to gamble and lose or gamble and win.

Any combination of two nines will play to a par 72 for men, from either the regular or championship tees. Women play to four different pars. Retreat is par 38 for women, Marshside 37, Plantation 36, and Seaside 39. Uniquely, there are two sets of ladies' tees—the Gold plays to the shortest length. Women can play from 5,232 yards to 5,991 yards; men, from 6,211 yards to 6,877 yards.

Besides being the venue of the Georgia PGA Championship, it was the site of the Ladies' Sea Island Invitational from 1957 to 1963. Also, in 1963 the USGA Men's Seniors was played there, and in 1971, the Women's Seniors. In 1958 the Plantation and Seaside Nines were used for a match of ABC's All-Star Golf, in which Sam Snead shot a 64 and broke Jones's record.

The Sea Island Golf Club actually is located on the southern tip of Saint Simons Island, adjacent to Sea Island—they are two

Mickey Wright blasts from the greenside bunker on the 7th hole to win her fifth Sea Island Invitational.

of seven islands off the Georgia coast promoted as Georgia's Golden Isles. Sea Island and Saint Simons are tongue-shaped, bordered on one side by the Atlantic and on the other by a maze of marshy inlets, and geographically located twelve zigzagging miles east of the city of Brunswick. They are islands of narrow, winding streets, dead-end lanes, drooping, moss-drenched oaks, fertile marshes, wide sand beaches with gentle surf and expensive homes.

A snug hideaway, they have been called many things. Aaron Burr, retreating to Saint Simons in the summer of 1804 after his duel with Alexander Hamilton, referred to it as idyllic. In 1838 Fanny Kemble, one of England's great Shakespearean actresses and then the wife of a prosperous United States plantation owner, called it all a teeming marshland bed of inhuman suffering.

The woman who helped to sway England from aiding the South during the Civil War, Fanny Kemble, the great actress and onetime resident of St. Simons Island.

More than a century later, in 1950 Vice-President Alben Barkley, honeymooning at The Cloister, called it his Shangri-la.

How such a remote area became such a patchwork of history is not all that mysterious. For Sea Island and Saint Simons have been unusually blessed and cursed by fate. That durable, famous long-staple Sea Island cotton originated on the islands, making millionaires of many plantation owners. When the demand for it declined in the early 1850s, fields were left fallow and plantations were deserted. The Civil War brought further doom.

Among those Southerners who refer to the Civil War as "The War of Northern Aggression," many still lament, curse, and mutter, "Fanny Kemble lost the war for us." If President Abraham Lincoln once re-ferred to Harriet Beecher Stowe, author of *Uncle Tom's Cabin,* as the little lady who started the great war, then Fanny Kemble helped to prevent it from getting greater.

Arriving in the United States in 1832 at the age of twenty-three, the glamorous actress, with long chestnut-brown hair framing a beautiful oval face, not only wooed theater critics but became something of a matinee idol. She eventually married a wealthy Philadelphian, and in 1838 they moved to the northern tip of Saint Simons Island to a plantation her husband had inherited, known as Butler Plantation, replete with several hundred acres of valuable long-staple Sea Island cotton and some four hundred slaves.

But plantation life hardly appealed to the spirited actress, who hated an indolent life and despised slavery. Her constant outrages over the inhuman suffering of the slaves caused a scandalous divorce, and Fanny Kemble fled to England and returned to the stage. However, she had kept a journal of her plantation days.

In the early 1860s, when England was on the brink of becoming involved in the Civil War—to such a degree that she was considering using her fleet to break President Lincoln's blockade of the South—Fanny Kemble published *Journal of a Residence on a Georgian Plantation,* a blistering attack on life in the South that so shocked England's aristocracy and Parliament that it swayed the country out of the Civil War.

Sea Island was cursed again, but would be unusually blessed a little more than a half century later. Blessing arrived in the visionary mind of industrialist Howard Coffin, a big, barrel-chested man who loved

The founder of The Cloister, Howard Coffin (*right*), with a visiting friend, President Calvin Coolidge.

duck shooting and giving lavish parties, and who wanted a grand resort where he could entertain some of his closest friends, including presidents Herbert Hoover and Calvin Coolidge, and Charles Lindbergh. His engineering career had begun just before the turn of the century, when he saw the future transportation as belonging not to railroads, but to automobiles and airplanes. It was no momentary flash. In 1897, at age twenty-four, he built his first automobile. At thirty-six he formed his own firm, the Hudson Motor Car Company. In 1916 President Woodrow Wilson appointed him president of the Aircraft Production Board for World War I, and Coffin innovated an ingenious engineering system which Henry Kaiser would employ in concept and partly in name during World War II. Coffin's invention was the Liberty motor for airplanes—a motor of such standardized design that all its parts were interchangeable from plane to plane. In 1925 he founded National Air Transport, later renamed United Airlines.

A year later Coffin launched his resort, propelled with the architectural zest of designer Addison Mizner. Coffin was by no means the first rich man to build his own resort. He had been preceded by the Clark family, who had built the Otesaga in Cooperstown, New York. Spencer Penrose, who had struck gold in Colorado, built what he considered the most lavish hotel in the Rockies—The Broadmoor, and there were the Tuftses of Boston, who founded Pinehurst in the Sandhills of North Carolina, and the Flaglers, who all but invented Florida. Other rich men followed. There was Arthur Winarick, who founded The Concord in the 1930s because a neighboring resort disliked the way he dressed. In the 1950s, Alfred Kaskel bought 2,300 acres west of Miami sight unseen and started the

Doral Country Club. At the same time, one of the richest of all resort builders, Laurance Rockefeller, started his chain of luxury resorts, Rockeresorts, which would spread halfway around the world, from the Caribbean to the resort hotel that may be the costliest per room in the world, Hawaii's Mauna Kea. However, of all the rich men who built resort hotels, few had humbler beginnings than a pushcart vender named Milton Hershey. He founded the Hershey Chocolate Company in 1902, and thirty years later he built the Hotel Hershey. If Mizner had not gone bankrupt building the Boca Raton Hotel, Hershey surely would have hired him to design his neoclassical hotel.

A decade and a half earlier, Mizner had changed the face of Palm Beach's Worth Avenue, giving its buildings a terra cotta-hued exterior, red-tiled roofs, turrets, arches, parapets, pillared corridors, and loggias. His enthusiasm for adapting classical Mediterranean architecture once spurred Frank Lloyd Wright to call him "nothing but a good stage designer." Maybe so. Other people irreverently referred to his flamboyant style as "Bastard Spanish," "Riviera with palms," or "Bull Market Renaissance."

The Cloister reflects Mizner's style at its best, and is still much as it was intended— a small, grand resort hotel—now with four elegant dining rooms, two lobbies, traditional afternoon tea, 61 high-ceilinged, airy rooms (with additional guest-houses, two ocean-front sections, the total room count is up to 220) overlooking courtyards and sculptured gardens. The best rooms, though all are good, are in the newer Retreat and Hamilton houses on the beach.

But wherever a guest is, the pervading feeling is one of elegance, from the finger bowls brought after each meal, including breakfast, to afternoon tea and the resort's extremely noncommercial atmosphere. Only one movie is shown a week, and none of the rooms has either radio or television. If a man feels he is someplace long ago and far away and has an urge to don a black tie and dinner jacket, that's just fine. Black tie is suggested for dinner Thursdays and Saturdays—though it is not mandatory and is not essential to one's dinner enjoyment, as the resort's cuisine is excellent, from its long-time specialties of Sea Island Shrimp Mill and Lynnhaven Oyster Pot Pie to its homemade pastries.

However, The Cloister is not stuffy. In 1972, when New Year's Eve fell on a Sunday—on which day Georgia law forbids the sale of liquor—the resort celebrated New Year's Eve on Hong Kong time (twenty-four hours earlier) with a dinner dance, and ended the party with a pantry raid in the dry hours of Sunday morning. It was, minus the pantry raid, almost like every evening, except Sunday, at the resort—just as danc-

ing before and after dinner has been for four decades. "It's a tradition," said the manager. "We will not change it."

Like The Homestead, where change cranks on slowly, The Cloister proceeds cautiously. Even if it does expand to the several thousand acres it owns on the northern end of Saint Simons Island, it will still be The Cloister that Coffin imagined in 1926.

Adjacent to that section of property is 1,700 acres known as Butler's Point, where Fanny Kemble spent her unhappy plantation years. It now is owned by a New Jersey conglomerate, which plans to develop it into a chic little resort residential community. A reminder that the greening of corporate assets produces not only dividends to stockholders but tees and greens jutting into a calm and blue Caribbean is Costasur's Casa de Campo, a new resort built in the Dominican Republic by that forward-pressing, mighty multinational conglomerate—Gulf + Western Americas.

COSTASUR'S

CASA de CAMPO

LaRomana, Dominican Republic

Every golfer who knows that golf can be a heroic game knows about Pebble Beach Golf Links. He knows about the Pacific Ocean breaking against the seawall on the 18th hole. He knows about the wind that comes screeching in off Carmel Bay. He knows it is where the U.S. Open or Amateur is played every decade or so, and where the Bing Crosby Pro-Am is played every January. But if asked to name the architect of one of America's very best courses, he would be hard pressed for an answer. It was Jack Neville, who was a fine amateur golfer but, before he designed Pebble Beach, never had designed a golf course. If he is one of the most forgotten of architects, he was one of the most blessed, being given what is perhaps the most dramatic piece of land for a golf course. Even Dr. Alister MacKenzie, who designed the neighboring Cypress Point Club, only got three holes in along the ocean; one, of course, being the famous 16th hole.

Pete Dye is one of the most renowned and innovative golf-course architects to come along since the mid-1950s. He was

almost as blessed as Neville by being given or, in his case, by having discovered one of the most exciting stretches of coastline terrain for a golf course. Costasur's course, Cajuiles, curves along the dramatic coast-

Pitching up to par. George Burns lofts the ball out of the deep Bahia grass on the 440-yard par-4 18th hole during the third round of the World Amateur Team Championship play at Cajuiles.

(*Left*) Sand, water and wind. Cajuiles's 198-yard par-3 7th hole, one of the three par 3s that play along the ocean. In all, seven tees sit on the ocean's edge.

line on the southeast shore of the Dominican Republic. The course evolved because Dye kept saying no to a resort developer who just would not take no for an answer. What resulted is a seaside course, but without the eerie fog and screeching winds, that is being called Pebble Beach-in-the-Tropics.

In 1967 Gulf + Western Americas, a multinational conglomerate, bought the South Puerto Rico Sugar Company, situated sixty miles northeast of Santo Domingo in La Romana, a city in the flat hinterlands, populated by fifty thousand residents who worked in the sugar mills or the cane fields. Besides the mill and cane fields, Gulf + Western acquired seventy thousand acres around the city. In 1968, G + W's president, Alvaro Carta, a Cuban exile, realized the country's politics were on a more stable footing and set out to build a resort that would become a showcase for the country's future tourist trade.

He immediately sought the counsel of architect Pete Dye and asked him to build, yes, a championship golf course. He first took Dye to a stretch of land on the outskirts of Santo Domingo. After three days of inspecting the land, Dye told Carta, no, the land was not suitable for a golf course, and he wanted to go back home to Florida. Carta then persuaded Dye to look at land around La Romana. Dye spotted a likely piece of land, but was told by Carta, no, part of the land was used by the kids as a baseball field. Dye started packing again.

Finally, an exasperated Carta ordered a company plane and flew Dye up and down the coastline—some four miles from the Hotel Romana. The land was either so thick with underbrush that one needed a machete to cut a way through, or so bald and rocky it was unfit for cattle grazing. But Dye showed interest—proof again that beauty is in the eye of the beholder. It was all the

encouragement Carta needed. Suddenly Dye had company planes, boats, and Land Rovers at his disposal.

For three days Dye boated up and down the coast, looking at the land, which rose sometimes gently and sometimes abruptly from the coral shore. What he first saw was a half-moon section of shoreline where the spray from the pounding waves at high tide looked like clouds of white smoke. This was the beginning. It would be maybe a long par 5 and a long par 3. After a few preliminary sketches, he decided on two long par 4s, sandwiching a long par 3. They would become the notorious and much-photographed 15th, 16th, and 17th holes. Dye said later, "This was the chance of a lifetime, to design a seaside course with so much of the sea actually coming into play, almost three miles of it."

What Dye had not counted on was the labor force. Not only had none of the natives ever seen a golf course, they had never heard of the game. Of the three hundred hired, only a score had ever ridden a bicycle; they eventually were taught to drive tractors. The rest of the work force sliced away the underbrush with machetes, cleared the fairways, and planted them by hand with Bermuda 320. To give the rough a rugged look and a different texture, they planted Behia grass, a wiry strain. To accent the teeing areas, coral called *dientes del perro*, translated as "teeth of the dog," was used.

Meanwhile, Dye kept redesigning each hole, reshaping a green, positioning a new tee, and, as he usually does, laying out each hole from the green back to the tee. What he ended up with is two elongated triangles that make up each nine. He also ended up with not only one of the best golf courses in the Caribbean, but with the best seaside course built in the Americas in decades—a

The spirit of the game. After shooting a third-round two-under-par 70, George Burns receives congratulations from teammates *(left to right)* Gary Koch, Jerry Pate and Curtis Strange.

course that out-beaches Pebble Beach in total use of ocean front.

Since Pebble Beach was built for competitive play, it is, for all its dramatic and peerless character, something of a horror for the average golfer. Cajuiles is a fairer test for the average player, and from the regular tees of 6,255 yards it is a stronger test than the Harbour Town Golf Links, also a Dye creation. From the ladies' tees, it is a course that champions women's rights, or in this case, women's drives. They play the course at a just 5,697 yards. This is not just because Dye is a quiet man who builds yawning bunkers, but because he is a man who listens. He listens to his wife Alice, a steady one-handicap golfer, nine times winner of

the Indiana Women's Amateur and a member of the 1970 U.S. Curtis Cup team. Once asked how long she thought a golf course should be for the average woman golfer, she replied briskly, "5,400 yards."

Alice Dye is basically responsible for the placement of the ladies' tees. To this day, she enjoys recalling how she persuaded her husband to change tees. "I just told Pete, 'Don't put the ladies' tees directly in front of the men's tees. Women don't like just standing around up there while their husbands shoot over their heads.'" So at Cajuiles, you could say a new shot has been made for Women's Lib. All the ladies' tees are off to the side, an advantage in more ways than one. The tees are angled so

29

The reigning 1974 U.S. Amateur Champion, Jerry Pate, displays a champion's putting touch, leading the U.S. team to victory in the World Amateur Team Championship.

women, on the par-4 and par-5 holes, drive to the largest part of the fairway—away from the majority of the hazards.

Conversely, the championship tees, from which the course plays to 6,843 yards, are angled to the narrowest part of the fairways, beckoning the golfer who is daring and wants an easier second shot to drive close to the hazards—deep, yawning bunkers and tall Guinea grass, for which one needs not a wedge but a machete, and the pale blue Caribbean. On no fewer than seven holes, waves break against the edge of the tees to unrest the quietest backswing. Seven greens rest by the shore's edge, surrounded by coral, sand, and sea-grape trees.

Yet for all the splashing surf, sand, the ubiquitous blond pampas grass twitching in the wind, and the coconut palms bent from the trade winds, the essential character of the course is its perfect balance, a rhythmic refrain that takes the best advantage of the coastline and the wind. The outgoing nine runs clockwise, beginning with four comparatively easy holes—made more difficult because they play into the wind. Holes five through eight, two par 3s and two long par 4s, play along the coastline, downwind with the sea at the left—a momentary reprieve for the golfer who slices. The incoming nine plays counterclockwise. The first four inland holes play downwind. Holes fourteen through seventeen, a par 5, and then the three holes running along the half-moon crescent, along the high cliffs, play into the wind. And alas, if the slicer felt up to this moment that he had found the perfect architect, who had unending sympathy for his weakness, he is sadly disillusioned. On the last three of the seven seaside holes, the sea is on the right. And what a plight it was for the golfer who stood on the 17th tee for ten minutes, driving a dozen balls into the Caribbean. Then in a fit of fury, he threw his driver into the sea, dove in after it, and damn near drowned trying to rescue it.

Holes fifteen, sixteen, and seventeen became known as Reload Alley by the men's U.S. team in the World Amateur Team Championship, a biennial event played at Cajuiles in 1974, in which each participating country sent its best men and women amateurs to compete in a 72-hole medal-play competition. The men play for the Eisenhower Cup, and the women for the Espirito Santo Trophy.

Though the United States won both competitions, they were not without dramatic mishaps. The United States's George Burns suffered putting woes for four rounds, and could manage only one sub-par round, eventually finishing nine over par for 72 holes. After three rounds Burns's teammate Jerry Pate finally got his driver working, and then only because he got a quick lesson from, you guessed it, former Curtis Cup team member, Alice Dye. Another American player, Gary Koch, was even par one round through sixteen holes and ended up with a 76 by pushing his tee shot into the Caribbean on the 17th hole and hooking his second shot into the pond guarding the 18th green. He lamented later, "This course will come out of nowhere, throw you down, and stomp on your head." A worse fate was dealt to a Canadian golfer who was even par after fifteen holes and

The reigning 1974 U.S. Women's Amateur Champion, Cynthia Hill, hits a wedge to the 9th green.

ended up with an 84, taking seven, eight, and nine on three of the last par-4 holes. From holes fifteen through seventeen the word was shoot and reload, because the local rule is that a tee shot hit into the water must be re-teed—one-stroke penalty.

Of the 560 rounds played by the best men amateurs in the world there were only six sub-par rounds, the lowest being three 70s. Of 198 rounds played by the women amateurs, there were only three sub-par rounds; the lowest was 71.

However, the most interesting record at Cajuiles is held by an ardent but average golfer who came to play golf for three days. He stayed on a fourth and a fifth day. Finally, on the sixth day, the manager politely asked him how long he was planning on staying. "I'm not going to leave," said the man angrily, "until I hit one of those greens on those damn par 3s with my first shot." Six days later, playing thirty-six holes a day, on the 13th, a 170-yard par 3 appropriately called the "Doughnut Hole" because the green is surrounded completely by a circular bunker and shaded by two black olive trees, the man hit the green. Not only did he not play the hole out, he left his ball on the green—a fitting testimony to his tenacity.

Four of the more scenic and perilous-to-play par 3s—three along the coastline, and one inland—lie in the hinterlands of the Dominican Republic, where half the roads

Casa de Campo's other ingenious architect, top fashion designer Oscar de la Renta, relaxing in his vacation home off the 16th tee.

remain unpaved and where the best shopping value in town is not cashmere or expensive crystal, but sugar at 7½ cents a pound. Situated near a sugar-cane mill, exuding its pungent odor of molasses, there is Costasur with two hotels: the Hotel Romana and the Casa de Campo (by the golf courses), with a total of 320 rooms, a championship golf course, an easier one, and a third on the drawing board. There are also a forty-court tennis complex, several swimming pools, and a secluded beach. Costasur is also one of the most fashion-conscious, most chic little resorts in the Americas.

With Cajuiles completed, Carta felt his resort now needed fashionable touches. He thus invited the Dominican Republic's top fashion designer, Oscar de la Renta, to take an active role in furthering the resort's sense of style. De la Renta, who had lived out of the country during most of the Trujillo regime, accepted immediately, built a vacation hideaway house adjacent to the 15th tee and then designed all the employees' uniforms. He dressed the chambermaids in red-and-white gingham aprons and white bandanas. Waiters got tan suits, white shirts, and dark brown ties, and waitresses wore de la Renta originals—floor-length white cotton skirts with close-fitting cotton blouses.

De la Renta also designed the interior fabrics. All the bedspreads and upholstery are simple repeating patterns in dark blue and white, a country-style look that blends with the rooms, which feature white stucco walls, red terra-cotta tiles (there is not a carpet in the whole place), mahogany furniture, and large louvered shutters.

At the Casa de Campo, one dines on an outdoor terrace or in the Tent Room, a high-ceilinged building with large quilts hanging from the beams. It is so informal

A green of inglorious security, the 4th of the Seaside
Nine at the Sea Island Golf Club, Sea Island, Georgia.

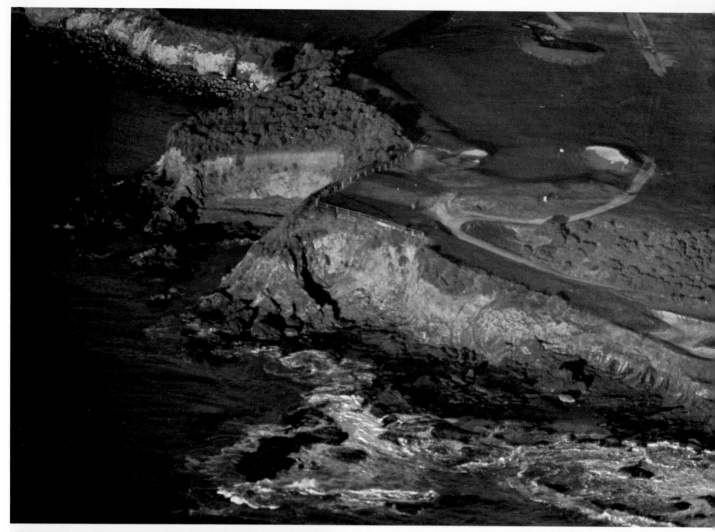

The imperious headlands that give Pebble Beach its peerless character. The finest stretch of oceanside holes in the world: (*clockwise from left*) the 8th green; a panorama of the 6th, 7th, and 8th holes; a lone golfer and caddie walking toward the 10th green.

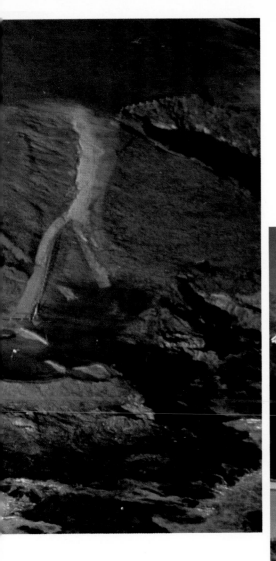

The spectacular beauty of two tropical resorts thousands
of miles apart. (*Above*) The par-3 16th hole of Cajuiles
at Casa de Campo in the Dominican Republic. (*Right*)
A dramatically beautiful beach on the Na Pali Coast on
the north shore of the island Kauai in Hawaii.

Precious little room for error. The penalizing aspects of
Harbour Town Golf Links, one of the greatest of the
new courses. (*Above*) The approach to the 8th green.
(*Right*) The green and sand of the par-3 7th.

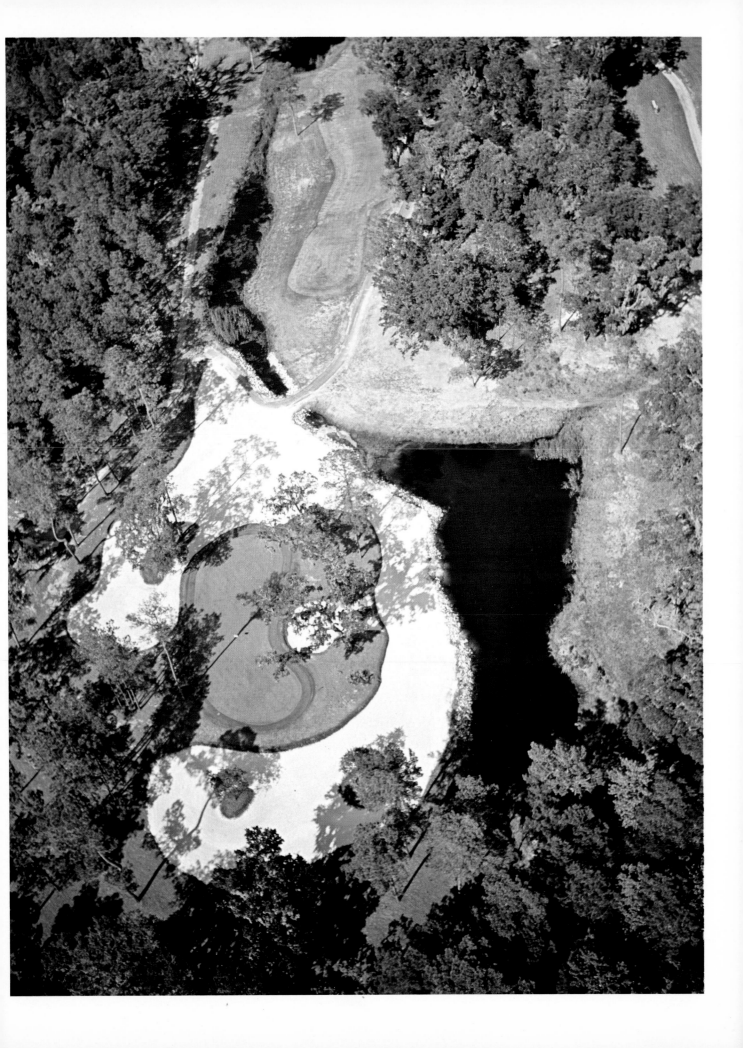

The 7th green at Casa de Campo, one of seven holes that
play along the beautiful Caribbean.

and relaxed that the only men regularly wearing neckties are the waiters.

Even the resort's manager rarely wears one, a fact that has stirred a few complaints and several embarrassing situations. A guest seeing him getting into his car mistook him for a cab driver and asked to be driven from Casa de Campo to the Hotel Romana. The manager, who sees to it that all employees extend prompt, courteous service to all guests, obliged. When they arrived at the hotel, the guest handed the manager two dollars. "I'm very sorry," said the manager, "I can't accept that. I'm the boss here." Apologetic over his mistake, the bemused guest quickly departed, money in hand, perhaps regretting that he had not bought Gulf + Western stock.

If there are any regrets, they come from guests in search of South American or Mexican cuisine—a hot chili, a spicy tortilla they will not find here. The basic cuisine is North American, except the black-bean soup made from a recipe from that once-famous Cuban restaurant, La Zaragozana. The onion soup is French, thickly crusted with cheese, and made from a native small sweet red onion.

Down to the last gimme putt, there is little to complain about at Costasur—not even the golf course. One reason is that for all its severe difficulty, its great shot value, it is an immensely fair test—half the fairways are over 75 yards wide. Also, the man the golfer might be complaining to could easily be architect Dye. He now spends over half the year there, nurturing his course as championship courses should be nurtured and making sure his finishing holes maintain their exciting character. For one of Dye's architectural principles is that, coming down the home stretch, the better golfer should win. But then, he just might be there to keep reminding people to call his course Cajuiles and not Pebble Beach-in-the-Tropics.

DEL MONTE
LODGE
Pebble Beach, California

The controversy is unending about Pebble Beach Golf Links. Where does the course *really* begin? Where does it really become Pebble-Triple-Bogey-by-the-Sea? "Pebble Beach," a PGA official once said after one of the Bing Crosby Pro-Am tournaments held there annually since 1947, "begins on the eighth hole, and from there on it is enough course for any golfer." "The course really begins on the sixth hole," claim most of those who have played it. Jack Neville, who designed it in 1916, told Herbert Warren Wind of the *New Yorker* just before the 1972 U.S. Open was played there, "The first six holes are something of a come-on, you could say. There's nothing especially hard about them. Then watch out. From there on in, you've got to play absolutely first-class shots or you can go for a bundle."

True enough for some. In the first round of the Open, pro Homero Blancas wiped through the first five holes in a neat four under par, but then had to struggle to end his round two over par. On the same day, Arnold Palmer bogied the first three holes

and ended with a 77. In the first national tournament held there, the 1929 U.S. Amateur, the first two holes, an easy-beginning 385-yard par 4 and an equally easy 507-yard par-5 2nd, proved the downfall of the

The inimitable host of the Bing Crosby Pro-Am. His tournament has been played at Pebble Beach since 1947 with all the style of a clambake and often in the foulest weather.

(*Left*) The scariest and most unnerving shot in golf, the second, third or quite likely fourth shot to the green on the 425-yard par-4 8th hole at Pebble Beach Golf Links.

Losing in the first round of the 1929 U.S. Amateur at Pebble Beach, Bobby Jones congratulates a victorious Johnny Goodman.

pillow and dream you are playing the course, which is probably America's finest. Or you can begin by tearing up the scorecard and just go out trying to enjoy your round as best you can. If you play to a 12 handicap or under, you do three things. First, go to the nearby practice range and work on your long game. Second, play the nine-hole Peter Hay par-3 course to tune up your short game. Third, try to score as many birdies as you can on the first five holes, because after that you will be giving away shots to par as easily as you can hit from the top.

Holes six through ten are the first of the ocean holes, stretching along the headlands, where the wind-seared cliffs drop one hundred feet into Carmel Bay. Tees and greens are pitched right there on the edge of the cliffs. Heroic in design, they are menacing to play, demanding length and accuracy, a par 5 and a par 3 followed by three awesome par 4s. Here one error breeds another. Though the 18th hole is acclaimed as the best finishing par 5 in golf—and it certainly is—serious students of Pebble regard the 8th, a par 4, 425 yards from the championship tee (400 yards from the regular tee and 360 yards from the ladies' tee), as the hardest hole on the course. Running along the headlands high above Carmel Bay, it demands a long drive to the top of a bluff. Then, perhaps the scariest shot on any par 4, a long iron or fairway wood shot is needed to carry the ball some 190 yards down over a rocky inlet to a small slot of a green perched hard by the edge of the cliff. A ball slicing too much ends up on the beach. At Pebble, being on the beach means just that—not in a sand bunker. Just how hard is the 8th? During the 1972 U.S. Open, the hole yielded only 28 birdies in 440 rounds played. Nicklaus played it in one bogey and three pars.

finest golfer in the world, Bobby Jones. In the first round he lost. How? He bogied the first two holes and never could get his game together. In fact his play was so inconsistent that day at Pebble that it prompted one sportswriter for the *New York Sun* to write, "Is Bobby Jones losing interest in golf?" From the 1st hole to the famous 18th, Pebble eventually humbles even the best.

Golfers on the Monterey peninsula suggest there are two ways for the average golfer to play the course. The easiest is to keep the head down and very still on the

Much tribulation and a rare moment of satisfaction at the famed 120-yard par-3 7th hole. Ray Floyd produces a cloud of sand blasting from a bunker during the final round of the 1972 U.S. Open, played at Pebble Beach. Gene Littler tosses his putter in utter frustration after missing a par putt during the 1975 Bing Crosby Pro-Am; nonetheless he won. Getting even, Jack Nicklaus grins with satisfaction after sinking a birdie putt in the final round of the 1972 U.S. Open. His two on the 7th hole helped earn him his third U.S. Open title.

A rare photo and an even rarer recovery from the rocky coast bordering the 540-yard par-5 18th hole. Harrison Johnston hit his third shot to the green on his way to victory in the 1929 U.S. Amateur.

After the 10th hole the course loops inland, becomes a bit more mellow, and then, with the 17th and 18th, it returns again to the ocean. In design, the course forms an elongated figure eight, a design that architecturally takes the fullest advantage of not only the dramatic coastline, but also the wind. Ah, the wind. It comes whirling in off Carmel Bay in so many directions that a golfer can play the course twice on the same day and it will not play the same. Take the tiny 7th hole. It is a mere 120-yard par 3 (110 yards from the regular tee and 100 yards from the ladies' tee) from an elevated tee down to a green hugging the cliff. On a calm day it is usually a wedge shot, but with the wind in the golfer's face, a full two-iron shot is not uncommon. During one Crosby the wind quartered across the green with such force it intimidated none other than Sam Snead, who simply putted the ball down the hill.

That screeching wind has produced some of the most absurd shots and scores in golf. In another Crosby the wind blew with such gale force that one pro played the front nine in 55 strokes. After one round played in gale winds, an exhausted and frustrated Dave Marr sat in the bar trying to recover. When informed that fellow pro Miller Barber was 19 shots over par Marr quipped, "Where did he make his birdies?"

Wind or not, the par-5 18th, at 540 yards (530 yards from the regular tee and 425 yards from the ladies' tee), has provided the most dramatics. It is a bow-shaped hole, with Carmel Bay splashing against the seawall down the left side from the tee to the green. On the right side are tall Monterey pines and out-of-bounds. A beautiful and spectacular golf hole it is, one of the precious few in the world that bestow upon the golfer a sudden impulse for heroics or the warrior's crucible of honor—

if he fails, he has failed while daring greatly. Indeed, no one should play the 18th at Pebble Beach unless he is willing to be lucky.

In the finals of the 1929 U.S. Amateur the eventual winner, Harrison Johnston, went for the green on the 18th with his second shot, a brassie that hooked into Carmel Bay, but the tide was out; he found his ball on the rocks, recovered magnificently with a spade mashie (six iron) to the green, saved par, and halved the hole. Architect Neville provided a dramatic ending to the 1929 California Amateur at Pebble when he went for the green with his second shot. It too hooked—not onto the rocks but into the bunker to the left of the green. From there he deftly holed out for an eagle and victory. Even more spectacular was the third shot by an amateur in the 1952 Crosby. One Bill Hoelle, teamed with pro Art Bell (the teaching pro at Pebble Beach), put his second shot in the long bunker hugging the seawall. A birdie by either would tie them for Pro-Am honors. Some 100 yards from the green Hoelle hit a crisp seven iron; the ball sailed onto the green and rolled into the cup.

But such heroic deeds are rare. In the 1959 Crosby, Gene Littler played a magnificent final round, making up eight shots on Art Wall, and reached the 18th tee needing one more birdie to tie Wall. Littler hooked his tee shot preciously close to the seawall. Unnerved, he lost control of his usually rhythmic swing, swung at the second shot and hit a horrendous hook into Carmel Bay. He finished with an unheroic seven.

Pebble Beach has been altered little since it opened for play in 1919. Only the famous 18th has undergone change. In the early years waves broke against the fairway so hard that some thirty yards of it were washed away. The original tee, protruding farther into the Bay than the present one, was being swept away, rock by rock. The bunker to the left of the green was in danger of being completely washed away. Finally, the officials of Del Monte Properties Company, the owners of the course, decided to construct a sturdy seawall, which they have maintained at considerable expense.

If Neville, assisted by Douglas Grant, designed what every golfing authority has ranked as not only America's best oceanside course, but perhaps the country's best (Jack Nicklaus has long considered Pebble Beach one of the two best courses in America— the other being Merion), then much of the actual credit must be given to the late Samuel Finley Brown Morse, one of the first men to entice home buyers with a golf course. He once told a real-estate salesman, "Don't sell property unless you feel that you are doing the buyer a favor."

It was a motto that would ripple through the Monterey peninsula for more than half a century, pushed by a wave of irony. In actual fact, Morse's first customer was himself. In 1915 he headed the Pacific Improvement Company, a subsidiary of the Southern Pacific Railroad, which had vast land holdings on and around the peninsula. Morse's task was simply to liquidate the holdings. However, the more he saw of the peninsula—125 miles south of San Francisco and 350 miles north of Los Angeles— the more he was convinced of its future. He formed his own company, Del Monte Properties Company, which he headed until his death in 1969, and bought out many of the holdings he was to liquidate. This included the luxurious Hotel Del Monte, which in the 1890s was referred to as the Newport-of-the-West, and the Del Monte golf course—the oldest course west of the

Mississippi, built in 1893 and long considered as the course for the golfer who cannot break 100.

To attract potential home buyers to the peninsula Morse knew he could not offer just another new golf course, but one that would make the peninsula a Pinehurst-of-the-West. He thus selected the most dramatic stretch of real estate, known then as Pebble Beach, not for posh homesites as originally intended, but for a golf course for competitive play.

The decision to hire Neville as the chief architect was a typical Morse hunch. One friend once described Morse as "a complete extrovert. He thinks from the skin out." By 1915 Neville had won two California Amateur championships and one Northwest Pacific Amateur. (He won the California Amateur a record five times and was a member of the 1923 U.S. Walker Cup Team.) The simple fact that before 1915 Neville had never designed a tee, fairway, green, or bunker did not bother Morse. He felt any man who could play golf as well as Neville did could design a decent course.

Neville walked the terrain for three weeks, made a preliminary sketch of the course, then consulted another California Amateur champion, Douglas Grant, who had just returned from touring and golfing in Great Britain. Grant's major asset was to give the course a linksland flavor. It was Neville's idea to build small greens. His feeling was that the shots that required the greatest skill were those with the long irons. He wanted to reward the golfer who could hit a small target with the long irons. The greens were judiciously contoured. The golfing adage at oceanside courses, that all putts break toward the ocean, is not true at Pebble. Some putts break away from the ocean; others even break uphill.

If the course fulfilled Morse's expectations down to the last slippery putt, it probably just managed to do so. He was a man of great expectations. He once attempted to move the California state capital from Sacramento to Monterey because he believed it rightfully belonged there, since it had been the capital when the Spanish and Mexicans ruled the territory. During World War II, when the U.S. Navy took over the Hotel Del Monte as a flight-training center, Morse thought that the Navy should extend its training operations there and promoted the idea of moving the United States Naval Academy from Annapolis to Monterey. Neither idea worked. Nor did his rather ingenious scheme in 1931 to fertilize his golf fairways with guano scraped from the rocks frequented by cormorants and pelicans. It not only proved damaging to the fairways, but once the rocks were cleaned, the seals took possession of them and never let the birds back.

Such an inventive bent ran in the Morse family. Samuel F.B. Morse, as he was called, was the grandnephew of the inventor of the telegraph, Samuel Morse—whom he disliked being associated with, because this Samuel F. B. Morse maintained an unexecutive disdain for hard work and perseverance. He once said, "Men do not get along in the world by hard work and perseverance—they only keep you from meeting the right people." Morse was one of the few men in the world who rode horseback with President Theodore Roosevelt and golfed with President Eisenhower.

A physical-fitness buff, he had captained the 1906 Yale football team, and even into his fifties he could prove his strength by tearing a telephone book in half.

If he was keen on his own fitness, Morse was equally vigorous at keeping the balance of nature on the peninsula intact. From the beginning, he ruled his domain, now 5,600 acres, as a lordly aristocrat. In fact, Morse most often was referred to as the Duke of Monterey. In his duchy residents are still told what they can build, plant, or move. To cut down a tree in the Del Monte forest is all but a sacrilege. The unspoiled, dramatic coastline through which the famous "17-mile drive" meanders has attracted more than home buyers. Movie producers in search of special effects—an angry sea, eerie fog, pristine beauty—have filmed the peninsula. Alfred Hitchcock photographed part of the road scenes in *Vertigo* along the "17-mile drive." The Riviera action in *Intermezzo* and scenes of the original version of *National Velvet*, starring Elizabeth Taylor, were shot there.

Morse liked to equate Pebble Beach with the rue de la Paix because, as he once said, "Everybody seems to get there eventually." Perhaps. Yearly more than 38,000 rounds of golf are played over Pebble, and that means two things: the course usually is in ragged condition, and the playing time is slow—usually over five hours. Pebble Beach is open to the public at a fairly steep weekend green fee, but the guests of Del Monte Lodge have preference in starting times and pay a lower green fee.

The Lodge opened in 1919 as a modest hostelry of only forty rooms built to handle the overflow from the Hotel Del Monte, and to serve specifically as a haven for those guests who just wanted to play golf. When the hotel was retained even after World War II as a Navy training center, the Lodge began expanding slowly and with great care to put up only low, spreading build-

(*Overleaf*) The all-too-frequent horrors of the 18th. Great Britain's Peter Townsend is seen returning to the tee after searching in vain for the ball he drove onto the coast during a Bing Crosby Pro-Am. Townsend hit his second drive onto the rocks, but recovered, taking a double bogey seven.

41

ings so that nothing would clash with the natural beauty of the area. The small main building with its yellow stucco exterior is of Monterey-Mediterranean design.

Compared to other major resorts, Del Monte Lodge is small, with only 140 rooms. It is also a cozy and friendly place with personal service. Though there are tennis, sailing, horseback riding, and swimming, all conversations usually lead to golf. Being a knowledgeable and educated player is definitely a social asset.

Most of the rooms are spacious, with high-beamed ceilings; many have balconies or terraces and even working fireplaces. The choicest rooms are in the main building and in several of the wings that spread from it: the Sloat, Vizcaino, Colton, Alvarado, Portola, and Fremont, all overlooking the 18th hole.

So do the two dining rooms—the main one and, below it, the Club XIX, which serves as a combination grill and 19th hole during the day. Then after six, it is transformed into a chic little restaurant with excellent cuisine. The menu changes frequently, offering fine meat and fish dishes. One feature of all meals is the vegetables and greens that grow just east of the resort, which refers to itself as "the salad bowl of the world."

Staying at the Del Monte Lodge is no guarantee that you will get to play Cypress Point Club. In their most benevolent mood, the board of governors of the club allow only four foursomes from the Lodge to play each day. All must tee off before 9:30 A.M. The green fee is moderate, but the caddie fee (with tip) is high—the club has only half a dozen golf carts—and the caddies only carry single. You play the course, and that is that. The club has no reciprocal playing privileges with members of other

clubs. Guests are not allowed in the clubhouse unless accompanied by a member.

When Cypress Point Club opened in 1928 the course achieved instant fame. One hole did it—the famous 16th, still one of the most awesome par-3 holes in golf, demanding a tee shot of 222 yards across the pounding surf to a green in the middle of a treeless, craggy piece of land protruding into the Pacific. If it intimidates the average golfer, it does the same to the pros. Most play it by hitting an iron safely around the inlet to the fairway and then pitching onto the green. Even Palmer, who has played some of the boldest shots in the game's history, once stated that if he had a two-stroke lead he would not play for the green.

Before the golfer gets to the 16th hole, he must play fifteen other holes, and here he will be pleasantly surprised. The inland holes at Cypress are of a higher playing value than those at Pebble, though they are not balanced within the rhythm of the course as strongly as Pebble's. Holes one through fourteen and the 18th stretch through a forest of cypress trees, and the golfer must negotiate some 120 strategically positioned bunkers. Who has negotiated them the best? A Texan by the name of Ben Hogan. He holds the unofficial course record of 63. Cypress was designed by Alistair MacKenzie, who codesigned Augusta National in 1931 with Bobby Jones—a course that would be updated slightly by another Jones, Robert Trent Jones.

Trent Jones also designed the newest course on the peninsula—Spyglass Hill—

The most famous par 3 is the 222-yard 16th hole at Cypress Point Club. Since 1928, only three holes-in-one have been made at the 16th. One was by Cypress Point member Crosby. Usually the tee shot is hit over a stormy Carmel Bay into twenty-knot winds.

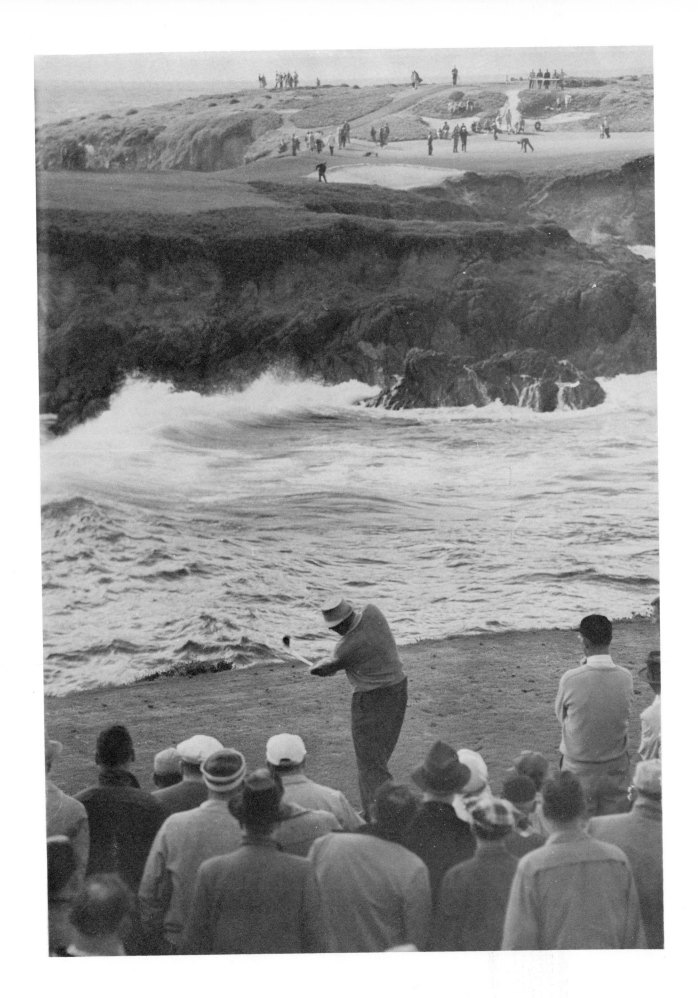

a redoubtable layout that first moves down to the sand dunes, then back into the forest. Jones, often accused of bulldozing the life out of nature when building a golf course, did not do so with Spyglass. The golfer wishes he had, especially after playing the first five holes. These run down to the sand dunes, or, more exactly, hopscotch through them. Fairways and greens are literally green oases surrounded by sand, wasteland, and ice plant. The first five holes are a Pine Valley-by-the-Sea. With the 6th hole, the course turns inland, with wide fairways cutting a green swath between thick rows of tall pines. The mood is the calm beauty of an Augusta National, minus the azaleas and wild flowers. But wildlife abounds. Deer and elk roam over tees, fairways, greens, and through sand traps on the peninsula, free from the threat of the stalking hunter. Sea gulls, geese, and ducks flock to the cliffs and litter the fairways. The untimely bark of a bull seal has caused many a putt to be yanked.

The preservation of wildlife and the protection of natural beauty by careful land use were all part of Morse's code. He may have hired an amateur golf-course architect to design what has become perhaps America's most famous and best course, but for architectural landscaping he retained the most experienced and the best: none other than Frederick Law Olmsted, that ingenious landscape architect of the most valuable piece of real estate in the world—New York City's Central Park.

A sandy panoramic view of the 4th and 5th holes of the redoubtable Spyglass Hill Golf Course.

DORADO BEACH
HOTEL
Dorado Beach, Puerto Rico

One of the better views of Central Park is to be had from the fifty-sixth floor of 30 Rockefeller Plaza. From there you can gaze north upon the 840 acres of Central Park, encompassing a network of six miles of bridle paths, two lakes, a reservoir, broad meadows, and pavilions. A striking view it is, and one afforded by hundreds of offices high above mid-Manhattan, all of which are considerably more accessible than the fifty-sixth floor at 30 Rockefeller Plaza. An unwritten law exists in the building that no one belongs on that floor unless he has a reason—a very good one. This is the floor of the offices and second offices of the brothers Rockefeller: David, John, Laurance, and Nelson. It is also the floor of their retinue of 175 specialists who handle the philanthropic, conservation, cultural, aviation, real-estate, and personal financial matters of the colossal Rockefeller fortune —one that boggles most people's minds. Few people extended sympathy to David Rockefeller in 1961, when he became president of Chase Manhattan Bank and, upon learning that the $150,000-a-year salary

was compulsory, said, "I'm afraid this is going to complicate my tax problem."

Laurance Rockefeller, long regarded as one of America's leading conservationists,

Sam Snead, the man who swings the golf club as it ought to be swung, practicing before capturing the individual honors in the 1961 Canada Cup Matches (now the World Cup Matches) played at Dorado Beach. Watching is partner Jimmy Demaret.

(*Left*) Part of the incoming nine of Dorado Beach's West Course. It is the best stretch of golf not only at Dorado but in Puerto Rico.

49

is probably best known today as the world's most prominent innkeeper, as well as one of the richest. He is chairman of the board of Rockeresorts Incorporated—an imposing empire of luxury resorts. Each reflects not only the typical Rockefeller architectural zest for simplicity and harmony with nature, but the feeling that on vacation all guests should be pampered as if they were Rockefellers. The Woodstock Inn in Woodstock, Vermont, has retained its quaint New England charm. Caneel Bay Plantation has become famous for its quiet, unspoiled splendor and equally so for what it does not have. It has no golf course, only a few tennis courts, and no night life. The rooms do not have air conditioning, radios, television sets, or even telephones.

The rooms at Dorado Beach do have air conditioning and telephones, but trying to put a call through beyond the front desk is a maddening experience. There is night life at Dorado—a gambling casino that stays open until 2:00 A.M.—but Dorado may be the only resort in the world where Monday-night bingo parties draw more people than the casino, which says much about the clientele.

The resort is located on a remote section on the northern coast of Puerto Rico, 20 miles above San Juan, but a good hour's drive and several snarling traffic jams from San Juan International Airport. It is best to use the shuttle airline, Dorado Wings, to Dorado Airport—a mere five-minute chauffeured drive to the main building. Arriving this way is the easiest and quickest means of capturing Dorado's mood—which appears to swing from prim and proper to utterly casual and informal. It is essentially low-key and maintains a temperament that has been stalwartly upheld through more than one trying moment. Nevertheless, it is a mood that attracts middle-and-corporate executives and their families, who at least

on vacation enjoy low-pressure atmosphere.

Conversely, Dorado has not become a favorite spot for celebrities—though many have been there to play golf and tennis, to swim, or to go deep-sea fishing. The rule that men must wear a coat and tie and women must be "appropriately attired" after 6:00 P.M. is hardly encouraging. Several years ago, Brigitte Bardot was asked to leave the dining room for arriving dressed in pants, a rule quite relaxed now. Ava Gardner once dove into one of the two swimming pools, not in pants, but in nothing at all, and was told in no uncertain terms that if she repeated the incident, she would have to leave.

When Robert Kennedy came to Dorado in an Air Force helicopter, he was extended the VIP treatment, but it was regarded as an incorrect manner to approach Dorado. Senator Edward Kennedy's visit caused considerable excitement after it was learned that he had been there for four days and no guest had known about it. Dorado is not a place where people go to meet other people.

Cleveland Amory, writing in *Travel & Leisure*, best summed up its social tone: "At the opening of the resort, Mr. Rockefeller, who built the place—it's now owned by Eastern Airlines,* but since Mr. Rockefeller owns a large piece of Eastern, it still —well, never mind—Mr. Rockefeller was told he would have to make an effort to meet his guests. A painfully shy and retiring man, this was not easy for him—but he agreed to give it a college try. He picked out a likely-looking couple at the opening-night party and determinedly advanced on the man.

" 'Hello,' he said, extending his hand, 'I'm Laurance Rockefeller.'

* Dorado Beach is now owned by Connecticut General Life Insurance Company and Teacher's Insurance & Annuity Association of America.

" 'Hello, yourself,' replied the man, 'I'm Napoleon Bonaparte.'

"Mr. Rockefeller has not tried again, and neither have many other people. It's all rather like an English party, where nobody is introduced and nobody minds not being."

It has been known that for years friends have gone there at the same time and have never met each other. One reason is that Dorado is spread out. Its 300 rooms fill 18 small units, low buildings hugging the ground and shrouded by tall palms and oaks, a specific aim of Laurance Rockefeller, who wanted a resort to bring people close to nature in a harmonious setting. Rates thus vary, depending upon location, cabana, ocean view, or fairway—not upon the room's size, since all are somewhat the same in size and furnishings, functional, and always clean, but hardly the luxury accommodations one finds at Mauna Kea, a sad fact that has disappointed many a first-time guest.

Once a wealthy Texan arrived late one evening after having had more than a sensible quota of drinks, and when he saw his room, told the bellboy not even to leave the bags, and promptly went to see the night manager. "Where I come from," the angry Texan said, "we've got broom closets bigger than that."

The night manager handled the problem with great aplomb. He had given the man not only one of Dorado's regular rooms, but, indeed, the last. So without fanfare he led the man out through the ocean front of the hotel rather than through the usual passageway to rooms, past the view of the multi-tiered dining room and the expanse of glass windows looking out on the night lights reflecting off the waves breaking against the rock jetties, then on past the elegant patio bar, and when they finally arrived back at the very same room he ushered the man in.

"Now these digs, son," the Texan said, "are more like it. Why the devil didn't you show me something like this in the first place?"

The 1,500-acre resort spreads over what once was a grapefruit plantation—the only evidence left is several groves of grapefruit trees along some fairways and the estate house, which is now converted into a Spanish restaurant. Over these grounds Robert Trent Jones, who designs all the golf courses for Rockeresorts, routed his two courses, the West and the East. He gave the golfer a menu of good golf by gearing the courses down to a level enjoyable for the average golfer and yet retaining a design that could be tightened up for tournaments. The Dorado Beach Invitational is held every December. In June 1961 the Canada Cup Matches (now the World Cup Matches) were played over what is now most of the West course (five holes were incorporated into the East Course), a flatish layout that can be stretched from almost 6,500 up to 7,000 yards for men. The course is played at sea level and the wind is a factor, but it is never as fiendish as at Pebble Beach, and only one hole, the par-3 13th, noses itself near the beach. Here, being on the beach means being in a bunker—not on the beach. The prevailing wind is from the northeast, and on all but two holes there is a crosswind.

Sam Snead, in winning the individual title for the United States in the Canada Cup Matches, played the course in 16 under par for 72 holes, and was never worse than two under par for any round. The 3rd hole (now the 12th on the West) received the most criticism from Snead. It is the kind of hole the pros refer to as a make-up hole, implying it is a birdie hole, a drive, and a wedge. The tee sits next to a large lake that borders the entire left side of the fairway—all 385 yards of it (365 regular and

Jimmy Demaret demonstrates how to hit a punch-wood shot from Bermuda rough during the first round of the 1961 Canada Cup Matches. Note that his right hand has not crossed over his left.

340 ladies' tee). On the right side are coconut palms and grapefruit trees, and just opposite, where the lake juts into the fairway, three bunkers march toward the green. If those aren't enough hazards, the crosswind usually is right to left. Though Snead played it in even par for four rounds, he claimed that it was unfair, too critical in the target area. One day his drive drew too much and rolled into the water. The next day he pushed it into the woods.

The 12th is characteristic of the incoming nine on the West, with the stress on shotmaking. One hole demands exact drives, while another, forgives off the tee but puts the premium on the second shot to a terraced green surrounded by traps. The 18th, a par 4 of 435 yards (413 regular and 405 ladies'), usually plays directly into the wind, and calls for a second shot, most likely a fairway wood to a green protected on the left and right sides by long bunkers. The left bunker is the key. It is diagonal to the green and not only catches shots that hook too much, but narrows the entrance to the green down to ten yards. It is an appropriate finishing hole for what is the finest stretch of golf not only at Dorado but in all Puerto Rico, the 10th through the 18th. Except for the greens —all replanted six years ago with Bermuda Tifton 320—the nine has not been altered.

It possesses neither the moody vagaries of a Pebble Beach nor the extreme subtleties of a Pinehurst No. 2. It is a fine, strategic nine that can be managed by the astute golfer. When President Eisenhower played it two days in a row in 1960, his first round was a ragged 97—the second, ten strokes less.

It is possible to hit a high, howling hook on the first hole of the East Course, find the ball resting near the 9th tee, loft a short iron shot over some bushes onto the green and make par. It is also possible to hit a slice into the coconut palms short of the fairway bunker, punch the ball onto the fairway, and hit a medium iron shot onto the green and make bogey. The golfer can even top his drive and end up with an easy bogey. A slight dogleg right, the hole measures only 360 yards from the championship tee (345 yards regular and 310 yards ladies') and serves as a good starting hole, testy enough to lure the golfer, but not so difficult as to ruin a round. The hole also sets the feeling of what the golfer can expect on the East Course. Though it measures almost the same distance as the West, it does not have the shot value. The fairways are wider than the West's, and most of the fairway bunkering is on the left side. There is no sequence of outstanding holes, and except for two holes, it is a good but ordinary layout.

When the golfer sets foot on the tee of the 8th hole, best played from the championship tee at 195 yards (160 yards regular and 105 yards ladies'), he looks across a section of a small lake running down to the green and around the left side—preciously close to the bell-shaped green. In back of the green are coconut palms, and its right side is protected by two bunkers. The surest shot is a straight one, which is of course the hardest to hit. In the Canada

A typical Dorado Beach guest, President Dwight Eisenhower, drives off the first tee in 1960. Ike improved his score the following day by ten shots: proof that course knowledge is a valuable thing.

Cup Matches, Jimmy Demaret, Snead's partner, took five the first round when he hooked his shot into the water. Instead of taking a penalty stroke, he waded in and took two more shots to reach the putting surface. Canadian golfer Al Balding fared worse. In the last round, he pushed his shot into one of the two bunkers right off the green, exploded his bunker shot over the green and into the water, took a penalty stroke, and finally made six.

Every golf course, be it a championship layout or just a good one, usually has one golf hole that shows the imagination of the architect, one that causes a golfer to complain or brag. The 13th hole on the East is such a one. A double dogleg, first left and then right, it measures 540 yards from the championship tee (505 yards regular and 475 ladies') and demands a long drive over the edge of one lake to set up a second shot that will enable the golfer to go for the green in two. His second shot must not only be good, it must be perfect. It must clear a second lake and a bunker in front of the green, and land softly. Low-handicap golfers who have played the hole several times rarely go for the green in two, but rather conservatively play around the lake and pitch on the green with their third shot. Going for the green in two is safest into a slight breeze; the reason naturally is that the wind holds the ball in the air and allows it to land softly. The green is wide but very shallow and pitched toward the water. A ball can hit on it and bounce unjustly into the rear bunker, leaving a delicate explosion shot to a green sloping to the water.

If there were caddies at Dorado, the golfer would be warned about such devious subtleties. Unfortunately, there are no caddies. And so for those golfers who still believe that walking is as much a part of golf as crisp five-iron shots and slick greens, Dorado in this respect is disappointing. In the beginning there were caddies. However, since they wore Dorado uniforms and were subject to the same security regulations as all employees, several, aided by a lawyer, declared themselves full-time employees, entitled to all benefits. Over a decade, the wages for all the caddies would have come to over a million dollars. Laurance Rockefeller settled out of court, and put the money he saved into eight rooms at Mauna Kea.

The 540-yard par-5 13th hole on Dorado's East Course, a double dogleg. To reach the green in two, you must first drive over the edge of a pond, then hit a perfect second shot. It must clear the pond in front of the green and land softly, in order to hold the narrow green guarded by a bunker in the back.

55

MAUNA KEA
BEACH HOTEL
Kamuela, Hawaii

Just before the new 102-room beach-front wing at Mauna Kea was to open in September 1968, Laurance Rockefeller made one of his customary inspection trips to his hotel. After looking over one of the new guest rooms, he went to inspect the bathroom. He looked at the bright orange shower curtain, the carefully hung white towels and orange washcloths, the Italian marble sinks and the white bathmat spread across the orange tiled floor. But the more he looked, the more troubled he became. He went back to the guest room, onto the balcony overlooking the crescent-shaped beach, then returned to inspect the bathroom again. He repeated the procedure several times. An hour and a half passed. What Rockefeller was pondering all this time was whether the bathroom should have one or two rolls of toilet paper.

The image of Laurance Rockefeller, or any Rockefeller for that matter, spending

an hour and a half deciding how many rolls of toilet paper each bathroom should have may seem strange, even eccentric. It is not a question of cost. The Rockefellers have been called many things, but cheap is not

The man responsible for creating the best modern resort hotel in the world, Laurance Rockefeller, with his wife Mary, receiving congratulations at the opening of Mauna Kea.

The wavy fairways and elevated greens of Mauna Kea. Arnold Palmer drills a five-iron shot to the green on the par-5 550-yard 17th en route to a final-round 67 in the "Big 3" television match against Gary Player and Jack Nicklaus. After Nicklaus pocketed the $50,000 first prize, he said, "This is the most fun golf course I've played."

one of them. The problem confronting Laurance Rockefeller was, would the sight of an extra roll of toilet paper produce a cluttered look; would it be aesthetically displeasing?

Rockefeller's visual sensibility, developed at Dorado Beach and at Caneel Bay Plantation in the Caribbean, matured to its fullest at Mauna Kea, the *grande dame* of Rockeresorts, located on a remote northwestern tip of the "big island" of Hawaii. The resort, which even has a par 3 similar in design to Cypress Point's 16th hole, covers 500 acres of a 12,000-acre tract and cost $36 million (excluding the worth of the art and religious objects displayed in the hotel), a figure that put Mauna Kea into the 1967 *Guinness Book of Records* as the costliest hotel per room—a neat $125,000 each—and there are 310 rooms. The new Garden Pavilion restaurant cost $2 ¼ million and seats 160 people, an average of $14,000 per seat.

Considerably less could have been spent, but one of the intended purposes of the resort was to get vacationers away from Waikiki onto the "big island." And the Rockefellers usually do not do things on a small or ordinary scale. And Mauna Kea is not your ordinary on-the-beach hotel. "Mauna Kea is the best resort hotel in the world," wrote the late Richard Joseph, travel editor of *Esquire*, who also ranked it as one of the three best hotels in the world. (The other two are New York City's Plaza and Venice's Gritti Palace.) *Fortune* selected Mauna Kea as one of the ten best buildings built in 1966. The hotel also received the Honor Award of the American Institute of Architects for outstanding architectural and decorative design.

From out on Kaunaoa Bay, the hotel looks like a beached oceanliner. However, the closer one gets, the less dominant the building appears, a deliberate architectural plan to play down the building, making it serve as a backdrop and frame for interior tropical gardens and courts. In essence, the building was designed from the inside out. Entering from the landward side, you see through the courtyards to the Pacific. The tiles you are walking on are as blue as the ocean. Looking up, you see that the building opens to the sky. You are, in effect, open to the environment at all times. Sprawling the length of two and one-half blocks, the whole building is like a tiered honeycomb. Interior corridors are actually balconies facing gardens with pools.

All rooms face either the ocean or the extinct volcano, Mauna Kea, the highest island mountain, rising 13,796 feet. Seven two-room suites look out on both. Though the rooms are not extraordinarily large, they are large enough, each with its own lanai (balcony), offering guests complete privacy without divorcing them from the landscape. The decor is simple, subtle, and luxurious. All furniture is made from tropical materials, cane or willow, and covered in a sturdy orange cotton. Woven mats of Samoan Lahalla tree straw cover a fourth of the tiled floor. Two original lithographs of bright tropical flowers and a framed collection of seashells hang in every room.

The atmosphere that pervades the resort is casual, highly personal, and sportive, toned to produce a salubrious feeling. Rockefeller and the architects of the firm Skidmore, Owens and Merrill wanted guests to feel that they were not in a hotel, but rather in a great country house, a place that would contain nothing to disrupt a guest's dignity and nothing to require him to maintain it if he decided to lose it. Even that matter has been carefully taken care of by a staff trained like gracious hosts and hostesses never to make people feel uncomfortable, a task that has had its strained moments.

At the top of a broad flight of stairs leading to the North Garden reigns a large pink-granite Indian Buddha set on a pedestal of Canadian black granite. It is a rare Buddha, one of seven of its kind in the world, and almost priceless. However, one guest who saw it did not think so. He entered the small gift shop, and pointing his arm in the direction of the Buddha, he said, "I want to buy that Buddha." Without so much as a gasp or a startled look, the salesgirl said, "May I interest you in something smaller?"

The Buddha is the most imposing of all the art and religious objects, a microcosm of culture of the Orient and the Pacific Basin. The Buddha is positioned in accordance with the Buddhist tradition—his heart always above the level of a man's eye. His mood is serene and compassionate. His hands form a cup, inviting the coins and small orchids placed there nightly by guests wishing, perhaps, that for the rest of their days they will par Mauna Kea's notorious 3rd hole or that their next movie will be distributed properly.

Unlike Dorado Beach, Mauna Kea does attract celebrities, directors, producers, actors, singers, agents, cameramen, writers, athletes, and government officials. In fact, the resort has become something of a way station, a place to recover from jet lag for the United States government officials going to the Far East. In October 1971 Henry Kissinger used Mauna Kea as a resting place on his first trip to China. In all, two U.S. Presidents, three Vice-Presidents, and enough Senators, Congressmen, and business tycoons to fill a *Who's Who* and a *Celebrity* and *Social Register* have stayed at Mauna Kea. And all guests are paying guests, even Nelson Rockefeller. The only guests who did not pay, but who were there as guests of the United States government,

A giant Buddha, the most imposing of all the art and religious objects at Mauna Kea. The Buddha is positioned in accordance with the Buddhist tradition—his heart above the level of a man's eye. (*Below*) A disciple of Buddha.

were the Emperor and Empress of Japan, who visited Mauna Kea in the fall of 1975.

Since the resort opened in July 1965 it has operated at eighty-five-percent occupancy annually. From mid-December to mid-May, it operates at ninety-five-percent occupancy. Besides the extraordinary character of the hotel itself, there is the island's wonderful climate: hot and dry, much like Palm Springs—with an ocean. In fact, Mauna Kea is the driest spot in the state, averaging only seven inches of rain yearly. However, the figures for occupancy are even more impressive when you consider the above-average room rates (which vary according to whether you have a view of the ocean or of the mountains). All rates include breakfast and dinner.

It is the wise guest who forsakes lunch—the daily buffet, a sumptuous feast of salads, meat, fish, fowl, and desserts. It would take a *Guinness Book of Records* eater to try everything twice. Dinner is the meal. It is a rare dining experience. The waitresses, shy and courteous, are dressed in colorful raw-silk shifts. There are three restaurants. The Dining Pavilion is a free-standing structure on the main terrace with three tiered levels. Next to it is the Garden Pavilion, also with three-level seating and featuring art objects, all of which represent some aspect of food. The Batik Room has a Ceylonese motif. Its unique dining salon was inspired by the Howdah, the throne-like canopied seat used by Asian royalty for riding on the backs of elephants.

The cuisine is a mixture of Continental and local dishes. Ribs of Beef and Deviled Rack of Lamb are offered with Macadamia and Sugar-Cane Brandy Pie. Saimin Chicken Broth is served with Sweetbread Marechale with Truffles and Madeira Sauce. All fish is fresh, caught that day. The produce, too, is fresh. When the resort was opened, the management told the local farmers of Kamuela that if they grew vegetables the hotel would buy them. Thus it has been.

Another tradition is that evening attire has been casual-chic. Neckties for men have never been required and are just not worn. Jackets are required, but they can vary from the admirable blue blazer to the safari jacket. Women do dress for dinner, usually wearing full-length cotton or silk dresses.

Dinner all but ends the evening activities. You can go to a rock ledge with spotlights shining into the water, where two giant manta rays swim around, turning somersaults—the ray's equivalent of half gainers. Or you can walk the crescent-shaped beach and maybe spot a young couple taking a nude swim, about which the hotel's manager only shrugs and says, "So what?" Better, the golfer should attend the only movie shown regularly at the hotel, Shell Oil Company's one-time successful television show, "Shell's Wonderful World of Golf." You will see Al Geiberger, Dan Sikes, and Peter Alliss playing Mauna Kea Golf Course. Sikes won, shooting an even par—72.

Every December the Mauna Kea Invitational is held. Until the Hawaiian Open was switched to February, there was a Mauna Kea Invitational following the Open. In 1964 the finals of another television series, the "Big 3" matches, were played at Mauna Kea, featuring the triumvirate of Jack Nicklaus, Arnold Palmer and Gary Player. Nicklaus won with 13 under par for four rounds. He later declared, "Mauna Kea is the most fun golf course I've ever played." The resort likes to quote Nicklaus in its brochures. What they do not say, however, is that Nicklaus said it just after he holed the winning putt in the match and won the winner's share of $50,000.

Another truth, be it known, is that

Mauna Kea might never have gotten off the lava flow, had it not been for Robert Trent Jones. When Laurance Rockefeller was considering the site in July 1960, he called in Jones to get his opinion about a golf course. They walked over the desertlike terrain, on which only cacti were growing, Jones looking here and there where he might place a green or a tee, while Rockefeller kept looking over anxiously at Jones. Finally Rockefeller said, "Trent, can you build a golf course here? If you can't, we'll have to look for another site. A golf course is vital to this resort."

"It all depends, Laurance," Jones answered, "whether the mudrock [volcanic stone] can be crushed and used as the soil base." After some experimenting, Jones discovered that the lava actually was quite porous, could be crushed and used as a soil base, and that with tender care Bermuda grass would grow on it. But it took cranes, giant bulldozers, one and a half years and $3 million, and, as still today, one million gallons of water daily to keep the course green.

The course follows the contour of the rolling land, which makes it hillier than the Cascades Course at The Homestead. The course is also long. From the championship tees it plays to 7,016 yards—5,831 from the ladies' tees. It is best for those playing to a ten handicap or higher to play it from the regular tees at 6,488 yards, for the course is hard, though it looks harder than it actually is. The standard remark at Mauna Kea is, "Once you're off the fairway, you don't need a caddie; you need a guide." Unfortunately neither is available. However, a local rule is somewhat redeeming. Any ball hit into the lava, lost or not, is only a one-stroke penalty.

Still, the course is not particularly kind to the golfer with a howling slice, hook, or alignment problem. Hawaii's former governor, William Quinn, not one of the best of Hawaii's golfing governors, with a handicap of 23, played the course one day and lost twenty-three balls. However, one golfer who played it, perhaps the day after Quinn, found fifty-two balls.

Periodically, for the first five years after the course opened, guests complained the course was too tough, too penalizing off the tee. Word got back to Rockefeller, who then made several requests to Jones to make it easier. Jones said he would rather break an ankle than change so much as a blade of the Bermuda grass. That was until the day when Jones was driving around there in a golf car, inspecting his course and looking at a green instead of where he should have been walking, stepped out of the car onto a piece of lava, fell, and broke his right ankle.

Ever since, the fairways slowly have been widened and much of the rough reduced. Then in 1975, Rockefeller told Jones that half the greens needed to be redesigned— too many were dome-shaped, and the green on the 3rd hole was unfair, because the golfer standing on the regular men's tee could not see the exact pin placement, because the green was too high in front. Anticipating Jones's answer, Rockefeller said, "Trent, if you don't do it, someone else will." Someone else did, Robert Trent Jones's older son Bob, who had designed the three spectacular nines of Princeville at Hanalei on the island of Kauai three years earlier.

The only other substantial change in the course occurred on the 3rd hole, which Jones likes to call his gem among eighteen jewels. Originally when the course opened for the "Big 3" matches, the championship tee was set back farther, pitched on the lava rocks, demanding a shot, all carry, to a

The might of Jack Nicklaus, seen hitting a long-iron shot on Mauna Kea's famed par-3 3rd hole during the "Big 3" match.

The 250 yards of hazards that Nicklaus, Palmer and Player had to cross. Over the years the tee has been moved up—it now demands a mere 215-yard carry. The cautious golfer can play to the right around the inlet.

green nearly 250 yards away. It was not too long for Nicklaus or Palmer, who, believe it or not, used irons to reach the green, but Player could not reach the green with a driver in four attempts. Now the championship tee demands only a 215-yard carry (175 yards regular; 143 yards ladies') over a horseshoe-shaped inlet of black lava and ocean. To the left of the green are three bunkers, lava, and the ocean. On the right of the green, on the side of a small hill, are two more bunkers. The green now rises from front to center and levels off toward the rear; it is not only the largest green on the course, but one of the ten largest single greens in the world, measuring 25,000 square feet.

The hole has the basic character of the 16th at Cypress Point, though less severe. The golfer rarely is hitting into a wind. The wind on the hole is a crosswind that shifts daily. In the morning it is out of the east, right to left; in the early afternoon it reverses. While the hole is the most dramatic, it is neither the hardest hole nor the hardest par 3 on the course.

That honor belongs to the 11th, a 247-yard par 3. From the championship tee, the hole measures 247 yards (198 regular, 167 ladies'). The championship tee sits on the top of a high hill surrounded by a kiawe tree and coconut palms. From the tee the golfer looks down over the tops of the kiawe trees behind the green and sees the Pacific. He also should look carefully at the green—it is long and narrow and slightly domed; a shot fading or drawing too much when it catches the green will roll off into bunkers on the right or in the left rear. The front of the green is guarded left and right by two large bunkers. Making matters worse, the hole usually plays into a wind (except early in the morning) that is more than a cooling trade wind. It whipped up with such force during one round of the "Big 3" match that Nicklaus was forced to use a driver. Now there are not many par 3s in the world where Nicklaus has to use a driver, and there are even fewer he cannot par in four attempts. In the four rounds of the "Big 3" match Nicklaus bogied the hole four times while he played the par-5, 535-yard 10th in two eagles and two birdies.

From the 11th green you can look across the Pacific to the hotel, whose trim cellular sequence of rooms appears to float above the treetops. Beneath it lies the beach. Even if you find yourself in one of the one hundred bunkers, you will find not sand, but crushed coral, and a bane it has been to the finest sand-wedge players, who do not use a sand wedge because the flange will bounce off the coral, resulting in a skulled shot that goes screeching across the green. A pitching wedge is used instead.

The cautious golfer can drive with a three wood, making sure he keeps the ball in play. However, it is the wise golfer who learns to swing away with the driver and to play for his draw or fade, because even from the regular men's tees, distance is needed. Jones elevated his greens—a shot must be all carry. Eight greens are placed on tops of hills, strongly fortified by bunkers. If you are not shooting up to a green, then you are shooting down to it. Only the 16th hole is flat. All this puts an added premium on club selection, and makes the yardage markers on the back of the scorecard meaningless. One hundred and fifty yards uphill is more like 170 yards—not a unique situation in Hawaii, where fairways zigzag along craters of extinct volcanos, or crawl up mountainsides, with Diamond Head off in the distance. Hawaii is a golfing state. Its first course was laid out in 1904, and the first Hawaiian Open was played in 1928. When Trent Jones's son Bobby finished his course at Princeville and gave the state its most beautiful par 3, it was the forty-sixth course in the state, which is approximately the size of Connecticut and Rhode Island combined.

PRINCEVILLE
AT HANALEI
Hanalei, Hawaii

Had Bob Jones, Jr., decided not to spend his honeymoon in the small village of Hanalei on the northern shore of the island of Kauai, on secluded beaches, looking up at green mountains with cascading waterfalls, at rainbows and sunsets, while humming tunes from the musical *South Pacific*, the golfing world would be considerably poorer. One of the best par-4 holes in the state, the backbone of the Woods Nine on the Princeville Makai Golf Course, probably would not exist, nor would the 3rd hole on the Ocean Nine, which is quickly gaining rank as one of the world's most beautiful par 3s.

Until a decade ago, few people had heard of Hanalei, though millions had seen it on film. It is out of the way, located on what could be said to be the westernmost paved road in the United States. The village is small, with a general store, a local museum, a small hotel, a church, two restaurants, a few bars with whirring overhead fans, and

a school where children attend barefooted and are given days off to go surfing. It is remote, relaxing, and enthrallingly beautiful. It is an enchanting place not only for a honeymoon, but also for a movie director seek-

Bob Jones, Jr., grins with satisfaction after completing the final design of his course. Bestowing rare praise is his father, Robert Trent Jones.

(*Left*) One of the most beautiful golf holes in the world, the 165-yard par-3 3rd hole of Princeville's Ocean Nine. It is usually a short-iron shot. Here, if you accidentally pull your head up too soon, you can blame the scenery, making the hole beautiful indeed.

ing the visual quintessence of the mystery and romance of the South Seas. Hanalei, with its coves and unspoiled beaches shaded by tall pine and palm trees, its moody emerald-green mountains pushing thousands of feet upward straight out of the sea, their peaks dashed against puffy white clouds, suited perfectly the mood for Joshua Logan's film version of *South Pacific*.

Somehow, young Jones never did quite recover from the beauty of the place—the calling of Bali Ha'i, with its special hope and dream. Ten years after his honeymoon, while commanding the San Francisco office of Robert Trent Jones, Inc., he heard that a land developer had purchased 11,000 acres above the village of Hanalei—a flat stretch of land, a former cattle ranch stretching from the craggy cliffs to the foothills of Mount Waialeale. It was to be a destination resort community, beginning with 27 holes of golf. Jones wrote to the developer, listing his credentials—a degree in history from Yale University, a 1 handicap (now up to 6), and six years of apprenticeship with his father, including working on the renowned Spyglass Hill Golf Course. He also wrote about his deep feelings for the Hanalei area, that a development should not be a blight on the horizon, that the golf course, the houses, and all those condominiums should blend into the look of the area.

Jones got the job. Yet for all his experience and worldly travels, he was not without self-doubt. He later recalled, "The developer drove me straight to the prettiest land in the package and said, 'The course goes here.' He wanted to maintain the integrity of the place. I got truly nervous looking at all that beauty and knowing it was mine to use."

Jones used the land to create three nines, each with its own character and hazards.

The Lake Nine weaves among lakes that front three greens. Ditches curl sinisterly along and across fairways. The Woods Nine plays among huge silver oaks and Norfolk Island pines, Hawaii's Christmas trees. The Ocean Nine runs down and across the edge of jagged cliffs above the Pacific. The Woods and Ocean nines are the best, and are best played in that order.

The three nines vary only 52 yards from the championship, 88 from the regular, and 117 from the ladies' tees. Thus, any combination the golfer will play adds up to just over 6,900 yards from the championship tees, from the regular tees just over 6,200 yards, and from the ladies' tees 5,400, a yardage that would delight former Curtis Cupper Alice Dye. The best par 3s are on the Ocean Nine, the best par 4s on the Woods Nine, and the best par 5 is the 9th hole on the Lakes Nine, demanding a drive over a lake, a second shot to the edge of a second lake and a third shot over more water.

However, where Jones created his scenic triumph was on the 3rd hole of the Ocean Nine, a par 3, which has taken on the name of "the postcard hole." A line that has become somewhat shopworn among the first-time golfers standing on the tee on one of Hawaii's golden afternoons is: "Do I use a seven iron or a fifty-millimeter lens [to photograph it]?" From the championship tee the hole measures 165 yards as the Maxfli flies (125 yards regular and ladies'), but it plays considerably shorter. The hole plays downhill and usually downwind. Standing on the championship tee, the golfer should be excused if he starts humming a few bars of "Blue Hawaii." First, the air is scented by the star jasmines that surround the rear of the tee. The golfer looks 60 feet down a hill covered with underbrush and guava trees to a dark blue pond that fronts a kid-

Water and more water. The two lakes must be crossed to reach the green on the 540-yard par-5 9th on the Lake Nine.

ney-shaped green further guarded by bunkers in the right front and left rear. The green lies in a natural amphitheater, surrounded on three sides by small hills. In the distance, off to infinity, the golfer sees the Pacific's frothy whitecaps, white beaches, and the mountains. It is an epic view, one to revere, the Hawaii one had always imagined whenever hearing Webley Edwards broadcasting "Hawaii Calls," the Hawaii expressed by lovely hula hands.

But sooner or later the golfer must hit some kind of shot. From the championship tee it is usually a six or seven iron; from the regular tee for men, a wedge. The shot looks more frightening than it actually is. A smooth wedge or seven iron will do. Thus the character of the hole requires, as do all good short par 3s, a deftness in judgment. Proper club selection is everything. The common fault is to overclub, and, of course, to look up. If the golfer has a chronic tend-

Hanalei, where enchanting evenings are both real and fictional. With its South Seas beauty, it was perfectly suited for director Joshua Logan's movie *South Pacific*. This was the site of the first romantic encounter between Ensign Nellie Forbush, played by Mitzi Gaynor, and the French planter Emile de Decque, played by Rossano Brazzi.

ency to do the latter, here he can blame the scenery and not his golf swing, making the hole beautiful indeed.

The 7th hole is the other par 3 on the Ocean Nine. It is heroic in design, and the hardest of all six par 3s. It is, in fact, something of a modified Pebble Beach 8th, with the cliffs running along the right side of the fairway and with the tee and green edging the cliff. Whereas at Pebble Beach's 8th the golfer is hitting down to a small slot of green, on Princeville's Ocean 7th the green is level with the tee, but the golfer still must hit over a rocky inlet that falls 400 feet to the Pacific. From the championship tee it is a 200-yard carry (150 regular; 115 ladies'),

hit with a long iron or full wood, preferably with a slight draw. The heart-shaped green hugs the cliff so tightly there is less than five yards between it and the edge of the cliff, room enough to place a bunker. Another bunker protects the left front of the green, and a third the left rear. Making the hole even harder is that the prevailing left-to-right wind will catch a slightly sliced or pushed ball and carry it over the cliff.

As with all seaside courses, Princeville's nines were laid out according to the prevailing winds, in this case, the northeast wind. On the Ocean Nine, the 2nd hole, a long par 5, and the 3rd play downwind, while the 4th, a short par 4, and the 5th hole, a par 5, play into the wind. On other holes on the nine, the wind is quartering. But about a dozen times a year, what is called a Kona wind whips up; it is a southwest wind, making the beautiful 3rd hole a terror, calling for a long iron shot. In such a wind, the 7th is hardly reachable from the championship tees with a driver, and even the best golfers tack their way carefully around the inlet. However, compensation awaits, for the best hole on the course, the 6th on the Woods Nine, plays downwind— a driver and a midiron. Normally, it is played into a breeze with a driver, a fairway wood, and a wish for some graphite muscles.

The hole measures 450 yards from the championship tee (400 yards regular; 355 yards ladies'). Left of the tee are Cassia trees growing along a narrow ditch, beyond which is out-of-bounds. The golfer has to walk to the right side of the tee to get a glimpse of the green at the end of a fairway doglegging right. At the corner of the dogleg, 225 yards from the regular tee, are two bunkers. Here the fairway slopes gently downhill to a deep gully fronting the green. No shot rolls onto the green, which is further defended by a half-moon-shaped bunker left of the green, a deep bunker on the right side, and a rear bunker. Behind it are tall silver oaks that cast devilish shadows on the green. The oaks are huge and ancient, planted nearly a century ago to mark the grave of anthrax-diseased cattle.

The trees almost caused the demise of Princeville's president, who one day stood anxiously on the adjacent 7th tee, gazing down the 6th fairway as the resort's pro consultant, Dave Marr, was about to hit his second shot but was in no hurry to do so. Instead of hitting his drive just to the left of the fairway bunkers, the ideal spot for a clear opening to the green, Marr had pushed his drive behind the right bunkers. After suggesting to his partner that perhaps the rough should be allowed to grow longer to make the hole even rougher, he slashed a four-wood shot, but instead of drawing, the ball faded, ricocheted smartly off the limb of an oak, and hit the president in the head. It was a shot that forever determined that the hole was hard enough as it was.

Just after young Jones had plotted his course, positioned his tees, shaped his bunkers and greens, and was ready to seed it, his father sent word that he was coming out from the mainland to look it over. The news that Trent Jones was coming out affected the developers as if they had heard a tsunami was heading their way. More than one developer has retreated to his jeep or Land Rover when Trent and Bob Jones began discussing how a certain bunker or green should be shaped. Their conversation would begin as a discussion and end up a stormy argument.

When Trent Jones arrived, he carefully inspected each fairway, kneeling here and there on a green to see that it sloped properly. The inspection took two days. The developers waited for the stormy outburst. Finally, in the makeshift clubhouse, Trent Jones turned to Bob and said, "You did a good job, son." It was rare but accurate praise from the most famous of modern golf-course architects.

Jones incorporated sound but subtle features into his course. Several of his fairway bunkers were positioned on man-made hills, presenting a double hazard. A drive hit directly to the bunker, but short of it, leaves the golfer behind a high-mounded bunker that partly obscures his view of the green. As for the greens, some are large, some small, some heavily contoured, others flattish. Jones wisely built flattish greens on those holes that are short and play predominantly downwind, making the golfer finesse his second shot, hitting a punch short-iron shot with bite, or a long pitch-and-run shot, because a shot hit directly to the pin does not hold, as the greens remain particularly hard and slope slightly toward the rear bunkers.

And, again, the old axiom that all putts on seaside courses break to the sea is not true at Princeville. The greens are very grainy, seeded with Bermuda 328, and it is the wise golfer who learns how to read the grain. The only time the greens are soft and

less grainy is during the rainy season, from December to April.

Rain on the northern tip of Kauai is either a fine mist that does not interrupt play or a downpour. It is not uncommon for two inches of rain to fall in an hour. So hard did it rain in the fall of 1971, just after the Woods Nine was seeded, that the 9th fairway was almost completely washed away.

Each nine begins and ends near the club-house, a low, two-story building (no building can exceed a height of 40 feet) that houses offices, a pro shop, a restaurant, and a bar, which overlook a swimming pool. It is also where all guests register. Princeville has no hotel (though two are planned for some time in the future), which makes it an anomaly among great resorts. However, it does offer more rooms than Mauna Kea and Del Monte Lodge collectively. There are 400 rooms in single-story fairway cottages, split-level cottages, and cliffside condominiums. Most have daily maid service and kitchens. The Pali Ke Kua condominiums, located above a secluded beach and the Golf Cottages, are the best accommodations.

All meals are served in the main clubhouse or the Beam Reach restaurant. The food is neither as good nor as varied as Mauna Kea's, but then few resorts are in that culinary category. Princeville's food is fair to good, and its menu changes little, with a balanced variety of meat and fish dishes, but its specialty is a surprise—it is Boston Clam Chowder. However, the atmosphere is so informal (men never wear ties, and not even jackets are necessary), and the help is so friendly and courteous, and the restaurant always seems to be filled with guests or residents looking so healthy, happy, and hopeful, that they compensate for the average quality of the food. Such

A rare moment of relaxation for Dan Jenkins, *Sports Illustrated*'s senior writer and Princeville's celebrated sometime resident. Because of its beauty and tranquillity, Jenkins selected Hanalei as a sanctuary from which to write three novels, including his best seller *Semi-Tough*.

enthusiasm is called the aloha spirit, and it is particularly infectious on the northern tip of Kauai, where everyone claims to have found paradise.

When the resort opened in 1972, Dan Jenkins, senior writer for *Sports Illustrated*, went there to write about it. A year later he returned, rented a house for his wife and children, and in the span of a few months wrote the best-selling novel *Semi-Tough*. With the royalties he bought the house, right on Hanalei Bay, contiguous to Princeville.

Not long afterward he was approached by writing colleague Charles Price, who had traveled and golfed almost everywhere in the world and wanted someplace new and different to spend his forthcoming honey-moon. Graciously, Jenkins lent him his house. It took Price and his new bride less than a week to realize that they, too, had discovered paradise, and when they saw a half-acre lot for sale in the village of Hanalei, that did it. They inquired at one of the local bars, which happened to be owned by a local realtor, about the price of the half-acre. When informed it was well into the six-figure category, it staggered even Price's imagination, and he was sadly reminded that if one chooses to live in paradise one must be able to afford it. And so the couple returned to their home, which they called semiparadise, on the 5th fairway of the Harbour Town Golf Links in Sea Pines Plantation on Hilton Head Island.

SEA PINES
PLANTATION
Hilton Head Island, South Carolina

Harbour Town Golf Links spreads moodily across the instep of the shoe-shaped Hilton Head Island. Thin fairways slither convolutely through woods of loblolly pine, live oak, elms, palmettos and pampas grass around lagoons and lakes, until they reach the marshy edge of Calibogue Sound with the par-3 17th hole, and finally skirt the salt marsh with the par-4 18th. The course is of such distinct character that it has been called Pebble Beach-East, Pine Valley-in-a-swamp, and a Scottish links with moss. Its designer, Pete Dye (Jack Nicklaus acted as consultant), once said, "It's different, but then so was Garbo."

What is different is that Harbour Town is an architectural collage of the above courses with its own unique personality—a mean Napoleonic complex. It is a short course by modern standards and often has a cruel way of humiliating long hitters. From the championship tees (the best length from which to appreciate its shot value) it measures a deceptive 6,655 yards (5,784 regular and 4,880 ladies'). There are only 12 fairway bunkers and 47 bunkers in all. The greens are small; the last two holes are similar in design to the last two at Pebble Beach. Like Pine Valley, it is target golf.

Railroad ties and planks—found on many Scottish links—are used to support greens and flank bunkers. However, the course's

The 1977 winner, Graham Marsh, watches intently after hitting a long-iron shot to the 18th green to win his first United States PGA tournament.

(*Left*) A scene that has been reenacted again and again over the past decade and a half: Arnold Palmer marches to victory down the 458-yard par-4 18th of Harbour Town Golf Links. In this case the tournament is the first Heritage Classic.

outstanding trait is inherited from the fundamental Scottish tradition that golf really is a point-to-point game. Playing Harbour Town, you are keenly aware that you must carefully tack your way down the twisting fairways to the greens. There are trees with fiendish overhanging limbs, greens nestled in groves of elms, and bunkers that strategically pinch the greens so hard they seem to bulge to odd shapes; they call for the golfer to hit the ball straight, from right to left, left to right, high and low. In fact, day in and day out, the surest shots at Harbour Town are poured at the 19th hole.

When the first Heritage Classic was played in 1969 Jack Nicklaus was accused of building a course to practice his talent shots on. "The truth is," said Nicklaus, "this is the kind of course I really like. The kind that makes you play good golf shots. You have to play a definite side of the fairway, depending on where the pin is, or you haven't got a shot. You have to play to the side of the green where the pin is, or you'll have to wedge over a bunker from one side of the green to the other. (Try it and you will have the greens superintendent after you.) You've also got the option of going with a driver and, say, an eight iron to a certain hole, or going with a one iron and five iron. This is what golf should be."

During the 1974 USGA Men's Seniors (age 55 and over), played at Harbour Town, former Walker Cupper and eventual winner Dale Morey voiced a similar opinion. "If they had bent-grass greens (they are Bermuda Tifton 320) I'd call it the best golf course in the world. And the yardage is meaningless. We played it at 6,500 yards. Well, take the ninth. It's three hundred and twenty-four yards. But you can't hit a driver here, because of the trees near the fairway. So you have to add twenty to thirty yards because you hit a four wood.

Then that skinny green with all the sand. Well, you do this all the way around, and it isn't a so-called 'short' course any more."

Harbour Town carries a course rating of 75, higher than Pebble Beach, Merion, Mauna Kea, or Costasur's Cajuiles. Its rating is one of the highest of any course its length in the Americas—and proof that, like Garbo, Harbour Town is different. The scores in the first Heritage Classic soared into the high 70s and low 80s. After 72 holes, only a victorious Arnold Palmer was under par, just barely, at 283. Par is 71. The next year, scores came down a little, but even designer consultant Nicklaus expressed his frustration, which has become universally shared by most golfers who have played the course. "I get angrier here than anywhere else we play," he said. "This place is designed for some shots I'm not supposed to be able to hit, and that's a challenge. Then when I can't hit them, it just burns my rear end." Bob Goalby won that year, with a score of 280.

Using a one iron off the tee on most of the par 4s and 5s, Hale Irwin, reputed to be one of the straightest drivers on the tour, won in 1971 and in 1973, breaking par by 13 shots in the latter year. In 1975, having learned to play a course of his own making, Nicklaus set a tournament record of 14 under par, aided by a second round 63, including eight birdies and no bogies. He birdied four of the 11 par 4s, all three par 5s—though he never reached a par-5 green in two, not even the 492-yard 2nd hole—but birdied only one of the four par 3s, the 167-yard 7th. He hit a six iron and sank a 14-foot putt.

Indeed, few courses in the world possess four so memorable and so penalizing par 3s as Harbour Town. They appear not to have been chiseled out of the woods and lagoons, but cut with a surgeon's scalpel

The making of Harbour Town Golf Links. Standing on the edge of Calibogue Sound, plotting one of the most penalizing modern courses in the world, are (*left to right*) codesigner Jack Nicklaus, architect Pete Dye, Donald O'Quinn, and the developer of Sea Pines Plantation, Charles Fraser.

(*Right*) Tom Watson deftly recovers from one of the plank-sided bunkers on his way to a second-place finish in the 1977 Heritage Classic.

and allowed to heal naturally in water, which comes into play on each hole—sometimes so effectively it seems that the pin is set on the water's edge. Other places, a brackish stream serves as a secondary hazard—only to catch the most errant shot, like on the 7th hole. You first must carry a narrow stream that runs in front of an omega-shaped bunker ringing all but 10 yards of the green. On the 4th hole, the tee

is pushed snugly into a grove of loblolly pine, palmetto, and elm, 180 yards back from a bell-shaped green. A lagoon flows from the tee to the front and left side of the green and then curls behind it. The green is supported by planks—no shot skips accidentally onto it. It is usually a full three-iron shot, all carry and ideally hit with a slight fade. The hole's sibling rival is the 14th; though shorter at 152 yards, it presents the same problem, but in reverse. A lagoon flows down to the right side of the green. During one Heritage Classic Lee Trevino took seven at the 14th, fading two short iron shots into the lagoon.

The tee shot on the 17th hole, a par 3, is best played with a two iron, a four wood, and a strong set of nerves. Incorporated into the hole is a mean nonpartisan design —nothing but a straight shot will do. For the golfer who draws the ball, there are hazards on the left, a lagoon flowing into Calibogue Sound, a long bunker completely protecting the left side of the green. A bunker on the right catches a pushed shot.

The 18th hole, a par 4 of 458 yards (412 yards regular and 305 ladies'), heads toward a red-and-white-striped lighthouse. Water guards the left side of the fairway from the tee to the green; out-of-bounds is on the right. Gambling to reach a patch of fairway protruding into the sound, the direct line to the green, you must fly the ball 230 yards; but even then you are faced with a second shot of over 200 yards to a green fronted by a long, shallow bunker. The green rises slowly from front to rear, where another bunker catches a shot that goes too long. The hole usually is played with a driver and fairway wood, unless your name is Palmer or Nicklaus. In the final round of the 1969 Heritage Palmer, playing downwind, hit a driver and an eight iron. In Nicklaus's second round in 1975, he drove with a three wood and hit a five iron to the green.

Appropriately, Harbour Town Golf Links bears the name of the town in which it is located, which, within the past decade, has become something of a regular port of call not only for golfers, but also for yachtsmen, tennis buffs, second-home and condominium buyers. Less than sixteen years ago this instep of Hilton Head Island was a vast swamp, a wasteland filled with alligators and rattlesnakes. The very prospect of turning it into a deluxe community was a dream of Charles E. Fraser, a young lawyer, southern historian, conservationist, and then a struggling developer trying to keep the parent firm, Sea Pines Company, from sinking financially—all 5,200 acres of it—into the loam soil of South Carolina Low Country.

In 1961 you could have bought a half-acre ocean-front lot for $2,500 (now up to $100,000), but with the deed went a forty-page set of restrictions to protect the environment and to support Fraser's architectural tenet that all parts be subordinated to the whole. Within Sea Pines Plantation, all stop signs are painted green—as are mailboxes and fireplugs. Most houses and buildings have bleached cedar siding. The very first restriction not only set the tone of all the others, but irrevocably stated who was in control. It read that any plan or specification for a home can be disallowed by Fraser for any reason whatever.

Jack Nicklaus learning to play a course of his own making. On his way to winning the 1975 Heritage Classic, he studies a delicate chip shot on the treacherous 152-yard par-3 14th.

(Overleaf) The calm, unspoiled beauty of Harbour Town Golf Links being enjoyed by two scorekeepers and an out-of-contention threesome.

Uncompromising, operating more on expectations than cash, Fraser made more than one textile baron conform. When a buyer did not adhere to Fraser's environmental planning concepts, Fraser bought back the land. He was obsessed with his vision that Hilton Head would not be given over to the high-rise buildings, hotdog stands, and parking lots so common along the Atlantic coast.

In maintaining nature's balance, Fraser was Hilton Head's counterpart to Pebble Beach's Samuel Morse. When the first bulldozers came, roads often were routed around trees. Fraser once spent $50,000 to save a gigantic oak and have it transplanted. To keep the native alligators, he fed them huge chunks of meat. They stayed. He tried the same with the bald eagles, but they fled, as did most of the rattlesnakes. At the Harbour Town marina he used concrete bulkheads that cost $750,000, when he could have used steel bulkheads for $200,000.

However, unlike Morse, who maintained a disdain for hard work and perseverance, Fraser's main recreation has been work. He is constantly concerned with numerous environmental causes and with attracting to his communities a coterie of residents who share his view of environmental controls on Hilton Head. At first a few textile presidents, generals, and admirals came to Sea Pines—Air Force General Nathan Twining, for example—then active and retired corporate presidents. Among the property owners at Sea Pines there is now a higher ratio of men listed in *Who's Who* than at Princeton. From 1961 to 1971, Fraser earned the tidy sum of $20 million, along with sundry awards; in 1968, Sea Pines Plantation was the first recipient of the American Institute of Architects's "Cita-tion of Excellence in Private Community Planning."

Thus, as a resort community, Sea Pines has few peers in the United States, but as a resort operation with personable, efficient service, excellent cuisine, warm ambience, and those extra resort services, it still is a four or five handicap, compared to Mauna Kea or The Cloister at even scratch. The Hilton Head Inn (not a part of the Hilton hotel chain) is named after William Hilton, the English sea captain who discovered the island in 1663. It is a modest structure of three wings, with 200 rooms on the ocean front. There are ocean-front cottages, shops, three restaurants, a wide beach, pool, and a playground for children. The rooms are average in size but unimaginatively decorated—one notch up from a better motel. The food is average. "One reason they have so many oyster roasts," said a former employee, "is that it's pretty hard to mess one up." It is all very informal, coat and tie are not required of men for dinner.

The best way to enjoy Sea Pines is to rent a villa or second home, of which there are 950, for a grand total of 2,500 bedrooms, which in terms of the number of rooms makes Sea Pines the largest single resort in the Americas. Maid service is available at villas and second homes. A variety of locations are also available: ocean front, fairway, or lagoon. Have breakfast in and all other meals out. There are 13 restaurants, five cocktail lounges, 39 tennis courts, 14 swimming pools (not counting private ones), 4½ miles of beach, 11 miles of bicycle paths, and three marinas.

The best restaurant is at the Sea Pines Club. The dining room is large and airy, with floor-to-ceiling windows facing fairways and lagoons. The atmosphere is what you might expect to find at a better restaurant, as is the cuisine. The fish dishes, especially the she-crab soup, are the best. The Irish coffee is matched only by that at the Buena Vista in San Francisco. Reservations are required, as are coat and tie for men at dinner.

The fairways you will gaze upon are part of the Sea Marsh and Ocean courses, two of ten golf courses on Hilton Head, and guests at Sea Pines have entree to both, since Sea Marsh and Ocean are part of Sea Pines. They were the first courses built and are geared for the average player. Wide fairways sweep between villas and second homes. Lagoons and streams are the main hazard. While most courses pride themselves on long par 4s, Sea Marsh and Ocean offer good short par 4s. If you do not think a 289-yard par-4 dogleg left with a green the size of an elephant's ear is not demanding, just play the 2nd hole at Sea Marsh.

Just beyond Sea Pines is the Hilton Head Golf Club, the most rolling of all the courses on the island and the one with the most water, which comes into play on sixteen holes. From the championship tees, it measures 7,003 yards—definitely a driving course, as are the two at nearby Palmetto Dunes, another resort community. There is the long Robert Trent Jones course; and the new George Fazio course has out-of-bounds left on 16 holes and has two acres of sand on the 18th hole. It measures 6,800 yards from the championship tees and gets shorter, as there are four sets of tees. Though Palmetto Dunes does not have the best courses on the island, it has the best hotel, Hyatt on Hilton Head.

On the northern tip of the island are Port Royal Plantation's Barony and Robber's Row courses. They are routed over high ground on sandy soil, with fairways lined with tall pine and elms. The courses have the playing value of Sea Marsh and Ocean, not an odd coincidence, since all four were designed by George Cobb. The courses are not great, but Port Royal's courses have one advantage over the others on the island. After a heavy rain, all other courses remain soggy and virtually nonplayable for at least a day, while Port Royal's courses drain quickly and are playable in a matter of hours after a rain.

Thus one can spend a week on Hilton Head and never play the same course twice. As the sea calls sailors back, championship courses call golfers back. Moody and beguiling is Harbour Town, but nevertheless very infectious, even if par is as elusive as Garbo. It is one of America's few championship courses where one does not need the power of a Nicklaus. What one needs more is Nicklaus's caddie. Disappointingly, there are no caddies (none, in fact, on the entire island), and few courses need them more. For the first-time golfer, a caddie could reduce the score by almost half a dozen shots and an equal number of golf balls.

Summing up the course in his wry way, as only he could, was former PGA champion and now television commentator, Dave Marr, who during one round of the Heritage Classic walked up to a PGA official and said, "Look, I never complain about the rough being too long or about difficult pin placements, but I want to tell you that you sure have put the fairways in some strange places today." The Prince of Wales, who never played Harbour Town, but frequently played Stanley Thompson's course, Banff Springs, in Canada, told the architect almost the same thing, after slicing eight balls across the fairway into the Bow River on the par-3 12th hole.

MOUNTAIN RESORTS

BANFF SPRINGS
HOTEL
Banff, Canada

In every direction, as far as the eye can see, rise the Canadian Rockies. A skirt of green pines covers their lower slopes; above the tree line the smoke-colored rock is jagged and creased with ridges climbing toward odd-shaped peaks sculptured by harsh north winds. This is the view from almost every tee, green, and bunker of one of Canada's unique mountain courses, Banff Springs Golf Course, a layout of noble birth, said to be one of the very first to have cost more than $1 million to build, and one of the very few courses Winston Churchill ever played, which helped shape his complete disdain for the game of golf, leading him at one point to pronounce: "Golf is a game of putting little balls into little holes with instruments very ill-adapted for the purpose."

Churchill's summary of the game of golf was neither original nor new. He had, in fact, cribbed it word for word from H. G.

Hutchinson, in the *Badminton Library* (1893). Nonetheless, it has been an accurate description of golf at Banff. Besides cascading mountain streams, bunkers, thousands of lodge pines, silver willows,

Cornelius Van Horne, the man responsible for bringing such splendor to the Canadian Rockies. He headed the Canadian Pacific Railroad in the late 1800s. He once said of himself, "I eat all I can, I drink all I can, and I don't give a damn for anyone."

(*Left*) One of Canada's great mountain courses, the Banff Springs Golf Course, stretching over a terrain as flat as Pinehurst No. 2. The course's main hazards are its 134 bunkers. Shown here are the 2nd and 18th fairways, and looming like a great baronial castle in the background is the hotel.

and white birches, there are a wandering stray coyote, a herd of elk, and a pack of black bears. Many a golfer has had to putt through an elk print, but before he finds himself in such a strange circumstance, he must reach the green—a noble task indeed. More distracting and hazardous than the roaming wildlife are the bunkers—some 142 of them—with no fewer than 90 guarding the greens, or an average of five per green.

Such intense pride does the operator of the course, the Canadian Pacific Railroad, have in each bunker that several years ago, when architect Geoffrey Cornish designed a new nine (scheduled to open in 1978) and informed an official of the CPR that four bunkers could be eliminated from the regular course without destroying its character, his request was met with such wrath that the beleaguered Cornish was all but run out of town. The bunkers stayed.

It was the kind of decision that would have pleased the architect of the course, Stanley Thompson, who was a lusty, full-broth of a man of six feet and two hundred and fifty pounds, who enjoyed good scotch, good poker games, and busty women. A scratch golfer, he won the medal of the 1924 Canadian Amateur with a borrowed set of clubs, his own set of only five clubs having been stolen on the eve of the tournament.

About golf-course design, he once said, "The most beautiful courses—the ones where the greens invite your shots—are the ones which hew most closely to nature." His imagination was streaked with the artistic belief that art imitates life. And to him, women were very much part of life and golf. In designing the course at Jasper Park Lodge, 180 miles northwest of Banff, Thompson contoured the 9th fairway, a par 3, after the female torso. Guarding

the green are two massive breast-shaped mounds. He aptly named the hole Cleopatra.

Equally imaginative though less stimulating is a series of mounds on the right side of the 1st fairway at Banff that resembles an elephant's trunk. With his bunkering, Thompson also was nature-conscious. At Banff almost every bunker was designed in the shape of the mountain peak it faced, which has made for an almost endless variety of bunker configurations. There are crescents, bunkers with jagged edges, half-stars, and crown-shaped bunkers. That many of these shapes have found themselves in much newer courses is hardly surprising. Geoffrey Cornish was once an employee of Thompson's, and Thompson's partner in the early 1930s was a fledgling architect named Robert Trent Jones.

Uniquely among mountain courses, Banff, at an altitude of 4,200 feet, is a flat course—flatter than The Broadmoor's East and West courses, flatter than The Homestead's Cascade Course and even the Otesaga's Leatherstocking Course. And because Thompson believed that playing only nine holes was a cardinal sin, he placed the 9th hole far from the clubhouse. Like the Old Course at St. Andrews, Banff runs counterclockwise, forming an almost perfect U shape, measuring 6,729 yards from the championship tee (6,282 regular and 5,977 ladies'). On the outgoing nine there usually is a following wind. The incoming nine plays into the wind, and to add to the golfer's plight, the strength of the course is its last seven holes, beginning at the 12th hole, a 138-yard par 3 (112 yards regular and 105 ladies') with water flowing in front of the green and the Bow River cascading down the right side of the fairway. The sound of the rushing water has caused many a golfer to rush his backswing. One who rushed his backswing several times was the Prince of Wales, who once unroyally sliced eight balls into Bow River and later told Thompson he had designed the course all wrong.

A shortish par 5, two par 3s over 200 yards long, and three par 4s varying in length from 400 to 430 yards follow the 12th, with the hazardous Bow River on the right. The 18th, a par 4 of 425 yards (411 regular and 397 ladies') is the tenth-handicapped rated hole. Depending on how much one is attracted to sand or on one's ability to get out of sand, it can be easier or harder. There are 25 bunkers on the hole.

However, the most spectacular hole on the course—and probably the most photographed golf hole in all Canada—is the par-3 8th of 173 yards from the championship tee (137 yards regular and 82 ladies'). The championship tee, sitting on the top of a cliff surrounded by tall lodge pines, faces 9,838-foot-high Rundle Mountain. At the bottom of the mountain, 80 feet below the tee, is a large bell-shaped green surrounded by seven bunkers. Between the tee and the green is a crystal-clear pond called the Devil's Cauldron. In the 1920s and 1930s the Reverend Charles Gordon would stand on the banks of the pond and preach fire-and-brimstone sermons to Scottish Highland gatherings. He could not have picked a better spot, for the golfer needs all the help from above he can get and had better keep his head down and pray he hits the green or else he will have the devil to pay.

Having confronted the honest face of evil, the golfer is playing a course with redeeming aspects. The fairways are wide—

Adding another touch of royalty to the royal and ancient game is the Prince of Wales, who was a frequent though erratic golfer at Banff in the 1920s.

87

some 100 yards—and the openings to the greens are wide, except on the par 3s. The greens are neither slick nor contoured with subtle breaks. Putts do break away from the closest mountain, but not as severely as at The Broadmoor's courses.

The course is public, and during the summer play is slow, over five hours. Also, the course is maintained in only average condition. Greens are hard to hold; a ball hit directly to the pin will often bounce off into a bunker. Playing to the front portion of the green and taking a club less is better. One reason the course is not put into tournament condition is that neither a major nor a minor tournament has ever been played on it (it was a site of "Shell's Wonderful World of Golf"), because the course is part of 2,564-square-mile Banff National Park, and the Department of Indian and Northern Affairs discourages major athletic competition in its parklands. However, movie producers have found the rugged scenery exciting. Part of *River of No Return*, starring Marilyn Monroe and Robert Mitchum, was filmed on the Bow River in Banff. The department has not discouraged the use of caddies on the course, but the resort did in the late 1960s (there are golf cars and pull carts), a further sign of the changing policy of the resort.

The original Banff Springs Hotel opened April 1, 1888. It was a grand hostelry built by the Canadian Pacific Railroad as it was thrusting westward. It was the men of the railroad who promised that they would tie up "the rags and ends of Confederation" from British Columbia to the Maritimes. The splendor in the wilderness of Canada's Northwest inspired Cornelius Van Horne, once described as "the ablest railroad general of the world," who realized the great marketing possibilities of the Canadian Rockies and built a small hotel in Banff to attract a wealthy international set. Thirty years to the day after the original hotel opened, it burned down; in 1919, the current hotel opened.

Its architecture has been described as "Scottish baronial castle," a style that reflects Van Horne's nature quite well. His self-indulgence was legendary. He said of himself, "I eat all I can, I drink all I can, and I don't give a damn for anyone."

Inside, the architecture ranges eclectically from medieval Gothic to Tudor to even a little Rocky Mountain Hunting Lodge. One has only to walk under one of the many stone arches to find oneself in a massive room with stone floors, refectory tables, ancient armor, and tapestries hanging from wrought-iron balconies.

The main lobby is paneled in dark walnut and rises two stories. On the west wall hangs a faded banner made by a contemporary of Florence Nightingale from pieces of uniforms worn in the Crimean War. On the south wall hangs a shaggy bison's head, and on the north wall the head of a fourteen-point elk.

In the hotel's heyday, between World Wars I and II, the lobby was graced with nobility of various ranks. More prominent than a bison's head was the turban-wrapped head of a certain maharajah, who arrived for a week's stay with a harem of thirty. He took two of the thirty large suites (the best rooms) and made his intentions appear epic when on the first night he ordered that the two double beds be pushed

A tender moment in the rugged adventure movie *River of No Return*, filmed at Banff. Matt Calder, played by Robert Mitchum, offers coffee and trust to Kay Weston, played by Marilyn Monroe.

together. The staff did not blink an eye, until it was discovered that the potentate was using the two beds only for himself and that the women were left to sleep on the floor.

It was a formal era in the hotel's history, complete with the harmonious big-band sound of Benny Goodman echoing through the stone-floored halls, while in the kitchen came the clanking of pots and pans thrown by a tempestuous chef whose quite literal downfall occurred one evening as he passed the dessert room and, noticing a girl not baking to his perfection, said, "Dammit, girl, whoever taught you to bake doesn't have the brains of an ox."

"Aye, you taught me," said the girl, "and don't speak to me that way."

It was enough to ignite the chef's highly inflammable temper. Brandishing the ladle he held in his hand, he vaulted into the dessert room, leaped over a counter, and landed ceremoniously on a lower counter filled with 360 dishes of gelatin, each topped with homemade whipped cream and a maraschino cherry.

The desserts are no longer topped with homemade whipped cream, because they are not as lavish, but neither are the entrées, appetizers, or soups. Most of the food is tasteless, prepared badly, and served worse. Of the three dining rooms, the Alhambra, Alberta, and Rob Roy, the Alberta is the best, serving food a notch better than your fast-food outlet.

If one gets struck with the nagging feeling that one is not truly a welcome guest but rather a number divided and subdivided to fill one of the 600 rooms and help pay the $4,000-per-day cost of running the hotel, this is an accurate feeling, not one bestowed by the largesse of the hotel, but rather by the fact that the resort has become a stopover station—a monument to see for what it once was—for a two- or three-day stay for those taking train or bus tours through Canada's Northwest. The atmosphere is charged with constant bustling.

The best way to enjoy the resort is to use it exactly as it now is intended, as a stopover. For a golf tour of the best courses of Canada's Northwest, the best time to go is July through September. A few days at Banff will suffice. The next journey, for the same amount of time, is to Jasper Park Lodge, smaller and better than Banff Springs Hotel. Make sure to stop at Lake Louise on your way, but avoid staying at the hotel. A good two days' drive from Jasper, 555 miles southwest, is Vancouver, where the best hotel is the Hotel Vancouver. The best course to play, one of the best seaside courses in the Americas, is Capilano Golf and Country Club, which extends playing privileges to members of clubs of the Royal Canadian Golf Association and the USGA, but only on a time-available basis, with only two guest foursomes allowed each day. All three courses, Banff, Jasper, and Capilano, were designed by Thompson, who was pioneering Canadian golf-course architecture as Donald Ross was doing in the United States. By the mid-1920s, Ross's courses at Pinehurst already were famous, as was his Scioto Country Club Course in Columbus, Ohio. And a course that was slowly gaining recognition for its beauty and its slick, undulating greens was Ross's course at The Broadmoor, in Colorado Springs, Colorado.

The fine Canadian golfer Stan Leonard hits a smooth short-iron shot over a pond called the Devil's Cauldron on the dramatically beautiful 175-yard par-3 8th hole in a match against Jackie Burke, Jr., for the television series *Shell's Wonderful World of Golf.*

THE BROADMOOR
Colorado Springs, Colorado

Initially, the Broadmoor course was built to be a good but not a great course, one of august beauty that would entice well-to-do Easterners to come west, to breathe the clear, dry Colorado air, to explore a rugged land, and to see what had lured one of the resort's founders, Spencer Penrose, from Philadelphia in 1891. In 1916 he set out to build the most lavish resort in Colorado Springs—then known as "the Newport-of-the-Rockies." He immediately hired Donald Ross to design an eighteen-hole course. The land Ross selected was in the scenic foothills of Cheyenne Mountain, and he routed his holes up and down the hills among the spruce, pine, American maple, and aspen trees. What his creation lacked in championship quality was compensated for by the majestic surroundings. Along the western perimeter of the course soar the Rockies, and on almost any clear day even in late June, you can stare toward the moun-

tains into a hard blue sky and see snow-capped peaks.

Colorado Springs no longer is called "the Newport-of-the-Rockies," though it is spangled with both new and old money, and there is still an avenue called "Millionaire's Row"—mansion after mansion built by those who had struck it rich in the

The coup de grâce: Nicklaus sinks an eight-foot putt on the last green to defeat Charlie Coe one up.

(*Left*) Even when Jack Nicklaus was nineteen, his concentration was intense. Nicklaus explodes from a bunker in the finals of the 1959 U.S. Amateur, played over The Broadmoor's East Course. A portent of things to come: Nicklaus's first-round victim was Robert Tyre Jones III, son of the great Bobby Jones.

93

gold rush of the 1890s in Cripple Creek. But The Broadmoor is becoming something of a Pinehurst-in-the-Rockies. It has not one but two first-class courses—a third, co-designed by Arnold Palmer, just opened; it has its own invitational tournaments—one for men, dating back to 1922, and one for women, since 1942. A Curtis Cup Match, five NCAA golf championships, and two U.S. Amateurs have been played there. The Broadmoor enjoys the rare distinction of having had the Amateur played on both its courses. In 1959 it was played over the East Course (though several holes of the nine-hole West Course were incorporated to make a sterner test) and in 1967 over the West Course. There is also a boutique called A Short Story which not only employs keen buyers and sellers but is a colony for some of the finest women golfers in America; three former winners of the Women's U.S. Amateur grace the sales floor, to say nothing of the fairways.

Women play the East Course at 6,081 yards and the West at 5,662 yards; from the regular men's tees, the courses measure 6,550 and 6,309 yards respectively. Each plays to just over 7,000 yards for the championship tees. The East is more forgiving off the tee, with wide fairways and only 10 fairway bunkers; it puts the premium on the shot to plateau greens guarded by deep bunkers—there are 45 greenside bunkers in all. The West Course is hillier, with several holes crawling up the mountainside. The fairways are narrow and severely bunkered, but there are fewer greenside bunkers. Neither course possesses a memorable hole or stretch of holes. There are very good holes, like the par-3 9th on the East Course, 220 yards downhill to a large green surrounded by five deep bunkers. There is the 11th on the West Course, an-

other par-3 downhill, over a pond to a green nestled in a forest of spruce. The 15th hole on the East Course is the best of the 54 holes. It measures 430 yards from the championship tee (385 yards regular and 340 ladies') and is a slight dogleg right that cannot be cut; a pond stretches across the bend in the fairway. A drive must be hit down the middle or left side of the fairway to leave a clear shot to the flat green.

Thus the difficulty of the courses lies not in a stretch of holes heroic in design, but rather in the natural elements of over-mile-high golf. The courses sit at an altitude of 6,000 feet, and in the thin air the ball flies farther—seven percent farther. A 225-yard drive, therefore, becomes a drive of 240 yards, putting an added premium on the club selection. As on most mountain courses, all putts break away from the mountains. The trick, of course, is to know how much. Also, because of the contours of the adjoining terrain, a putt that appears to be level is not. The greens on the East and West courses are not only large, but fast, faster than any championship green, except Oakmont's. The usual advice from The Broadmoor's pro shop is that guests coming to the resort for the first time should practice putting on a tin roof.

Of course, Robert Trent Jones would rather be seen in his underwear than putting on a tin roof. When he went to The Broadmoor in 1957 to remodel Ross's East Course and continue his work on the West Course, three members persuaded Jones to play a friendly match with them one morning. But when it came time to team up, a problem occurred. Since Jones had never played the complete course before and a rather sizable Nassau was at stake, he was not the most desirable partner. One man resolved the problem by going into the pro shop and asking the pro, Ed Dudley, how he thought Jones would do on the greens. "Don't take Jones," Dudley replied. "He has never putted these greens. He'll three-putt all the way around."

The man returned to the tee and, when another member said he would take Jones as a partner, told Jones what Dudley had said to him.

"If I can't read a green," roared Jones, "who the hell can?"

Jones not only read the greens almost perfectly, but putted with an uncanny ability, three-putting only once, and finished with a one over par 73.

When he returned to the pro shop, Dudley said "Trent, how in God's name did you do it?"

"Well, Ed," answered Jones, "whenever I lined up a putt, I pulled my golf cap down just above my eyes, to block out any view of the mountains that might distort the line of the putt. It was simple, Ed."

The first tournament that brought nationwide golfing prominence to The Broadmoor and also to the eventual winner was the 1959 U.S. Amateur. When 199 of the country's finest amateur golfers arrived that September, it was as difficult to win the Amateur as to become a Broadway star, and the Broadway adage held true: to become an overnight star takes years of hard work and lucky breaks. The cast was steeped with veteran performers. There was the venerable Chick Evans, back for the forty-seventh time; defending champion Charlie Coe; Harvie Ward; Billy Joe Patton; Dick Chapman; Bill Campbell; Bill Hyndman III; Bob Gardner; and Drs. Ed Updegraff and Bud Taylor. The chorus consisted of talented youth, whose destinies would cross and change the direction of golf in the world. There was a striving young blond attorney named Mark McCormack; defending British Amateur winner Deane

Beman; an insurance agent from Indiana named Pete Dye; 1956 Southern California Amateur Al Geiberger; and 19-year-old Jack Nicklaus, competing in his fourth Amateur and sixth major championship.

Under match play, first rounds in the U.S. Amateur are always full of surprises, and the 1959 event was no exception. Dr. Ed Updegraff was defeated, as were Al Geiberger and Mark McCormack. Coe won easily, as did Nicklaus. But Nicklaus's victory rang with irony, a portent of what was to come. Nicklaus had defeated Robert Tyre Jones III, son of the great Bobby Jones.

Holding the trophy of his first major championship, Nicklaus receives congratulations from runner-up Coe. Such high-quality golf was played in the finals that more than a decade later, after Nicklaus had won two U.S. Opens, three Masters, a PGA Championship and dozens of other tournaments, he said of his match with Coe: "It was the most exhilarating and exhausting duel I have been engaged in."

As the week wore on, many of the favorites fell victim to the slick greens. In the second round, Deane Beman went, and so did Bill Campbell and Bob Gardner. In the quarterfinals, Coe defeated Hyndman, Nicklaus, and Dick Yost. Joseph C. Dey, then executive director of the USGA, who is always on the scene at major championships, is fond of recalling what the youthful Nicklaus was like. "Whenever Jack had time," Dey says, "he would talk about the rules of golf. He was constantly surprised that they contained a lot of rights rather than prohibitions for the player."

In the finals it was Nicklaus and Coe, in what has been described as one of the classic matches. Coe had won the U.S. Amateur twice and a year before had finished thirteenth in the U.S. Open and sixth in the Masters. Earlier that year Nicklaus had captured the North and South and Trans-Mississippi amateurs. After the first three holes, Nicklaus was two under par, but for all his efforts was one down in the match. Coe had gone birdie, birdie, birdie. At the end of the first 18 holes, Coe stood two up. At the 21st hole (the current 18th on the East Course), a long, straight 573-yard par 5 with a pond fronting the green, Nicklaus reached the green in two, birdied the hole, and evened the match. Over the next fourteen holes, the lead changed five times, with neither player gaining more than a one-up margin. At the 35th hole, with a precious one-up lead, Nicklaus bogied, and Coe parred to even the match. Both drove perfectly on the 36th (the current 15th on the East Course) with three woods. Coe was then first to hit, and struck an eight-iron shot; the ball hit pin-high but bounced hard to the back of the green, into the high USGA rough. It was Coe's first of two errors on the hole. Nicklaus hit a nine-iron shot eight feet short of the pin.

The difficulty of Coe's third shot was reported incisively in *Golf Magazine* by Ross Goodner: "Coe faced a shot that none of us has the skill to play, the kind where an easy stroke leaves the ball right there in the heavy grass, and a crisp stroke sends the ball skidding clear across the green. However, Charley played it with the touch of a Willie Hoppe nursing the shot down the rail, and the ball rolled gently down the green only to die right on the edge of the cup. It not only almost was one of the great shots, it was one of the great shots."

Then Coe committed his second error. Instead of leaving the ball there or asking Nicklaus whether he could tap in, Coe marked his ball. Suddenly realizing his error, he looked at Joe Dey, then at Nicklaus, because then, under the rules of match play, he had no right to lift the ball, and Nicklaus, ever conscious of the rules, could have called the infraction. Instead, he conceded the putt to Coe. Nicklaus then began to look over his eight-footer as he always studies such putts, took his stance, and stroked the ball into the middle of the cup. He had won his first of two U.S. Amateurs and his first major championship. More than a decade later, after he had won two U.S. Opens, three Masters, a PGA championship, and dozens of other tournaments, he said of his match with Coe, "It was the most exhilarating and exhausting duel I have ever been engaged in."

However, Nicklaus was not the first athlete to give a sporting luster to The Broadmoor. When the resort opened in 1918, its managers hired the current PGA champion, "Long Jim" Barnes, whose $15,000 fee for the summer made him the highest-paid golfing professional. He promptly golfed himself into successfully defending his PGA title the following year. In the 1920s Jack Dempsey trained at The Broadmoor for one of his fights with Gene Tunney. And in the 1950s President Eisenhower was a frequent visitor and playing partner of pro Ed Dudley. In the 1960s the resort's skating rink, the World Arena, became the training center for figure skaters, including Peggy Fleming and Janet Lynn. If golf dominates the resort in the summer, skating does in the winter. The World Figure Skating Championship has been held there six times, and the NCAA Hockey Championship eleven times.

The man responsible for giving The Broadmoor its sporting character is William Thayer Tutt, a stocky, ruddy-faced man in his mid-sixties. He presently heads El Pomar Foundation, a conglomerate that operates The Broadmoor and sundry other firms. A devout sportsman, he is a director of the United States Olympic Committee and president of the Amateur Hockey Association of the United States. He is the grandson of the other founder of the resort, Charles Leaming Tutt.

In 1891 Spencer Penrose, fresh out of Harvard, informed his wealthy Philadelphia family he was going west to seek his fortune. He was soon regarded by his parents as the black sheep of the family for preferring the west to the east, but Penrose was determined, and he persuaded Charles Tutt to join him as partner. However, Spec, as Coloradans called him, soon found the going financially rough, and within a year after his arrival in Colorado Springs he wired his brother Bois for $1,500 so he could get into a mining deal. His brother sent him $150 instead and sternly warned against such a deal. But Spec would not be denied his fortune. He struck gold in Cripple Creek. Years later, he returned to Philadelphia and handed his brother $75,000 in gold coins. The amazed Bois told Spencer he had not gone into the deal and had only

sent him $150. "That's why," said Spec, "I'm only giving you $75,000. If you'd sent me $1,500, I would be giving you three quarters of a million dollars."

For Spec had not only struck gold, he had parlayed his strikes from gold into copper in Utah and formed the Kennecott Copper Corporation. Legend is that Spec Penrose built The Broadmoor because the management of the Antlers Hotel in Colorado Springs took exception to his shooting a revolver in the bar. Outraged over what he considered such unwestern protocol, he set out to build a hotel where his guests and friends, usually indistinguishable in his lifetime, could do as they pleased, which included some spirited gambling. Sparing no expense at the grand opening in July 1918, Penrose not only invited most of America's most distinguished and wealthy families, he rented a complete train to bring his guests from New York and Chicago. Among the guests was John D. Rockefeller, Jr.

Architecturally, his hotel is often described as millionaire baronial. In fact, it is Italian Renaissance, pale pink soaring nine stories high, backdropped by the purple Rockies. Inside there is della Robbia tile, an Italian-marble staircase, hand-painted beams, intricate plaster latticework ceilings, palm courts, and four dining rooms. Two of the dining rooms are casual—The Tavern, with a glassed-in garden, and The Golden Bee, a reconstructed eighteenth-century English pub, complete with issues of *Punch*. More formal dining is at the main dining room, with windows facing Cheyenne Lake. It was here that the renowned writer Lucius Beebe was banned because

(*Overleaf*) Barbara McIntire watches the flight of a drive during the 1962 Curtis Cup Matches, played at The Broadmoor. The United States beat Great Britain eight to one.

The Broadmoor Golf Club in the 1920s. Its creator was Spencer Penrose, a man who had discovered gold in Cripple Creek. He wanted his resort to be "permanent and perfect."

The Broadmoor today, and the green of the 430-yard par-4 15th hole.

the maitre d' judged his McAfee riding boots, whipcord breeches, and English tweed jacket incorrect attire for dining. Regulations have changed somewhat, but men still must wear a coat and tie in the dining rooms and lounges after 6 p.m. With its Edwardian decor, the Penrose Room is the most elegant, situated on the ninth floor of the new Broadmoor South, a complex of 234 rooms; the restaurant offers dinner dancing, views of the mountains, and far away, the twinkling lights of Colorado Springs. The ribs of beef and fresh mountain trout are the excellent specialties. Breakfast and lunch are served in the golf clubhouse, the resort's oldest building and one-time gambling casino. The quick and courteous service has not changed through the years. "We tell the staff," Tutt said, voicing one of his operating principles, "we haven't anything to sell but service." Of the 650 employees, one-third have been there over a decade. "I came for the season," says one bartender, "and stayed seventeen years." Several have been there almost from the beginning. "I was hired as temporary help," says one maitre d' of forty-five years' employment, "and nobody's ever told me I was permanent." In June 1968, when the resort celebrated its fiftieth anniversary, the feast was planned by the same chef who had supervised the hotel's opening in 1918.

Unlike most resorts, The Broadmoor offers nightly entertainment other than year-old movies. Besides a piano player who plays excellent ragtime in the Lake Terrace Lounge, there is the appearance in the International Center of top names in show business, concert pianists, stand-up comedians, and even a folk-rock group or two.

There are 600 rooms in the main building and two wings; there are 60 two-room suites. The best accommodations are the penthouse suites in the Broadmoor West. None of the rooms is small or cramped, because when Penrose started to build his hotel he said, "I want it to be permanent and perfect."

Unfortunately, Donald Ross's course at The Broadmoor was neither permanent nor perfect. It was not a unique situation in the 1920s, when most resort developers had yet to grasp the great promotional value of being able to advertise that they had a "championship course." Samuel Morse of Pebble Beach and the Tuftses of Pinehurst were exceptions. But with the advent of big-time tournament golf—televised to millions —resort developers began having courses designed specifically for tournament golf. Greens set in natural amphitheaters became more common, as did wide areas between fairways for galleries. Some developers succeeded. At the Doral Country Club, Alfred Kaskel had the now-famous Blue Course built for a tournament—the Doral Open, which began in 1962.

In 1960 the owner of The Concord, Kiamesha Lake, New York, hired Houston architect Joe Finger and told him to design a championship course that Palmer or Nicklaus would not chop up. Neither has had the opportunity, because the course has yet to be the site of a big televised tournament. Nonetheless, "the monster," as it is justly called because of its vast length and treacherous water holes, has gained a solid reputation as one of the best courses in the northeast and has helped make The Concord a major golfing resort.

THE CONCORD

Kiamesha Lake, New York

At first glance, the 10th hole at The Concord's Championship Course appears to be neither permanent nor perfect. Kiamesha Creek runs down the right side of the fairway, then cuts diagonally forty yards in front of the green and flows into a big blue lake that borders the left side of the fairway. Even in the heart of a dry summer, it looks as though both will swell over their banks and engulf the whole fairway, the 11,000-square-foot green, and four bunkers, a happening that would delight thousands of golfers. For the hole is not the perfect one with which to begin the incoming nine.

The 10th tee is perched near the top of a high hill, and the golfer looks down to the fairway below. The more he looks, the narrower the fairway seems. There is water everywhere, and where there is no water, there is sand. Soon the fairway begins to look like a narrow green ribbon tied to a distant green 419 yards from the championship tee (376 regular; no ladies'). First the

golfer is asked to hit his longest and best drive, preferably one drawing slightly, as the fairway doglegs around the lake. This done, he must hit a bold second shot over Kiamesha Creek and over two bunkers

Jackie Burke, Jr., literally burning up the course. Serving as a consultant to golf course architect Joe Finger, Burke is about to drive from a makeshift tee on the 10th hole to determine whether the routing of Kiamesha Creek across the fairway would be too penalizing for the average golfer.

(*Left*) The beautiful but often troublesome 417-yard par-4 10th hole of The Concord Championship Golf Course. The landing area for the drive is actually much wider than it appears from the tee.

guarding the front of an enormous green filled with heavy swells. In short, The Concord's 10th may be one of the scariest 10th holes in the United States. And making it even harder is the fact that from the tee the golfer can look over the tops of the tall evergreens, oaks, and maples behind the green and see more water on the par-3 11th and par-5 12th holes.

So the 10th hole does not serenely lure the golfer with hidden delights of what awaits. On almost any other course, views of such fierce forthcoming dangers might send the golfer to the 19th hole or to the gin-rummy table, but at The Concord, the view is needed to keep the golfer in the bold frame of mind he needs to play the incoming nine.

After all, he already has played a long, tough outgoing nine on which he had to lean into four- and five-wood shots to get home on par 4s. He also has played three memorable holes—a par 5, a par 3, and a par 4. The longest and best of the par 5s is the 4th hole, measuring 586 yards from the championship tee (557 regular). Oaks, elms, and evergreens line the right side of the 80-foot-long tee. The first 200 yards of the fairway plays slightly uphill, and the golfer must keep his drive on the right side of the fairway, though the hole is a dogleg left. Beginning at the crest of the hill and running diagonally across the fairway is a lake, and a long drive that draws too much will catch the front edge. A drive just short of it will leave a 205-yard second shot over the left side of the lake to a narrow stretch of fairway, bordered on the right side by a long finger of the lake and on the left side by woods. The golfer who plays more cautiously can play around the lake, but instead of a third shot with a short iron, he will be hitting a long or midiron to a large green guarded in the front by a steep-walled bunker. Though the par-3 11th and 14th holes play over water, the hardest of the par 3s is the 7th hole. The tee is slightly elevated in a funnel of evergreens and elms; from the back of the tee to the back of the green, the hole measures 243 yards. To the front of the green from the regular championship tee the hole plays to 224 yards (201 from the regular tee). The fairway gradually rises to a green elevated 15 feet above the fairway and fortified by a deep bunker in front and on the right side. The green itself is 34 yards deep and slopes slightly from right to left. The shot, all carry, calls for anything, if the back is strong, from a full four wood to a driver, and preferably hit with a slight fade, as left of the green there is a rock ledge above a steep bank and thick woods. In the various men's and women's tournaments played on the course, the 7th has received its share of complaints. The players said that when the pin was set up front they could not see the exact location. Many took a club too much and ended up in the bunker guarding the rear of the green.

The 432-yard par-4 9th (422 yards from the regular tee) received more complaints. The hole plays uphill for the first half, then doglegs left. The tee is open except for a large maple on the left side. From the tee, the golfer sees a large fairway bunker on the left side at the crest of the hill. The ideal drive, some 230 yards, should be slightly right of the bunker, leaving an open shot to the green. A drive pushed too much means you must negotiate a large twin pine in the middle of the fairway, just 54 yards in front of the green, which is kidney-shaped and 50 feet deep.

Four years after the course opened a pro-am was staged, and pro Tommy Bolt was asked after he finished the second round two over par whether he thought the tree was properly placed. "It's in a perfect position," proclaimed the typically angry Bolt, "to hang the course's architect from!"

During the same pro-am an even angrier Jim Ferree, on his way to a 36-hole score of 11 over par, hit a good drive and then tried to hit a five-iron shot over the top of the pine: the ball caught a top limb and fell straight down. As Ferree approached to hit his third shot he started to curse the tree; suddenly he stopped 30 paces in front of it and threw his five iron at the top limbs. However, the five iron went where the ball should have gone, completely over the top. It is one of the dubious records held on the 9th.

Venting such fury may be the best way to approach the 10th hole. Such an approach will be with either a caddie or a golf car, as there are no pull carts. The Concord's Championship Course is one of the few courses where golf cars cannot be driven on the fairways; they must at all times remain on the cart paths, one reason the course is always in excellent condition. It is the wise golfer who, not wishing to slow down play and still undecided over club selection for his next shot, leaves his golf car with several clubs and also a ball retriever in hand. Water comes into play twelve times, twice on three holes. The cruel fact is that there are 34 acres of water, and each year a skin diver dredges 30,000 balls from the eight lakes.

The hole where more water comes into play than on any other is the controversial 17th. It is one of only two holes that play under 400 yards from the championship tees; the 17th just makes it, playing to 399 yards (381 from the regular tee). Evergreens and oaks border the right side of the long tee. Ten yards in front of the tee runs a branch of Kiamesha Creek. Standing on the tee and looking at a landing area only

Architect Finger on the fairway of the 432-yard par-4 9th. In the middle of the fairway is a twin pine. Four years after the course opened, when pro Tommy Bolt finished a pro-am tournament at two over par, he was asked whether he thought the tree was properly placed. "It's in a perfect position," proclaimed a typically angry Bolt, "to hang the architect from."

(*Overleaf*) The very controversial 399-yard par-4 17th. The fairway is S-shaped, with water on both sides. The two-tiered green, fifty feet long, is protected by six bunkers.

105

40 yards wide, the golfer also looks at how to get there, and a frightening sight it is. The fairway is S-shaped, and for the first 270 yards it is flanked on both sides by two lakes. The highly punitive character of the hole is that it will punish the aggressive and the cautious player equally. In brief, no matter how the golfer plays the hole, his drive must be perfect, or splash. Playing aggressively, the golfer can drive over the lake on the left; it is a 210-yard carry, but the distant shoreline runs diagonally from right to left. A 230-yard drive that hooks too much will catch the lake. The same drive pushed too much will catch the lake on the right. Playing safely, the golfer can drive to the narrow fairway, best done with a four iron, but if he hooks or slices, he will catch either lake. A perfectly hit four-iron shot will then leave another long iron shot to the most severely bunkered green on the course, a two-tiered green 50 feet long, protected by six bunkers.

Though complaints about the harsher aspects of the hole have reached The Concord's owner and general manager, Ray Parker, an assertive cigar-smoking man in his early sixties who now rarely plays golf, he refuses to change the hole. "I want people to talk about it," he once said sternly. "If we ease up too much, we'll be just another golf course." He then points with pride to confirming statistics to prove that the hole is not too difficult. During the first pro-am tournament, records were kept on how many of the sixteen pros decided to drive over the left lake. Fourteen did, and nine made the fairway.

Ray Parker is responsible for what The Concord's Championship Course is, especially for its stress on power and aggressive play. In 1960 he hired Houston-based golf-course architect Joe Finger, and at their first meeting Parker told him exactly what he wanted. "I want a golf course," Parker said, lighting a cigar, "that Arnold Palmer and Jack Nicklaus can't chop up. Just build us the greatest golf course in the world." Finger reflected for a moment, then replied, "Mr. Parker, that type of course would be entirely too tough for the average resort golfer, not to mention some of the best amateurs."

"Dammit, just build the course and leave the rest to me," barked Parker, relighting his cigar. "We already have a resort course, the International Course, and a nine-hole course, the Challenger. Give me a course that'll be the Pebble Beach of mountain courses."

Construction of the course took three years and cost $1.5 million. And to help carry out Parker's concept, Jimmy Demaret and Jackie Burke were hired as consultants. They hit drives from makeshift tees to make sure hazards would not be unfairly placed. Finger, to make sure his course would not be chopped up by Palmer or Nicklaus, used all 267 acres, designing a long course, then one of the longest in the United States. From the back of the championship tees he stretched the course to 7,780 yards, but designed it to play from the regular championship tees at 7,205 yards. A third set of tees was built, further reducing the length to a mere 6,793 yards, which is the best length for the average golfer to play it from.

But from any length, the course, which rightfully has been called "the monster," has produced numerous bets in the New York Metropolitan area. One is that a seven handicapper could not break 85 on it his first try. A foursome, not from New York but from Texas, arrived one day and got into a match with some spirited betting. The worst player had a four handicap. Not one broke 90. The competitive course record from the championship tees is two 67s; the highest recorded score is 169. The dubious record for the most balls lost on the 10th and 11th holes is held by Sammy Davis, Jr., who plunked an even dozen into the ponds. Owner Ray Parker holds one of the more extravagant records of any builder. During the construction of the course, three times a week he would drive down from the hotel and onto his course. In the wake of bulldozers and tractors, he would drive up and down the hills. In three years he destroyed the wheel alignment, shock absorbers, and countless tires on four Cadillacs.

In 1968 the first bona-fide tournament was played on the course: the Ladies' Concord Invitational. The women professionals played the course from 6,900 yards to a par 77. Only the winner, Shirley Englehorn, broke par for 54 holes, with a stunning 230. A year later the LPGA Championship was played there on a course with a new set of tees that reduced the length to 6,306 yards and the par to 73. No one broke par for four rounds. Winner Betsy Rawls won with a one over par 293, and there were only five rounds under 300. In 1971, the Liggett & Myers Concord Invitational, a second tour tournament, was played there. The pros played it from 7,205 yards, par 72. Again, no one broke par for 72 holes. Winner John Lotz picked up first-prize money of $12,000 with a 289. The course also has been the site of three New York State Men's Amateur championships.

It has changed little since it opened in October 1964, the most obvious change being the flow of the holes. The nines have been reversed. The notorious 10th hole used to be the first hole.

Both nines begin and end at the clubhouse, a rambling two-story motel-like building overlooking the course. It is where

the serious golfer will want to stay. It has 42 rooms; it is a comfortable and sporting place with a large bar whose floor-to-ceiling windows face the practice putting green. The restaurant serves breakfast and lunch.

Dinner is served at The Concord Hotel, a massive hostelry that rears up like a modern airline terminal with a swimming pool. It is equally busy and impersonal. Nonetheless, guests come to the resort year after year, and even generation after generation. To many it is an institution; they would not vacation elsewhere.

The resort was built by another rich man, Arthur Winarick, who amassed a small fortune as founder of Jeris Hair Tonic and Powder. He was a spirited and aggressive businessman, who after acquiring a fortune also acquired the attitude that he should have the best of everything. That The Concord since its beginning until the early 1960s was known as a very dressy hotel was none of Winarick's doing, for one of the few things on which he would spend as little money as possible was his own clothes. He was an abominably bad dresser.

Legend is that before he founded The Concord he went to vacation at what now has become the resort's chief rival in the Catskills, Grossinger's. He arrived at the front desk dressed in old, wrinkled clothes and in need of a shave. The registration clerk took one look at him and said, "I'm sorry, we have no reservations in the name of Winarick." Arthur Winarick argued that he had made reservations, but the clerk stood his ground, and Winarick went off to another hotel. The following summer he purchased the Kiamesha Ideal Hotel, a resort catering solely to families.

As times changed, so did the hotel. Originally a three-story structure, five stories were added. A new wing was added, and then another, until finally, in the late 1950s,

The perfect follow-through of pro Betsy Rawls as she drove to victory in the final round of the 1969 LPGA Championship, played over "the monster." Although the course was reduced for the women from the usual 7,205 yards to a mere 6,306 yards, no one broke par for seventy-two holes.

the total number of rooms was 1,250. The executive rooms with twin baths are the best, but all the rooms are large, with twin beds. A full house is just over 2,500 guests, which the hotel can easily accommodate. Its nightclub holds 3,300 people and the dining room seats 3,000, a figure to which Winarick pointed proudly.

When the initial plans for the Championship Course were being discussed, the resort's pro at that time, Jimmy Demaret, and architect Joe Finger were having dinner there with several wealthy associates of Demaret's. When Winarick came into the dining room, he spotted Demaret and came over to the table. Demaret, always a gracious host, introduced Winarick to his associates. Quickly the conversation turned to golf courses, and Winarick started boasting that he was going to have one of the largest golfing complexes in the United States, 45 holes. When one of Demaret's associates said he owned a couple of golf courses, Winarick said, "How many?"

"Five," said the man.

"Where?" asked Winarick.

"Chicago."

"All in one place?" asked Winarick.

"Yes, ninety holes," answered the man.

Winarick, knowing he would not have the largest golfing facility in the United States, was suddenly crestfallen. But after a few moments of looking around the dining room he asked, "How many people does your dining room seat?"

"Four hundred," answered the man.

"Four hundred!" roared Winarick. "Hell, our men's room seats more than that!"

The story has provided comedians who come to play The Concord with endless material. Another source of material is the food. Jokes are not made about the quality, which is good, but the quantity, which is copious. Annually, the hotel serves over 2¼ million meals, using 450 tons of meat and over 4 million eggs. What accounts for such staggering figures is that guests can eat as much as they want. They can have everything on the menu, including all the entrées, at no extra charge. Though there is a wide variety of entrées, dishes incorporating lobster, shrimp, pork and bacon are not served.

Except for those in Las Vegas, The Concord is without peer among resort hotels at providing the guests with the best after-dinner entertainers from Broadway and television. Before shows, or instead of them, guests can go to a variety of bars; there is the Night Owl for singles only, and a discothèque for teenagers only. The main nightclub, which holds 3,300 people, is the Imperial Room, and it is packed whenever the likes of Diahann Carroll, Tom Jones, or Sammy Davis, Jr., perform. And for those entertainers on the way up, The Concord is one of *the* places to play in the Borscht Belt. The comedians who got their start at The Concord include Alan King, Buddy Hackett and Joey Bishop.

They return over Christmas week, New Year's week, Easter, or any long weekend. And as is the tradition at The Concord, when they leave that night or the next day they depart through the main lobby to sign autographs, a procedure that can take an hour, as the lobby at any time of day or night is usually jammed with guests.

The long lobby looks as though it were encased in marble. "It's a mausoleum," said one long-time guest. Others have described its decor as neo-Catskill with smatterings of Miami Beach. Though the lobby has been redesigned, redecorated, and repainted so many times that any definite architectural theme has been lost, it justly reflects the management's view that function—providing a place where guests can walk and talk and sit—take precedence over form and that order and grace and grandeur are things of a past era. The management of The Homestead cringes at such viewpoints, but then The Homestead is one resort that proudly testifies that it catered to such illustrious figures as George Washington, Thomas Jefferson, and Alexander Hamilton.

THE HOMESTEAD

Hot Springs, Virginia

The lobby of The Homestead is called the Great Hall. It is a room of grandeur and grace, soaked in the soft white light from 18 crystal chandeliers and 10 high windows that make the hall appear even longer than its 240 feet. Marching down either side of the hall are eight Corinthian columns. At the north end ticks an antique grandfather clock that has chimed in every hour since the present hotel and hall were opened in 1903. The clock's face stares at 26 overstuffed chairs, a concert grand piano, and on the west wall, two fireplaces which, in keeping with a Homestead tradition, crackle with roaring fires even on the hottest days of August.

Walking through the lobby, one senses a great feeling of order and tradition, a place where change grinds slowly against the millstone of the past. The days are gone when the black waiters in the dining room carried trays on their heads in order to leave their hands free to serve; but it was not until 1968 that the younger waiters, feeling the policy was demeaning, successfully

(Left) The 371-yard par-4 6th hole on The Homestead's Cascades Course, site of forty-five Virginia Men's State Amateur championships, the 1966 Curtis Cup Match, and the 1967 U.S. Women's Open.

protested and caused an unusual breach in the two-century-old cradle-to-grave employment practice.

Though the management often looks upon change as more of a blight than a de-

The famed tower of The Homestead Hotel, a spa that dates back to 1766.

light, it takes unrelenting pride in treating all guests equally. Inspired by the resort's proximity to Washington, D.C., 170 miles to the northeast, it has also used plenty of ingenuity when handling visiting Senators, Congressmen, and various members of foreign diplomatic corps, who have a penchant for abusing that worldwide luxury: the expense account. What has become a classic case of bookkeeping juggling at The Homestead occurred in 1935 when Japan's ambassador, Hirosi Saito, rented a cottage for the summer. When the ambassador was ready to leave, he was presented with the usual itemized bill, which included considerable charges for champagne. On seeing the bill, an attaché informed the manager that, while the Japanese government was to pay for the rent of the cottage and incidentals, the ambassador had far exceeded his expense account, and if The Homestead expected to get paid, it would have to conceal the champagne charges. An imaginative bookkeeper realized that among the incidentals, the cottage would have to be put back in proper order after the ambassador left. So a new bill was drawn up to include among the sundry incidentals the amount paid to a cleaning woman, which came to the unrealistic sum of $1,800. Nonetheless, the bill was paid.

And like it or not, every guest is a paying guest, whether he is the Secretary of State or a lumber salesman from North Carolina. In the view of the management, to change the hotel's policy would be, well, downright un-American, considering its

The Duke of Windsor, about to tee off on his one and only visit to The Homestead in 1948. His style was more than a knot. Later, on being presented his bill, the Duke asked, "What do I do with this?" From then on he vacationed at The Homestead's rival, The Greenbrier.

114

The Homestead's greatest contribution to golf, Sam Snead. It was on The Cascades Course that Sam shaped his game, which brought him 135 tournament victories. In 1936 he left The Homestead to become The Greenbrier's teaching pro for $45 a month. At the Greenbrier, watching in awe as Snead swings, is a golfer named Ike.

history. The first hotel in Hot Springs to be called The Homestead was built in 1766 as a small grand spa. It catered to such fighters for colonial independence as George Washington, Alexander Hamilton, and Thomas Jefferson, who was a regular guest and whose charges for whiskey were substantial, proof that our American forefathers not only took the waters with great zest but also partook of the spirits.

But not all guests have left The Homestead sensing a grand feeling of tradition.

One was none other than the Duke of Windsor, who after spending a two-week vacation there in 1948, was presented with a bill his last day. "What do I do with this?" the duke asked, quite unaccustomed to paying bills. He was informed very politely that he must pay it. He did, but never returned, preferring to vacation at The Homestead's rival, The Greenbrier, where he was treated as he was accustomed to being treated.

The rivalry between the two resorts is

legendary. In unkind moments The Homestead calls The Greenbrier commercial, while The Greenbrier calls The Homestead stuffy and old guard. But both have their loyal clienteles as well as their defectors. Sam Snead, who was born in Hot Springs and shaped the game that won him 135 tournaments on the Cascades and Homestead courses, went over to The Greenbrier in 1936 when its management offered him $45 a month to be its teaching pro.

In the 1920s, both vied to be the number-one springtime vacation spot of high society, the nesting and mating place of the Southern belle. The single woman who arrived then was called in the local newspapers merely Miss L or Miss W. Even among the belles, there were the defectors. However, none made a more spectacular defection than a Miss B, who arrived one Saturday afternoon at The Homestead with her mother and father. Her mother was not at all pleased that her daughter had taken to dating a local jockey, and to ensure that there would be no meeting of the pair that evening, she made the fatal mistake of locking her daughter in their cottage, dressed only in bloomers, with no clothes to wear. When the jockey arrived late that afternoon, he asserted not only his ingenuity but his cavalier spirit by loaning the girl his silks and white breeches, and off they rode to The Greenbrier.

At every resort there are those memorable moments—a famous actress banned from a dining room for arriving in short shorts, a temperamental chef slipping, in a fit of anger, onto a table filled with gelatin desserts, a portly woman being told she is an ass by an attendant at the spa—but for first-rate farce, few resorts can match the scene that occurred on the Fourth of July, 1926, at the award ceremonies after the

qualifying round of the Virginia State Amateur, which was held on The Homestead's Cascades Course. A frequent visitor to the resort that time of year was New York's Senator Chauncey Depew, and since the ceremonies had always had a regal air about them, Senator Depew was asked if he would officiate at the presentation and hand out the prizes. The Senator consented, though he admitted he knew absolutely nothing about golf. Upon being given the first trophy that was to go to the medal winner and seeing an eager audience, the Senator could not resist the temptation to make a speech. "I really have wondered," the Senator said, "at the hold the game of golf is gaining on Americans, but it was not until this moment that I realized what this game has which others do not. In most games the prize is awarded to the best player, the one who accomplishes the most. I see that with golf it is different. Here I am about to award the first and most important prize to the man who made the lowest score, in other words, to the absolutely worst player. It is obvious that rewards in golf do not go to the most skillful performer, but to the most diligent and earnest, laboring under the greatest difficulties. . . ."

Golf came to The Homestead not for the diligent or earnest player, but so the resort spa could advertise complete sporting facilities. Finally, in 1899 the Virginia Hot Springs Golf and Tennis Club was formed and a six-hole course was laid out. It soon was expanded to nine holes, then to eighteen, revamped and lengthened to its present 5,922 hilly yards, par-71 (5,212 yards from the ladies' tees). Though the first tee is situated less than a hundred yards from the hotel—convenient for the guests who want to get in a quick 18 holes—it occupies an even rarer place in American golfing history as the oldest first tee, date 1892, still in existence.

However, the course's greatest glory began one brisk spring day when four top-level managers of the resort experienced the plight of the public-course player, having to wait almost an hour on the tee of one of the par 3s while several foursomes played out. Then and there it was decided the resort needed another course.

Fortunately, a 1,702-acre estate two miles south in Healing Springs was for sale. Golf-course architect William S. Flynn, who a year before had designed the Cherry Hills Country Club outside Denver and had consulted with George Crump on Pine Valley, was called in from his home in Philadelphia to see whether any of the land was suitable for a golf course. His decision had to be made in a day. Starting off at dawn, Flynn marched over the land, through the woods, down a rock-filled ravine, over boulders and along the streams. Finally, sipping scotch with the managers at dusk, Flynn took a sheet of paper, drew some preliminary sketches of holes, and said, "I don't know how the holes will run, but if I have two extra sites for greens, I can build you a course." The sites for the two greens, the present 4th and 10th, were acquired at considerable cost. This done, Flynn curved his fairways around streams, cut them on the bias of mountain slopes, and designed no two holes alike, making a definite right and wrong side of the fairway to drive to. In fact, so penalizing are the natural hazards that a shot hit to the wrong side of a fairway or green will bound off down a slope into the woods or into Swift Run Stream, which curls devilishly among eight of the holes. This splendid use of the terrain makes The Cascades the most thoroughly nature-bound of all mountain courses, so much so that few fairway bunkers are needed. There are only six on the outgoing nine and 22 in all, with an average of two guarding each smallish green.

The course stretches 6,568 yards from the championship tees (6,234 regular and 5,586 ladies') and plays over two different levels. Holes one through thirteen spread over hilly ground, and then holes fourteen through eighteen move over flattish terrain. If the course is unconventionally short by modern championship standards, it also contains other unconventional features. There are only three par 5s, two back to back, and five par 3s, three on the incoming nine. Even the finishing hole is a 190-yard par 3, over a pond to a green sitting on the side of a hill. For years the hole was a favorite hustling spot for Sam Snead, as foolhardy gamblers would wager ample sums of money that Sam could not hit the green three consecutive times. A surer bet would be that the next day Sam would have a full head of hair.

Snead may be the Cascades's major contribution to golf, but since the course opened in 1924, some of the game's great players have walked the fairways. The first major tournament played there was the 1928 U.S. Women's Amateur, won by the great Glenna Collett. Since 1924 and up until 1973, except for three years during World War II and in 1946, The Cascades has been the site of the Virginia Men's State Amateur, and since 1934 the Virginia Women's State Amateur has been played there. In 1966 the Curtis Cup matches were played there, with the United States winning, 13 to 5. A year later, it was the site of the U.S. Women's Open.

After the first round, defending champion Sandra Spuzich recorded a ragged 77, then treated the press to some crisp midiron

rhetoric. "No amateur could ever win this tournament, and they know it," she said with the divot flying in the direction of one of the first-round leaders, amateur Catherine Lacoste, daughter of the famous French holder of the U.S. and Wimbledon tennis titles, René Lacoste. (He is now famous as the designer of the polo shirt with the insignia of the crocodile.) Three days later, Spuzich no doubt wished she could have retracted her first-round score and remark. Lacoste not only won the Women's Open, but broke three records doing it, becoming the first amateur, the youngest woman and the first foreigner to win it.

Her victory was not without its hour of high drama. Going into the final nine holes, Lacoste held a four-stroke lead, then played as if she indeed had a crocodile by the tail. On the short par-4 dogleg 10th, where the green sits just beyond Swift Run Stream, she missed the green with her second shot, pitched on, and missed a putt for a par. She bogied the par-3 11th. Three bogies later, her lead had dwindled to one stroke. On the 16th, where the first day she had put her third shot into the pond fronting the green, she shanked her second shot. Another bogey. But fortunately for Lacoste, her closest contender, the great Louise Suggs, hit her third shot into the pond in front of the 16th green. Then on the 17th, shortened from 408 yards, its usual length for women, to 355 yards, Lacoste hit an eight-iron second shot 10 feet from the pin and sank the putt. She won by two shots, but her winning score was 10 over par, 294. In all, there were only three sub-par rounds.

Great Britain's Elizabeth Chadwick leans into a wood shot on The Cascades 190-yard par-3 18th during the 1966 Curtis Cup Matches. The United States won again, thirteen to five.

Catherine Lacoste blasts from a greenside bunker on the 200-yard par-3 4th during the final round of the 1967 U.S. Women's Open. Lacoste set three records in the contest, becoming the first amateur, the first foreigner, and the youngest player to win the Open.

If the 16th was almost Lacoste's Waterloo, it has been one of the most conquerable golf holes for Marvin M. Giles, four-time member of the U.S. Walker Cup Team, winner of both the U.S. and British amateurs, holder of the dubious record for being runner-up three consecutive times in the U.S. Amateur, and unprecedented six-time winner of the Virginia Men's State Amateur, winning it five times at match play and

once at medal play—in 1968, when he won with eight under par. Helping his cause were four birdies at the 16th.

The 16th hole is a classic, strategic par-5 slight dogleg right, measuring 522 yards from the championship tee (485 yards regular and 457 ladies'). The tee is surrounded by small evergreens. Looking down the right side of the fairway, you see tall oaks and elms and a branch of Swift Run Stream

Vinny Giles, one of Virginia's finest amateurs, holes a putt on the 18th green to win the 1966 Virginia Men's State Amateur. He would go on to win it an unprecedented six times.

that will catch a badly sliced drive or second shot. Exactly 242 yards from the tee, at the right elbow of the dogleg, are three bunkers forming a triangle. Of course, if you harbor any hopes of reaching the green in two, you must first drive safely over the last bunker, 278 yards from the tee. Even after this Nicklaus-length drive, you must hit a second shot that will carry more than 230 yards over the pond to the green, which, though large, is flat and hard to hold. Going for the green in two is not the best of gambles. The hole is best played by driving

just left of the three fairway bunkers, laying up with a midiron and pitching on. Giles, who has played the hole more than 150 times in competition, has gone for the green only nine times and succeeded four times.

Until 1973, the 36-hole qualification for the Virginia Men's State Amateur took place over The Cascades and the newer Lower Cascades, designed in 1963 by Robert Trent Jones. You can stand on the first tee, or on any of the seventeen others, and see most of the fairways sweeping over the mountainside. If the openness invites you to spank the ball with every ounce of energy, you can do so without fear of slicing or hooking out of bounds, losing every ball you own, or finding your ball deep in a fairway bunker, of which there are only thirteen. Cedar Creek and the Cascades Stream may add a few penalty shots to your round, but not too many, as they come into play decisively on only four holes. So at the Lower Cascades you can hit the ball hard, find it, and hit it hard again, which is the way to play the course, since it can be stretched from the ladies' tees of 5,943 yards to the championship tees of 6,769 yards. The Lower Cascades gets less play than the other two, so if you must have a 9:10 starting time, you usually can get it there.

Besides a variety of golf courses, The Homestead offers a variety of accommodations. The Cascades Inn, located halfway between the Lower Cascades and the Cascades courses is ideal for the golfer or trout fisherman who likes his vacation without frills. The surroundings are homey and informal (jackets are required for dinner), offering average-size but comfortable rooms. The food is the same as that served at the hotel, though not as varied, and all guests of course are regular hotel guests and can use all the hotel's facilities.

If you enjoy modern decor, there is the new South Wing of brick, chrome, steel, and tinted glass, with a number of small balconies and thirteen duplex suites. It was all built as a self-contained conference center, and while it contains the conventioneer quite well, keeping him from sneaking off to the golf courses or tennis courts on company time, it also discreetly separates convention guests from those regular hotel guests who champion The Homestead's grandeur and grace. The main hotel's accommodations, the best, tie in well with the classical architecture of the Great Hall. Most rooms are quite large and traditionally furnished, with high ceilings and intricate wainscoting.

Evenings are still rather dressy. Men wear suits more than sport jackets. Women wear long skirts or conservatively styled dresses. Dinner is served in the huge, softly lighted main dining room, which has arched mirrors and windows, and is separated into three sections by Doric columns. More informal dining can be found at the Grille. At both places, the cuisine is good, especially the trout, which is usually freshly caught and served boned. However, those seeking old-time all-winter-cured Virginia smoked country ham will be disappointed.

The saying among old Virginia families is that one is going to The Hot, which is a synonym for The Homestead. For Hot Springs is not a resort town like Palm Springs, Palm Beach, Colorado Springs or Cooperstown. It is a rural, backwoods town where the residents still speak with a hillbilly twang, farm the land, and frequent the local hardware store as much as the ABC liquor store. But the major industry of the area is not farming, sheep or cattle raising. Hot Springs's industry is The Homestead, which is to the town what museums are to Cooperstown.

THE OTESAGA
HOTEL
Cooperstown, New York

Cooperstown, population 2,600, elevation 1,264 feet, lies seventy miles west of Albany, and at least one hundred light-years east of the industrial society. It has no train station or airport, and though there is a bus stop, there is no terminal—only a small country general store. Streets are named Elm, Chestnut, and Pioneer. The major thoroughfare, running east to west through the compact village, is Main Street, of course. It is narrow and two-laned, beginning at the foot of Mount Vision, crossing the Susquehanna River at its source, pushing straight through the village, and then rising gently to the ridge of Hannah's Hill in the west. Aging hard maples, sugar maples, linden and locust trees line the street along with the turn-of-the-century lampposts, from which hang huge baskets of blooming petunias and geraniums.

Along the broad sidewalks rise nineteenth-century buildings of Victorian and neoclassical design. An ordinance prohibits parking meters and gas stations on Main Street. There is one small movie theater and a dozen antique stores, but no sprawling shopping complex. In fact, the low profile of the village equals its pace. Even in midsummer, there is seldom the febrile social activity associated with most resort towns, which makes the whole place something of a village of paradoxes.

Doubleday Field in the 1920s. The first game played there in 1919 attracted five hundred people. Today more than ten thousand people jam the stadium every August for the Hall of Fame game.

(*Left*) In the 1870s, a lone sculler rows on Otsego Lake, once described by Cooperstown's famed novelist James Fenimore Cooper as "a broad sheet of water so placid and limpid that it resembles a bed of pure mountain atmosphere compressed into a setting of hills and woods."

An almost changeless scene in the American landscape. This rare photo of Cooperstown was taken in the 1870s, but little has altered in the village in over a century.

Cooperstown is properly called the "village of great museums." There is the granddaddy of all sports museums, the National Baseball Hall of Fame, Museum, and Library, and Doubleday Field. There is the Carriage and Harness Museum, the Farmers' Museum, and Fenimore House, where James Fenimore Cooper is honored and revered more than in his lifetime. It is here where Abner Doubleday, it is claimed, invented baseball in 1839.

As the story goes, on one fine spring day Doubleday—a student at a local military academy—scratched a diamond in the dirt with a stick, decided on the number of players, defined some rules, and gave the game its name; it is a spin-off of a game called town ball and a game played in Great Britain called rounders. Though at Fort Sumter Doubleday earned a footnote in American

history as the first Union soldier to fire a shot in the Civil War, he is best remembered as the father of baseball.

His stadium was built in 1919, and the first game played there, on August 20 of that year, was witnessed by five hundred fans. Today more than ten thousand fans jam the stadium for the Hall of Fame game held each summer. The closest the village has come to having one of its own inducted into the Hall of Fame was with John D. (Happy Jack) Chesbro, who played briefly for the Cooperstown Athletics in 1896. The first black to play professionally was born in Cooperstown—John Jackson, who played under the name Bud Fowler.

But Cooperstown's first claim to fame is tied to the life and work of James Fenimore Cooper, whose vivid accounts of late eighteenth-century life in America made him the first American novelist to achieve worldwide fame. The setting for *The Deerslayer*, the last of the five-volume Leatherstocking series, is Otsego Lake, referred to as "Glimmerglass." In 1840, Cooper described it as "a broad sheet of water so placid and limpid that it resembled a bed of pure mountain atmosphere compressed into a setting of hills and woods." The village was founded and named by the author's father, Judge William Cooper, in 1786. Today, in a pocket park near the baseball museum, where in 1798 Judge Cooper built "the noblest mansion west of Albany," there is a statue of the author, hat and cane in hand, gazing toward the lake he loved. In a special wing of the Hall of Fame hang bronze plaques honoring baseball's greatest players. Yet the most significant name in Cooperstown today is not Cooper, Doubleday, or Babe Ruth; it is Clark.

The Clark fortune began with Edward Clark, a small-town lawyer who moved to New York City in 1838 as a partner of the firm Jordan and Clark. In the early 1850s, a journeyman inventor arrived with his latest invention, a wood-carving machine, and sought legal assistance from Clark. So impressed was the man with Clark's astute business mind that he returned a year later with another invention. This time Clark was the one who was impressed, and a year later they became partners. The client's name was Isaac Singer, inventor of the first practical sewing machine.

As the Clark fortune grew, so did the Singer family. In all, Singer had twenty-five children. His most famous offspring was his illegitimate son, Paris Singer, a one-time traveling companion of the famous dancer Isadora Duncan. Singer financed Palm Beach's neo-renaissance face-lift. The designer was Addison Mizner.

While Paris Singer was displaying a conspicuous use of wealth, the Clark family did not put their trust in money, preferring to put their money in trust, and provided Cooperstown with perhaps the finest understatement of wealth that money could buy. It was mostly the efforts of Stephen Clark, grandson of Edward, who in the early 1930s inherited from Edward S., his older brother, the Fenimore House and a farm across the street. Discovering that operating both was impractical, he invited the New York State Historical Association to move to Cooperstown from Ticonderoga. The offer was accepted. The farm became the Farmers' Museum, with a section displaying a re-creation of the early-American rural life of the region. The Fenimore House, besides housing the archives of James Fenimore Cooper, features an outstanding collection of American academic art of the first half of the nineteenth century and folk art of the nineteenth and twentieth centuries.

Stephen Clark is remembered today for one thing—he founded the Baseball Hall of Fame. It was one of those happy accidents. In 1935 he learned that a nearby resident of Cooperstown had found a baseball ostensibly made in the Doubleday era. Clark bought it for five dollars, and the Hall of Fame began.

Museums are not the only legacy of the Clarks. There is the brick- and limestone-trimmed Otesaga Hotel, built by Edward Clark in 1909, sitting on the south shore of Otsego Lake. Massive white pillars support the porte-cochere at the main entrance. It is a huge building, a sort of Homestead of the North. On its sprawling verandas, neat rows of rocking chairs afford a sweeping view of the lake.

From the exterior the hotel appears to contain at least 300 rooms, although there

The plaque of one of baseball's immortals in the Baseball Hall of Fame, the granddaddy of all sports museums, founded in 1935.

are actually only about half as many, 135 regular rooms and 12 suites. All rooms are furnished alike with reproductions of early-American maple furniture and of early-American prints, mostly Currier and Ives. For regular returning guests, rooms are furnished with fresh flowers. In fact, the hotel abounds with arrays of flowers: on the verandas are huge hanging begonias; in the lobby, decorated with floral chintz drapery and sofas, there are bouquets on almost every table. In the entrance to the elegant Georgian dining room is a huge bouquet of chrysanthemums. There is a small band playing nightly—mostly slow, flowery waltzes. Though the service also borders on slow, the food is consistently good, espe-

cially in midsummer, when all the vegetables are fresh.

For fifty years black tie was recommended on Wednesday and Saturday nights. Wednesdays were dropped first, and finally Saturdays in the early 1960s. But the hotel held out stalwartly against the newest women's fashion in the 1960s, forbidding pants suits in the dining rooms, a rule which has since been revised. Neckties are recommended for men, but that regulation too is being relaxed. One that definitely is not is that any guest caught taking an impulsive moonlight nude swim in the pool is evicted immediately. Two people have tried, and each left within the hour.

"I guess," said the night manager, "you could sum up the tone of The Otesaga as conservative. In none of our advertisements or brochure pictures do we show young girls sunbathing in skimpy bikinis. It just isn't our image."

In such a serene setting, you might expect the golf course to be one of fairways lined with daffodils and tulips, a course as calm as the lake. The Leatherstocking Golf Course, next to the hotel, fits into the scenery for the reason that opposites attract. It is a fierce little course, not as penalizing as Harbour Town Golf Links, but with a shot value almost as good as The Cascades' at The Homestead. From the regular tees, it measures 6,554 yards, and the course plays to every yard of it. From the ladies' tees, it measures 5,857 yards. It has been the site of the New York State Women's Amateur (1958 and 1962), the New York State Men's Amateur (1964), the New York State Senior Men's Golf Association Amateur, and, each July, the Otesaga Open, an 18-hole event for pros. The winning score usually is three or four under par, and less than fifteen percent of the field of 150 is par or under.

The reasons the scores are so high for such a relatively short course is that the pros play from the championship tees—some 200 yards more than the regular length. The rough is usually up to the height it is in the spring and fall—four inches, U.S. Open rough, you might say. Then there are the natural hazards—menacing dips in the fairways that unkindly conceal yawning greenside bunkers, two-tiered greens, or greens creased down the middle. Creeks meander across and along the fairways. Several greens are nestled in a grove of short needle pines or fir trees. Most greens are elevated, too, making every shot to a green all carry. A chipping course it is not. An errant shot to a green will leave a pitch shot over a series of chocolate drops or a bunker. When the course was built in 1909, some 145 bunkers were put in, but even the golfers of Cooperstown and the Clark family considered that too many, and through the years 34 have been removed—mainly the fairway bunkers—to favor the shorter hitter.

The course was designed by Devereux Emmett, best known for designing the Women's National Golf Links on Long Island's North Shore, a chic all-women's club. Legend is that as Emmett walked along the rolling ground above the shore of Otsego Lake, staking out the course, Stephen C. Clark, Sr., followed in his footsteps and instructed him to bunker the fairways in a way that would be an advantage to his game, mediocre at best, and a disadvantage to his opponents—to most of whom he frequently lost. It could be said that the course reflects the thought that there is only one fury worse than the wrath of a sore loser on the golf course.

In the 1920s the course was revamped by the pro/superintendent, Len Rayner, who shifted the tees and greens to bring into

Devereux Emmett, the architect of The Leatherstocking Golf Course.

(*Overleaf*) The Leatherstocking Golf Course in the 1920s. Over the years it has matured into a fierce course, though shortish by modern standards. It is one of the best-maintained resort courses in the country.

127

On his way to winning the 1964 New York State Men's Amateur Championship, played over The Leatherstocking Golf Course, amateur Don Allen watches a birdie putt drop.

play a row of willows, as on the 7th hole, or sometimes a clump of evergreens. The current pro, Ed Kroll, changed the 3rd hole from a meek par 4 to a fearsome 206-yard par 3 (same yardage from the ladies' tee). From a slightly elevated tee, you look down to a bow-shaped fairway that swings from right to left, with a series of bunkers staggered down the right side—seven in all— which must be carried to reach the green. A shot drawing too much catches a bunker left of the green. The green itself is large and filled with heavy swells. Just beyond the green is a stone wall and out-of-bounds.

During the Otesaga Open, the pros have played the hole at an average of 3.6 shots, which makes it the third-hardest hole on the course. The easiest par 3 is the 12th hole. The tee sits on a high hill, level with the tops of the evergreens beyond the green, a mere 132 yards (same yardage from the ladies' tee) straight downhill from the tee. The green is ringed with bunkers. It is usually a wedge or nine-iron shot, although it can be a wedge, another wedge, a sand wedge out of a bunker, another bunker shot, and two putts, which is exactly how former New York Yankee pitcher, now golf pro Ralph Terry played the hole in the 1975 Otesaga Open. His first shot flew over the evergreens and out-of-bounds into the parking lot of the Farmers' Museum. His next shot caught the front of a bunker, from which he blasted out into a rear bunker. On the green in five, he two-putted. When questioned about his misfortune, he replied philosophically, "In this game I'm on my own; I don't have Mantle, Maris, or Skowron backing me up."

The next three holes could be described as Jack Neville described the beginning holes at Pebble Beach—something of a come-on. Here is an easy par 4 followed by an easier par 4, where one does not need the power of a Jack Nicklaus to drive to the green. The 15th is a short 475-yard par 5 (410 yards ladies'), easily reachable in two shots; the green sits invitingly at the bottom of a small hill. After that, as Neville would say about the last twelve holes at Pebble, "You can go for a bundle." Here is the backbone of the course—a short but fiendish par 4, a long par 3, and a par 5 over and around water.

The 16th is a timeless masterpiece that plays as hard today as it did in the 1920s, when golfers played the game with wooden-shafted clubs, golf balls that floated, caddies, and fore-caddies. The tee sits on the ridge of a hill, open and exposed to the mountain breezes. From there, the fairway slopes downhill for 150 yards, then levels out straight to a green 375 yards from the tee (242 yards ladies'). Down the right side of the fairway is a row of willows and maples; on the left side, to catch only the most horrendously hooked drive, is the lake. However, curling into the left side of the fairway, 235 yards from the tee, is a wide U-shaped drainage ditch. The ideal drive, of course, is down the left side, leaving an open second shot to the small green.

In the right front of the green is a pond. And on those days when the pin is set on the right front section of the green, the pond claims innumerable golf balls. The pin was placed in the right front during the finals of the 1958 New York State Women's Amateur. Two holes down with three holes to play, Barbara McGhie had to win the last three holes to defeat Mrs. Harry Nevil. McGhie cut her second shot too close to the pond and went in. She dropped in front of the pond, hit her wedge fat, and put her third shot in the pond, at which point she conceded the hole, match, and tournament.

The 17th is a 180-yard par 3 (same ladies'), all carry over water to a green with its right side surrounded by water. A local rule states that the water is not just a lateral hazard but, adding insult to injury for the golfer who slices, it is also out-of-bounds. A potential three can quickly turn into a five or six. The cautious golfer can play down the fairway, swinging in from the left. This, however, leaves a delicate pitch over a bunker to a heavily contoured green. And as on all the greens, all putts break toward the lake.

In the early 1920s the 18th also was a par 3, but redesigner Rayner changed it to a 550-yard par 5 (same ladies') with much of the character of the 18th at Pebble Beach. To achieve this, he built an island tee in the lake, 100 feet from the shore. It was built with 22 junked automobiles, debris from an old Methodist Church, and 2,000 pounds of rock, and was topped off with clinker cinders. The original tee stood for three decades until muskrats began nibbling away at its foundation, causing it to slowly sink. Better it had sunk, or had not been rebuilt, for the golfer must drive at least 130 yards to reach the fairway (the ladies' tee is adjacent to the 17th green). Of course, he can, if he so dares, cut off more in order to reach the bow-shaped fairway running along the shore. In fact, the golfer can stand on the tee until he has put every golf ball he owns into the lake. Another cruel local rule is that there is no drop area: you either drive the fairway or try again. The green can be reached with two mighty shots, after which you might think the golfer would be justly rewarded with a possible eagle—a cinch birdie. Not so. The green is pear-shaped and steeply two-tiered, with the final ten feet of the upper half sloping slightly away from the golfer. Making matters worse, the pin is usually set in the upper left corner. Standing on the green and looking back across the water to the tee, it is easy to imagine that James Fenimore Cooper's deer slayer stood on this very spot when he saw the lake for the first time and said, "This is grand! 'Tis solemn! 'Tis an education in itself to look upon!" And a helluva one to play over, too!

Even Ed Kroll, who for a decade held the course record of a 64, attempts to reach the 18th green in only two out of every ten rounds. Too risky, he says. He inherited such golfing savvy from his cousin, Ted Kroll, the tournament pro other pros would go to for a lesson in the 1950s. It was Ted, however, who took one risk too many and lost the 1956 U.S. Open at Oak Hill. It was at the same open that Hogan missed a short putt on the 71st green in his attempt to gain a tie with Cary Middlecoff, who won at even par of 281. Six strokes back was a young golfer still seeking his first U.S. pro-tournament victory. His name was Arnold Palmer. A month later, he would win two tournaments, and four years later, on a bright, sunny afternoon at Cherry Hills Country Club, he would come up from seven strokes back of the leader in the final round to win the open.

It was there he became the golfer who, for almost the next decade, would make the golfing world forget there was anyone else playing professional golf. A complete wall in the grill of his Bay Hill Club and Lodge in Orlando, Florida, is filled with photos of Palmer. Each photo captures not only that indomitable Palmer spirit, but that stuff of champions—that they can be as gracious in defeat as in victory.

INLAND RESORTS

BAY HILL
CLUB & LODGE
Orlando, Florida

Orlando, Florida, currently ranks sixth in the world in number of guest rooms available—30,000. It has more available rooms than Paris, Rome, Dallas, or Los Angeles. The golfer might like to imagine, in a flight of fantasy, that this is because Arnold Palmer owns Bay Hill and because several times a year his fans converge upon Orlando to get a closer look at their leader in action. Of course this is not true, but then fantasy fits well in Orlando, site of Disney World, and Arnie, even without an ailing hip and putting woes, and giving two shots aside, could not beat the better ball of Mickey Mouse and Donald Duck for sheer drawing power.

Yet one has only to wander into Bay Hill's pro shop, which is spangled with large four-color photos of Palmer, then into the grill—with one wall completely covered with black-and-white photos of him—to realize that not even the great imagination of Walt Disney could have created a character whose face so clearly expresses all the emotions—from anguish to elation and the

hundreds in between—that the game of golf produces. There is Palmer walking the fairways, his shirttail hanging out, hitching up his trousers, wincing over a missed putt, squinting into the sun—the antithesis of the precise, cool Hogan.

Arnold Palmer slashes a long-iron shot to the green of the 14th. Though Arnie owns Bay Hill, he doesn't always play the 14th as if it belonged to him.

(*Left*) Bay Hill's best par 3, the 218-yard 14th hole, exemplifies the precise bunkering done by the great golf course architect Dick Wilson.

135

Palmer's impact on the game, recalled by Dan Jenkins in his book *The Dogged Victims of Inexorable Fate*, began the moment he ceased being another golfing pro and became the hero of a rooting army. It was after he had won the 1960 U.S. Open at Cherry Hills Country Club:

"There have been other major victories, as we know, and scores of lesser ones, and precisely because of him the professional tour has tripled, quadrupled in prize money. He has become, they say, something immeasurable in champions, something more than life-size, even though he has turned into his forties, the hip hurts, and a lot of other big ones have slipped away.

"This is true, I think. He is the most immeasurable of all golf champions. But this is not entirely true because of all that he has won, or because of that mysterious fury with which he has managed to rally himself. It is partly because of the nobility he has brought to losing. And more than anything, it is true because of the pure, unmixed joy he has brought to trying.

"He has been, after all, the doggedest victim of us all."

You might expect Bay Hill to be something of a shrine to the nobility of Palmer, but like Mauna Kea, which shows Laurance Rockefeller's zest for simplicity and harmony with nature, or The Broadmoor, which reflects Spencer Penrose's idea of what elegance should be, in the Colorado Rockies, Bay Hill incorporates Palmer's feelings of what a golf resort should have: a tradition-bound golf-club atmosphere and a great course, always in peak condition. To achieve the latter, Palmer hired the course superintendent of golf's holy ground of beautification—Augusta National. In essence, Bay Hill is a private club. It has a tight and loyal resident membership, which has preference of starting times, and a large

nonresident membership. However, in 1975 guests of Bay Hill's lodge were extended playing privileges at a minimal membership fee of five dollars a day.

The course was less than a year old in 1961, when it began to be a favorite golfing spot of Northeasterners, many of whom like Florida, but have a mild disdain for the usual flat Florida courses, even the good ones. Bay Hill is different. It rolls gently over 155 acres of what is perhaps the most exciting golfing terrain in Florida this side of the Seminole Golf Club. The fairways rise from 115 to 170 feet above sea level, sweep dramatically around orange groves, small forests of evergreens and seven man-made lakes. The fairways are amply wide, the greens narrow, and no two fairways run parallel. A howling slice or hook lands not in another fairway, but deep in the woods, water, or scrub land.

It is what the pros like to call a good driving course, demanding both length and accuracy off the tee. Palmer boasts, "This place [Bay Hill] is a good tune-up course for any tournament. You can run into any shot here that you would have at the Masters or the U.S. Open. As a training ground for the circuit, it's probably one of the best courses in the world." Such affection for the course is due in part of course to the fact that Palmer owns it and likes to promote the place. But his statement is not without truth. Nearing the end of the 1969 tour without a victory, in what the media came to describe as the Palmer "hip slump," he retreated to Bay Hill to work on his game before the last two tournaments. He played twenty-seven holes of golf three days in a row, then went off and won the Heritage Classic, driving like the Palmer of Cherry Hills on a course supposedly not suited for his game—the Harbour Town Golf Links. He followed up his victory at the Heritage the next week by winning the Danny Thomas Classic.

Palmer is not the only golfer to come away from Bay Hill with a sounder golf game. In August 1974 the course was the site of the Southern Amateur. Finishing at one under par for 72 holes, in fourth place, was Jerry Pate. A month later he would win the U.S. Amateur.

The scores in the Southern Amateur are proof that, from the championship tees at 7,055 yards (or near them, as the Southern was played at 6,888 yards), the course's four-round shot value is one of the best in the southeast. In the Southern only four players broke the par of 288 for four rounds, and in the 208 rounds of the tournament there were only 20 sub-par rounds. Palmer's best from the championship tees is a lone 66.

There are four sets of tees: championship, regular at 6,583 yards, seniors' at 6,103 yards, and ladies'. Women play the huge course, with its 119 bunkers and nine water holes, more to the liking of Sandra Palmer, at 5,318 yards. So far in front of the championship tees are the ladies' tees that on the 12th hole, a slightly uphill 568-yard par 5, one's drive must not only avoid the bunkers on either side of the fairway, but must be of the Palmer length (Arnold, that is) of 253 yards just to reach the ladies' tee, from which the hole measures 315 yards.

Like most of the holes at Bay Hill, length and accuracy are needed off the tee, while the shot into the greens demands great finesse. On the 12th, five bunkers jealously guard the green on the left side; on the right side, one yawning bunker pinches the entrance to the green to a mere 35 feet. It was at the 12th in 1965, when Palmer first played the course, that he slashed a magnificent three-wood shot between the bun-

The championship form of Jerry Pate en route to a mere one-under-par fourth-place finish in the 1974 Southern Amateur, played at Bay Hill. A month later he captured the U.S. Amateur.

kers. The ball stopped 12 feet from the pin, and he dropped the putt for an eagle. And right then, he thought about buying the course. Like all great golfers, Palmer understands the vagaries of the game—in the hundreds of times he has played the 12th, that has been his only eagle.

However, his most spectacular shot was hit on the par-3 17th, where the championship tee sits on the top of a small hill surrounded by evergreens. The golfer looks across a blue pond to a two-tiered green 223 yards away (185 yards regular and 134 yards ladies'), with two bunkers strategically placed at the front and rear of the green. In the resort's brochure, Palmer suggests that if you hit from the championship tee on the 17th, you should use a driver. One day he ignored his own advice and asked his caddie for a three iron. "That's the club for you," announced the caddie affirmatively. But Palmer caught the shot fat, and the ball sailed into the pond, one of four hundred balls the pond claims each week. Palmer then took a two iron and said, "Well, this is for my par," and holed out. With immense satisfaction he handed the two iron to his caddie, who promptly one-upped his boss, saying, "It's a three iron, Mr. Palmer."

The other par 3s are not as dramatic as the 17th, though they are equally difficult. The 2nd hole is 230 yards (212 yards regular and 181 yards ladies') downhill to a green pitched on the side of a slope. The 7th and 14th are similar in character, both slightly uphill, making them play longer than the actual yardage. Of the two, the 14th is better. The tee is open and rests on the edge of a pond. The hole measures 218 yards (194 yards regular; 169 yards ladies')—a long iron or fairway wood. A rise in the fairway prevents the golfer from seeing the exact pin placement. Two long, serpentine-edged bunkers extend 40 yards down the fairway from either side of the green. It is a memorable hole, one of many that characterize what is best about Bay Hill—magnificent use of terrain and strategic bunkering that further defines the holes, each of which requires great skill to play. Even more, it is a course where not only Arnold but Sandra Palmer can feel at home.

There are an additional nine holes geared for the less enthusiastic player. The fairways are wider, the greens are larger, and the bunkering is not as severe. It is called

the Charger, after Palmer's many legendary last nine charges. From the championship tees it measures only 3,090 yards.

Though Palmer owns Bay Hill, he is not the pro and is not available for lessons. Even when he is there, he is treated more like a resident member than the owner, and often participates in the regular members' Saturday Morning Florida Scramble Tournament, in which he is subjected to the first-tee verbal sparring of the weekend golfers working out a match.

When Palmer is there (he owns a condominium just across from the main lodge), the whole place seems charged with electricity. When he is not there, a feeling of expectancy pervades Bay Hill. But there is always the aura of his presence. Of all the greatest golfing resorts, Bay Hill exudes the strongest masculine atmosphere. It is an informal and friendly place where, if one is not playing golf, one is talking about it or playing gin rummy, the major evening entertainment. And Bay Hill fits into the category of those country clubs where golf is what really matters. Drinks are hearty and good, but the food is below average compared to that in most resorts. The staples are meat and potatoes. Even the orange juice, which one would expect to be fresh, is not. Though the management is trying to improve the culinary department, the basic attitude is that Bay Hill's members and guests are golfers, not eaters.

A two-story 72-room lodge adjoins the clubhouse. It has six suites and 66 large rooms, half with two double beds, thick wall-to-wall carpeting, balcony or patio, and color television—the same as what you

The notorious par-5 568-yard 12th. When Palmer played it for the first time in 1965, he eagled it, and then and there he decided to buy Bay Hill.

might expect to find in any one of Orlando's more than 30,000 guest rooms. For more homey and better-decorated accommodations, there are 16 two- and three-room condominiums for rent.

The condominiums are the best accommodations, because Bay Hill does a brisk convention business, especially from January through April. Since the resort is small, a convention in progress dominates it. The bar and restaurant are noisy and frenetic.

And if Palmer happens to be around, there is no mistaking the burden of fame he has accepted and pays for dearly. He is a gracious and hospitable host. Though Florida's other major golfing resort, Doral Country Club, steeped in the whims of its founder, Alfred Kaskel, is larger and more luxurious, it does not have Arnold Palmer, who made the word charisma part of the golfing vocabulary.

The ever-recognizable follow-through of Palmer, golf's most immeasurable of champions.

DORAL
COUNTRY CLUB
Miami, Florida

In memory he is called Mr. Kaskel. Not Al. Not Alfred. It is always Mr. Kaskel did this or Mr. Kaskel did that whenever people west of Miami talk about the late Alfred Kaskel. He was the man with the vision, money, power, and temperament to create a first-class resort west of Miami's International Airport, where there had been nothing but wasteland—acre after acre spreading in unimaginative flatness westward to the Everglades.

In the late 1950s Kaskel came to Miami, an interloper, a tycoon who had amassed a $200-million fortune in New York City real estate. He bought 2,300 of those flat acres at $2,000 each, to create a resort catering to families. It was to have maybe two golf courses, a few tennis courts, a swimming pool, and enough rooms for 300 people. The Miami Beach men called the plan "Kaskel's follies." They knew Miami was Miami Beach. It was the Eden Roc, the Fontainebleau soaring upward, basking in the sunniest sun of the Sunshine State. It was the climate people came for; it was Col-

lins Avenue running the length of Miami Beach that had attracted tourists for over half a century; it was the sun, the nightlife. To divorce a resort from Miami Beach would be a disaster.

The founder of Doral, Alfred Kaskel. The resort's name is a combination of his own and his wife's first names.

(Left) What more can be said? A photograph worth not only a thousand words but a whole book. This photo of Ben Hogan was taken at the first Doral Open in 1962.

Yet for all its facilities, Miami Beach did not have a convenient golf course for guests. As with so many golfers, Kaskel's enthusiasm for the game was not equaled by his playing ability. At best, he was an average golfer. It could be that all he wanted was a quiet place to play golf. "I put myself in the shoes of the tourists," he once said. "I could never come to Miami Beach or any other resort if I couldn't play golf whenever I wanted." A man of less insight and less money never would have bought 2,300 acres of wasteland sight unseen as Kaskel did. On his first visit to his newly acquired property, Kaskel got lost for two hours and never did find the place. But with the confidence that goes with becoming a millionaire by the time one is thirty years old, Kaskel remained undaunted.

Nearly two decades after the grunt of the first bulldozer was heard, one of Florida's largest resort complexes thrives far from what the natives call "the strip"—Collins Avenue. The 2,300 acres are now valued at about $40,000 each. There are five golf courses: a par 3 and four regulation courses, of which the Gold and Blue courses are of championship caliber, with one hole—the famous 18th on the Blue Course—that has gained the rare distinction of being, according to IBM statistics, the hardest par 4 on the golf tour. A fleet of 400 golf cars yields an annual revenue of over $1 million; the pro shop does almost as well. A full house now is just over 1,300 guests in 660 rooms.

Relentlessly sports-conscious, Doral has become the favorite playground of several players of the Miami Dolphin football team, a few jai alai players, and jockeys from Hialeah and Gulf Stream. In fact, Dolphin coach Don Shula once negotiated a rather sticky contract with one of his running backs while playing golf on the Blue Course, further proof that "the monster,"

as it is called, eventually brings not only golfers but also football players to their knees.

During Christmas and Easter weeks, Doral signs on a contingent of famous athletes to teach children sports: Bob Griese, football; Willie Mays, baseball; Arthur Ashe, a regular staff pro, tennis; and Tom Shaw, golf. Doral even has a touring backgammon pro, Paul Magriel.

Besides the five golf courses, there are 19 tennis courts, an Olympic-size swimming pool, seven tennis pros (Arthur Ashe gives only group lessons, but they are gratis), and eight golf pros, including one woman. One shortcoming is a scarcity of caddies—they are available by written request only in season, from mid-December to mid-April.

While other famous resorts usually have names derived from their surroundings—the pines of Pinehurst, the sea of Sea Pines—Kaskel was faced with the reality that there already was a Miami Country Club and, in Palm Beach, the Everglades Club. He therefore decided to name the resort after his wife, Dora, and the first syllable of his own first name, Al. However, the Al has dominated. The resort now is steeped in the exuberance and whims of Kaskel himself.

While walking on the clubhouse veranda one day, he thought there was too great an expanse of grass between it and the golf courses, so he ordered the staff to lay out a garden similar to one he had seen at Versailles. Inspecting it several months later, he found one wall too high, so he took a bulldozer and knocked it down, and ordered

An unusually pensive look from Lee Trevino as he watches a putt for a birdie slip by the cup on the 246-yard par-3 13th on his way to victory in the 1973 Doral-Eastern Open.

the whole garden rebuilt. It now takes one caretaker six hours a day to maintain it. During the 1963 Doral Open, begun in 1962 and now named the Doral-Eastern Open, a PGA official quietly approached Kaskel and informed him that in a few years, as the gallery expanded, a bridge over a stream between the 3rd and 14th fairways would be nice for crowd control. With his greens superintendent, Kaskel went to the site. He ordered that a bridge be built that very night—"Use mahogany, nothing else," he said. Once while playing a round of golf with Kaskel over the Blue Course, Palmer suggested that a row of palm trees be planted between the 7th and 11th fairways to mark the dividing line. "What's more," Palmer added, "when they've grown, they will add more beauty to the course." Kaskel just nodded and continued playing. But that night, under the beams of floodlights and with the aid of cranes, a row of fully grown palms was planted exactly where Palmer had suggested. "Sure, it cost a lot of money," Kaskel later said, "but it was worth it the next day when Arnie and I reached that spot. It was worth every damn cent just to see Arnie's double take. He had suggested I plant a few small palms."

Doral is one of a few resorts that have a team of skin-divers under contract. They come at dusk each day to retrieve balls from the thirty man-made lakes. The average take is five hundred balls, which not only explains why the pro shop does such a brisk business, but says a lot about the courses and their architects.

Dick Wilson designed the Blue and Red courses, while his one-time disciple Robert Van Hagge designed the White and the Gold. They fitted their courses nicely over the flattish, unimaginative terrain. What are today hundreds of different varieties of palms, flowers, and shrubs were all imported. Every year a hundred new trees are planted. The small mounds on the fairways, providing proper alignment for comparatively safe, if not properly positioned, drives, were manufactured.

Wilson believed it took a better man to build a golf course than to lay one out, and that an architect should use the existing terrain. "Look at it this way," he once said, "you can put a beautiful woman in an expensive dress, but if the dress doesn't fit, neither the woman nor the dress is going to look any good at all. It's the same with building a golf course. You've got to cut the course to fit the property."

If the saying is true that there are no ugly women, only women who do not know how to look pretty, then Doral's courses are a testimonial that even the homeliest piece of land, with enough corrective surgery, can be made into an exciting and beautiful golf course—one that has the quality Wilson considers essential to any course. "A golf course," he once said, "should look more vicious to play than it actually is. It should inspire you, keep you alert."

Unfortunately, the Blue Course is as vicious as it looks. There are eight lakes, a network of streams that make this the best use of water of America's inland courses, and 100 bunkers. Half the greens are fronted by either bunkers or water. Few shots roll onto the putting surface; once on the green, you must work to get down in two putts. On many of the greens, there can be a difference of three clubs from the front to the rear. Putting from that distance can be a maddening experience, as it was for Jack Nicklaus, who three-putted four times in the 1964 Doral Open.

From the championship tees, the Blue Course measures 7,065 yards, but unless you play to under a five handicap, you should play it from the regular tees at 6,627 yards (from the ladies' tees it measures 6,189 yards). Even at that somewhat modest length, it can be beguiling. In the 1967 Doral Open three rounds were played at 6,700 yards, and though there were several 66s, the winning score by Doug Sanders was a respectable 13 under par—not a tournament record. However, his motive for winning might be one of the most unusual ever in the history of the game. Sanders, then regarded as one of professional golf's lustier drinkers, had not won a tournament in a year, and a month prior to the Doral Open, he vowed he would not take a drink until he had won a golf tournament or until his birthday in June. "I wanted to win," Sanders said at the winner's ceremony, "because I wanted a drink." His victorious return to the 19th hole was helped by three birdies at the first hole.

One reason the pros get off to such a good start on the Blue Course is that the first two holes are easy birdies. The 1st is a relatively easy par 5 of 533 yards (508 regular and 483 ladies'), with no trouble down the left. Four woods to three irons are what the pros use to reach the green in two. Three shots by a mediocre golfer will make the green. The 2nd is a shortish par-4 slight dogleg right, again no problem down the left side of the fairway, another easy hole. After that, like a coquettish lady showing many early promises, the course displays a nature that shows it can take care of itself. The next 16 holes weave through the eight lakes, crowded by 90 bunkers. The course fights back the hardest on the last hole. It is a variation on the architectural theme of the 18th at Pebble Beach; there is water down the left side from the tee to the green—all 437 yards (412 regular and 387 ladies')—and mounds and clusters of palms run down the right side of the fairway. A

drive or second shot hooked too much is in the lake. A perfect drive leaves a four wood or a long iron shot to a green that runs 175 feet from front to rear.

As anyone who owns a driver and a television set knows, it is at the 18th where the Doral-Eastern Open is usually won or lost. Since the first Doral Open in 1962, all but three have been decided on the 18th, and not always in a professional manner. In thirteen tournaments, the winners played the hole the last day in five pars, six bogies, two double bogies, and only one birdie; in 1975, Nicklaus rammed in a 20-foot uphill birdie putt.

The Gold Course often is used as a qualifying site for the Doral Open. Opened in 1970, it was originally dubbed the "Gold Bachelor," since it was to be of herculean length—for men only. It can be stretched to 7,258 yards, 6,655 yards from the regular tees. Women can now play it, but there are no ladies' tees, no ladies' par or course rating.

Von Hagge, one of the United States's more experimental golf-course architects, has built courses over some of the most abominable land: a course over roller-coaster terrain fit only for mountain goats, a land-fill course over what once was a city garbage dump. He also has an ingenious way of describing golf courses. On the Gold Course, he describes his fairway bunkers as not just hazards (wait until you get in one), but signposts with fingertips pointing to the spot on the fairway where the golfer should drive. Such a well-positioned drive will never bring a greenside bunker into play. The problem is staying out of the forty-some signpost hazards and the water that comes into play on thirteen holes.

Though the White Course is ranked next in degree of difficulty, it usually plays several shots harder than the Gold for the aver-

Water, sand, and an easy three putt await the golfer on Doral's famous 437-yard par-4 18th. Two golfers in the process of paying their dues at the hole: (*far left*) Gardner Dickinson explodes ever so carefully from the right greenside bunker; (*left*) Arnold Palmer pitches from the water's edge.

age golfer. The reason is narrow fairways bordered by thick clusters of palms and oaks, bunkers, and series of evil mounds that can leave delicate side and uphill lies. It is the most penalizing of all the courses, especially when the wind blows and for long hitters who hit high howling hooks or slices.

The Red Course is where you can work on such problems without finding your ball in a water hazard or buried in a bunker. It is the easiest of the four regulation courses and is geared not to discourage the average player, while presenting just enough challenges. It too is ideal for the golfer who has come down from the north after not having swung a club in several months. It is an excellent course to begin your golfing vacation on. If you are in good golfing form, you should play easily to your handicap; if not, just a few shots over. The ideal order of play is Red, Gold, White, and Blue. Neither the White nor the Blue should be attempted the first day.

Tee times are mandatory. One can be booked when you make reservations; thereafter, they must be made a minimum of twenty-four hours in advance, up to three consecutive days. If you miss your starting time, you go to the end of the line. This policy is one of the major complaints of guests. Another is that Doral lies beneath the final landing approach of Miami International Airport, and the sporadic roar of jet airplanes has caused many a putt to be yanked.

Neither the noise nor the mandatory starting times prevent people from returning. Doral does a seventy-percent repeat business. Christmas and Easter always bring a full house; reservations for either holiday must be made a minimum of six months in advance. Even at those times there is a sporting country-club air, minus the formality. Though men must wear coat and tie in the evening and after-five attire is appropriate for women, Doral is not dressy. Black tie is never suggested.

You can spend all day and half the night dressed in either golf or tennis attire. The Gazebo, a coffee shop just off the veranda, serves breakfast, lunch, a casual dinner, and late-night snacks. The Conquistador Room is somewhat more formal, demanding coat and tie, but compared to other resort dining rooms, it is not an intimate or serene place to dine. The room is too large, noisy, and brightly lighted. This is more eating than dining. The service is efficient but not great; worse is that the guest feels he is being rushed through his meal. The food is plentiful (especially the desserts) but, again, not great. For excellent dining, one needs only to go to the Starlight Room at the Doral Hotel-on-the-ocean in Miami Beach (shuttle-bus service available)—a luxury highrise hotel on Collins Avenue, which includes such extras as a telephone in each bathroom.

The rooms at the Country Club are almost as luxurious, even without the bathroom telephones. There are no small rooms; all are spacious, furnished with either one or two double beds, color television, and a balcony or terrace. The best are the suites in the lodges just beyond the Blue Course's 18th green.

Doral's nightly entertainment is bingo, which outdraws the showing of old movies. Just after the last bingo card is filled, the first of two nightly shows begins in the Blue Room, a cozy bar just off the lobby. There is usually a stand-up comic or singer—no big names; the big names usually are in the audience or have gone to bed. Keeping its distance from Miami Beach, Doral closes early.

Kaskel himself provided Doral with perhaps its most memorable nightly entertainment. In 1965 and much of 1966 Jackie Gleason lived at the Doral while his show was being televised from Miami. In that time he won several hefty Nassau bets from Kaskel. One night Kaskel decided to recoup his losses and challenged Gleason to a putting contest on the practice green situated between the formal garden and the colorful fountain. The bet was substantial, reportedly $1,000 per hole. Kaskel putted as though he were Billy Casper and pocketed more than $5,000 of Gleason's money.

He used it to buy more art objects for his lobby and to add more multi-colored underwater lights for his fountain, which sprays water high into the air, producing a rainbow of colors; it is even more spectacular when the grounds glitter with a full Miami moon. Kaskel bought the fountain from the 1964 New York World's Fair. It is another monument to a wealthy man's self-indulgence. An even more opulent monument has been erected to the American people's indulgence in sweets; it is in Hershey, Pennsylvania—Chocolate Town, U.S.A.

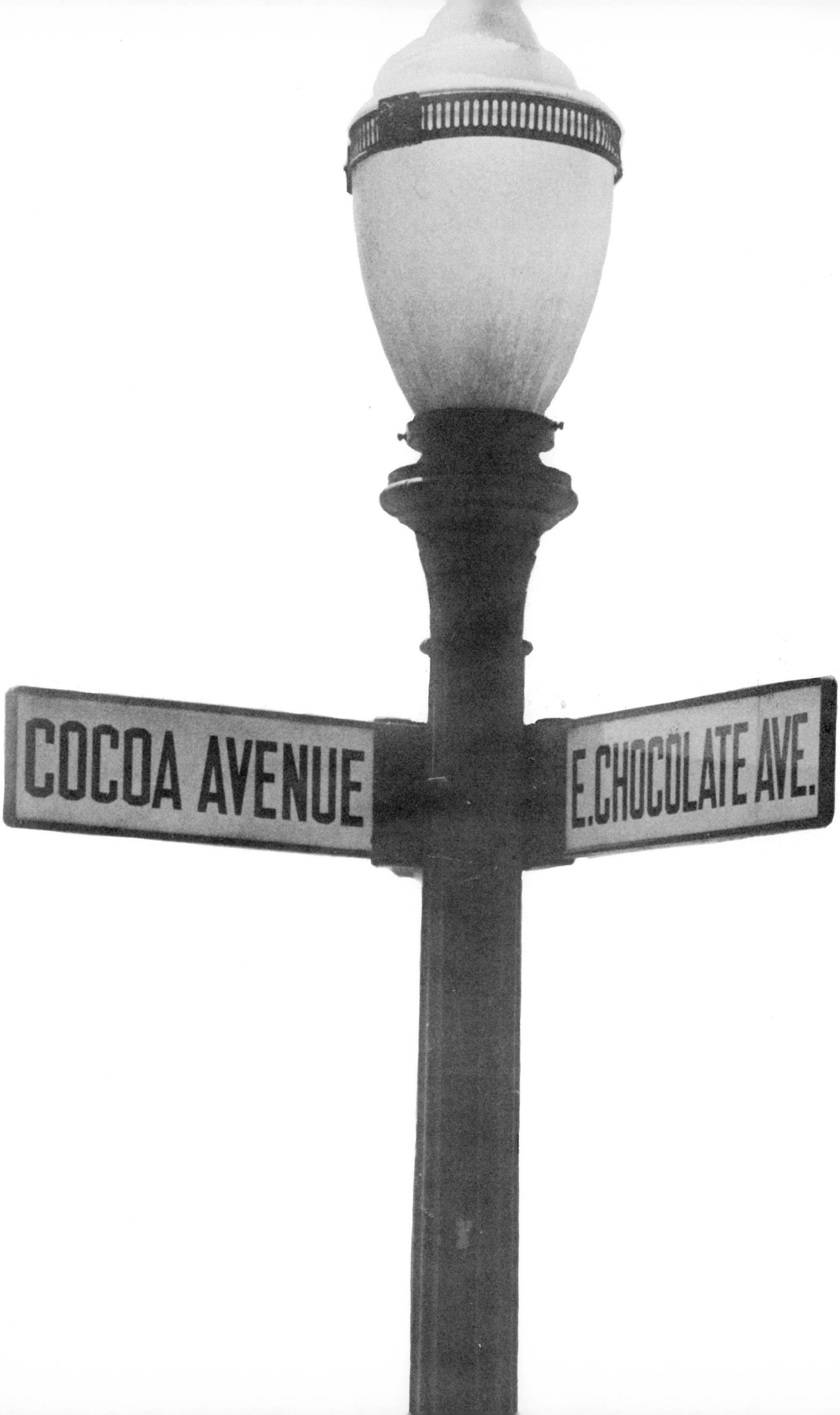
COCOA AVENUE
E. CHOCOLATE AVE.

HOTEL HERSHEY

Hershey, Pennsylvania

Set on the crest of a hill thick with ever-greens, on the north edge of Hershey, Pennsylvania, is a monument to the American people's unending hunger for chocolate —the Hotel Hershey. Cast in the grand mold of hotels like The Broadmoor, The Cloister, and The Otesaga, the Hotel Hershey is the ornate work of yet another rich man, one who had developed an affinity for opulence and the attitude that price is no object. The hotel was built over an eighteen-month period from 1931 to 1933, during the heart of the Depression, by 800 men. The cost of the hotel—reported to be $1.5 million—was actually closer to twice that much.

At whatever cost, it was only a small drop in the financial vat of Hershey Estates, whose sister firm, the Hershey Chocolate Company, reported sales of $32 million in 1930. While other corporations were stubbornly fending off bankruptcy, and bread lines were growing longer in every city, and most people could not afford lunch but could afford a chocolate bar for a nickel, a chocolate factory was becoming a money

factory. In 1934 Hershey's sales were $30 million; in 1941, $55 million; and in 1971 sales were over $401 million, a figure that would not place the present Hershey Foods Corporation in America's top twenty-five

Milton S. Hershey with one of the wards of the Milton Hershey School for Boys, the world's richest orphanage. It retains the controlling stock in the Hershey Foods Corporation.

(Left) The chocolate crossroads of the world. Two avenues meet in the center of Hershey, Pennsylvania.

153

The green on the 310-yard par-4 4th hole on the West Course, epitomizing the character of the course: small flat greens, bunkers, trees and more trees.

corporations. However, in the orbit of corporate trusts, the Hershey Orphanage for Boys is in the top ten, with funds conservatively estimated at $500 million. It was one of the many legacies left by Milton S. Hershey, a man who never went beyond the fourth grade and claimed he made only one great business deal in his life.

Milton Hershey was born in 1857, the son of a strict Mennonite mother and a wandering, failing inventor of a father, Pennsylvania's unsuccessful answer to Isaac Singer. For the first two decades of Milton Hershey's business life he appeared to be following in his father's footsteps. He began his business career as a newspaper printer, failed at that, and then went into candy making. He opened candy stores in Phila-

delphia, Chicago, and New York, and every one of them failed. Like Spencer Penrose, he even went to Colorado to strike it rich in silver, but where Penrose succeeded, Hershey failed. He finally returned to Lancaster, Pennsylvania, as a pushcart vendor of the caramels he was manufacturing. When success came in the early 1890s, Hershey pushed ahead without looking back, and by 1894 his Lancaster Caramel Company was the largest caramel factory in the United States. In 1893 he visited the World's Columbian Exposition in Chicago and saw chocolate being made. He promptly declared, "Caramels are only a fad." He soon started manufacturing chocolate along with his caramels. In 1900 the president of the American Caramel Company approached

Hershey with the idea of a merger to form a monopoly, but said that if Hershey refused, American would ruin his business. Hershey refused. American changed its mind and offered to buy him out. Hershey mulled over the idea and decided to sell his caramel business. Negotiations lasted more than six months; and the final outcome of Hershey's one great deal was that he would sell all his caramel business, patents, and machinery, and keep his chocolate business. The price was $1 million in cash. Hershey was forty-four at the time.

A year later he decided to start not just a chocolate factory, which would become the world's largest, but a town—his own Utopia. Hershey laid out the town and named streets Chocolate and Cocoa avenues. He ran a contest to name his town. Suggestions were Chocolate City, Etabit, Ulikit, Hustletown, and of course, St. Milton. The winning name was Hersheykoko, but the United States Post Office rejected it and reduced it to Hershey, a decision that delighted Milton Hershey.

His politics could have been described as "Pennsylvania Land Baron." Once, when a local barber did not adhere to one of Hershey's policies, he simply had the barber's shop removed. If things had to be done, Hershey paid for them. He was the autocrat who set the rules, though he often claimed otherwise. In the 1930s he told a friend, "We can all find plenty to do without wasting time on rules and regulations. It has been my experience that the expectation of trouble is often one of the chief causes of it."

For all he had accomplished, Hershey remained acutely sensitive to criticism. In 1934 *Fortune* reported what a Pennsylvania Dutch farmer called the smell in the Hershey air, "Da chockle stink," and the article continued: "The moral atmosphere of the town is pervaded by another odor—the sweet and oppressive odor of charity." To this Hershey replied, "You'd think I'd get a little credit for what I have done, wouldn't you?"

When he died in 1945 at the age of eighty-eight, Milton Hershey had done a great deal for his town. Besides building the world's largest chocolate factory and establishing the world's richest orphanage, he built two hotels, a resort, four golf courses, an airport, a lumber company, a department store, a professional hockey team (called the Hershey Bears, but locally called the Hershey Bars), a sports arena, a stadium, a soap division, an elaborate zoo and amusement park, a garden with 120,000 varieties of plants, a campground, a real-estate operation, and a bank. All this was done by a businessman who hated telephones (he would not have one in his office), seldom held business conferences, wouldn't sign his name to letters or documents, wrote pithy telegrams, seldom made speeches, and until his dying day hated media advertising.

A few more important business facts should be noted. The Milton Hershey School for Boys retains the controlling stock of the Hershey Foods Corporation. The price of a Hershey chocolate bar remained a nickel from 1903 to 1970—though since World War II it had changed size twelve times. And, much to the chagrin of Madison Avenue, it was not until 1969 that the first media ad for a Hershey product ran. However, point-of-purchase advertising was first used by Hershey in 1900, when he introduced the first automobile to Lancaster, Pennsylvania, with his logo, Hershey's Cocoa, imprinted on the side. Hershey's success without mass-media advertising was once analyzed by a New York advertising man, who claimed that Hershey had had unnaturally good sales luck because of the pleonasm in his name, the double feminine of her and she.

The Hotel Hershey overlooks the town, including the tall gray smokestacks of the chocolate factory. The original plan was to design the hotel like the Heliopolis Hotel in Cairo, and those blueprints were even bought for several thousand dollars. But the architects estimated the cost to be well over $5 million. "We could cut out the marble stairways, some royal suites and handmade rugs," said one of the architects. "Cut out the marble," answered Hershey. He then ordered that the hotel have 150 rooms (which it does to this day), a Spanish patio, tiled floors in the lobby, and a fountain. It was to have formal gardens and an Italian-Romanesque swimming pool.

The dining room posed an architectural problem. "It," ordered Hershey, who was a small man and often had been seated behind pillars, "is to have no pillars. Furthermore," he added, "it is to have no corners. In some places, if you don't tip well, they put you in a corner." So a large circular dining room was designed, with a domed ceiling, seating for 350 people, and no pillars.

Essentially, the hotel is Spanish Renaissance in style, resembling the work of Addison Mizner, whom Frank Lloyd Wright once called nothing but a good stage designer. Here, however, the lobby of the Hotel Hershey outdoes the mightiest efforts of Hollywood. There are the colorful inlaid tiles, huge bronze urns, hanging lanterns, striped awnings, archways leading off to long halls, a railed balcony running above three sides of the lobby. Only a dueling Errol Flynn is missing.

Nowadays there is fencing of another kind in the lobby—verbal fencing—the kind heard outside corporate board rooms. The hotel has become a favorite eastern convention center. Eighty percent of its business is convention business, which does not help give it the air of grandeur that once induced Lowell Thomas to pronounce it a "palace that out-palaces the palaces of the Maharajahs of India." Unfortunately, the hotel is geared more for convention business than resort trade, offering a menu that varies little from day to day for the "dinner-only" customers. Guests of the hotel on the American plan (the hotel is one of the few that offers all three plans) get treated to some 21 menus, some offering the hotel's specialties—Shrimp and Scallops Bonne Femme, Filet of Beef Perigourdine. The hotel's Swiss chef describes the cuisine as mostly French and part Italian, with a touch of American grill. The dairy products that used to be fresh daily from the Hershey farms now are not. At dinner men must wear jackets.

July and August, when the convention business is not so brisk, are the best time for a visit. Even then, three to four days is a sufficient stay. The hotel is a bustling place, if not with conventions, then usually with sightseers in town to visit the amusement parks or to take the fascinating tour of Hershey's Chocolate World—a simulated world of cocoa and chocolate manufacturing visited by a million people annually. Rooms at the hotel are all good and of ample size, with prices depending on the guest's choice of plan rather than on location. Each room has twin beds, air conditioning, and color television. In the 1940s and 1950s, the resort's heyday, it was open year-round (it is now closed for two weeks in December), operated in a grand manner, mostly in the red financially, and supported by Hershey Estates. In the winter of 1950, *Life* sent a photographer and a staff of reporters to the hotel to report on the operations of a luxury hotel out of season.

They found that rarely had so many served so few. A staff of 85 waited on 13 guests, who paid seven dollars a day without meals.

If the hotel is not what it once was, the Hershey Country Club (open to all guests of the hotel) is one of the most lavish and modern in the United States. It sports a new $5-million clubhouse, carpeted at every dogleg of its two stories. It has exercise rooms, saunas, three curling sheets, 18 guest rooms (the best place for the golfer to stay, but reservations should be made five months in advance), and six dining rooms, including a men's and a women's grill. There is the new East Course and the old West Course, which was originally built by Maurice McCarthy in 1915 as Milton Hershey's private course—why is unknown, as Hershey played infrequently and was a notoriously bad golfer, who took more pride in the maintenance of the course than in maintaining his own game.

Though the West Course has been revamped and redesigned, and holes have been rerouted several times in more than half a century, the course has essentially retained the character of an old course, and is death to golfers who hit howling slices and half-topped fairway wood shots. The course demands more accuracy than length and de-emphasizes putting. The greens are circular, flat, and of moderate size, measuring just under 7,000 square feet. The fairways are narrow, twisting, and thickly lined with trees, almost 17,000 of them, which reduce driving landing areas to 30 yards wide. It is the trees and the bunkering that give the course its great character, for there are no fewer than 117 bunkers on the course, which stretches over 200 acres of rolling terrain, with the outgoing nine forming the perimeter of the course and the incoming nine running inside it.

The course is also steeped in a rich golfing tradition. Since 1963 it has been the site of the annual Pennsylvania State Junior Championship. The Pennsylvania Men's State Open Championship has been held there seventeen times. In 1940 the course was the site of the PGA Championship. The finals were a promoter's dream. After a week of late-August rain, the sun came out, and on a clear, windless day the two finest players of the time were pitted against each other—Byron Nelson and Sam Snead. It was the sort of competition that makes match play so dramatically stimulating. The match went down to the final hole. On the 16th tee (the 34th hole) Nelson stood two down, after frittering away a three-hole advantage. He played the last three holes (the current 10th, 11th, and 12th) in birdie, birdie, and par—a neat nine strokes—to win one up. It was his second major championship.

The West Course is kept in near-tournament condition. The rough graduates off the fairway from two to four inches and up. The fairways are lush (except in the early spring, when they can be extremely soggy), guaranteeing excellent lies and little roll. A team of twenty-five workmen maintains the course, spending eighty hours weekly just hand-raking the bunkers.

It is best to play the course from the regular tees at 6,696 yards (6,928 championship and 6,244 ladies'). Even from the regular tees, all five par 5s play to over 500 yards. Though wind is not a hazard, the West Course incorporates one of the best principles of golf-course architecture—every par 3 runs in a different direction.

The 8th hole is the hardest of the par 3s. It measures 240 yards from the championship tee (230 regular and 220 ladies'). The green is small and elevated, guarded on the left by a long bunker and on the right by two bunkers. There are out-of-bounds and pine trees down the right side of the fairway. The outgoing nine plays shorter by almost 200 yards than the incoming nine, but is at least three strokes harder.

Aside from the 8th, most of the difficulty outgoing is on the first three holes, which are terrors. The 1st hole is the number-one handicap hole; the 2nd, the seventh; and the 3rd, a fiendish short par 4, the eleventh.

The tee on the 1st hole is two-level, with a 15-foot hedge shielding its back half.

From there the golfer can gaze into the distance and see the smokestacks of the chocolate factory puffing away, a reminder that he should try to hit the ball on the sweet spot. The hole is a slight dogleg right stretching 434 yards (423 regular and 412 ladies'). One hundred yards from the tee, down the right side, is a cluster of Norway spruce. At the elbow of the dogleg, 235 yards from the tee, are a large maple, an oak, and a yawning bunker. The left side

Sam Snead in pre–straw-hat days digs the ball out of deep rough during the finals of the 1940 PGA Championship, played over Hershey's West Course. Note how Snead keeps his head down after impact and extends well through the shot.

(*Right*) The graceful driving form of Byron Nelson during the 1940 PGA finals. After being two down on the 33rd hole, Nelson finished with three 3s, to beat Snead one up. It was Nelson's second major championship.

Henry Picard, Hershey Country Club's touring pro in the 1930s. The press dubbed him "the chocolate soldier." Here he demonstrates how to clear the left side as he draws a five-iron shot.

of the fairway is lined with white birches and more Norway spruce, and at the corner of the dogleg is a large, spreading elm. The ideal drive is just to the left of the right fairway bunker, or, drawing just slightly, over it. But even such a sweet drive does not leave the golfer with an easy second shot. Fifty yards in front of the green is a bunker to catch a topped four-wood shot. The green is large and flat and guarded by two deep bunkers on either side and by tall Australian pines and Douglas firs at the back.

The 2nd hole is a straightaway 570-yard par 5 (548 yards regular and 533 yards la-

dies'). You drive from an elevated tee sparsely surrounded by Australian pines, elms, and Ailanthus trees. The fairway slopes gently downhill from the tee, runs flat for 400 yards, then rises sharply for 50 feet, making it almost impossible to hit the green in two and leaving a blind third shot to a large green that slopes slightly from right to left. The fairway is narrow, hemmed in by dozens of Australian pines, blue spruce, and larches. Out-of-bounds runs down the right side from the tee to the green.

The 3rd hole is the most deceiving on the course, one of those great short par 4s where you either make a birdie or take a double or triple bogey. It is only 355 yards long (305 regular and 277 ladies'), a straightaway hole with an array of trouble left and right off the tee and around the green. The championship tee is recessed in a shaded chute of tall poplars, beeches, and ashes that also run down the right side of the fairway, mingling with elms and maples and concealing most of the fence that marks out-of-bounds. The first of three fairway bunkers begins 194 yards from the tee on the left side of the fairway; another is placed 30 yards beyond it. Between the bunkers there is a deep gully. On the right is another bunker. Provided you have driven the ball perfectly, with either a three wood or a two iron, between the three bunkers to a landing area 29 yards wide, you are then faced with a delicate short iron shot. If you come off the ball just slightly, the ball will catch a bunker right of the green or sail out-of-bounds. Pulled, the ball catches a bunker left of the green. Hit too firmly, the ball will land on the back of the green and roll off, for the small green rises from front to center, then falls away.

For the golfer who prefers more room for error, there is the East Course, designed by

George Fazio and opened in 1969. It is a big course, measuring 7,240 yards from the championship tees (6,515 yards regular, but only 5,680 ladies'). The fairways are wide, and the greens are large, heavily contoured, and rigidly protected by bunkers, making every shot to a green all carry.

Hershey likes to advertise that it has fifteen miles of golf, and rightly so. Besides the two courses at the country club, there are two 9-hole courses—one at the Hotel Hershey and one at the Spring Creek Course in the center of town. Also in town, adjacent to Chocolate World, is the Parkview Course, one of the state's best public courses, where the Pennsylvania State Public Links Tournament is held every year.

By no small effort, Hershey has become Pennsylvania's golfing capital. Helping to spread the word that the town of Hershey had more than chocolate bars were two golfers who represented the Hershey Country Club on the pro tour. The first was Henry Picard, who served as the club's tournament pro from 1934 to 1941. He was dubbed the Chocolate Soldier by the sportswriters. When he left, he recommended the position to his friend, Ben Hogan, who held the post for a decade. The name Hogan, followed by Hershey, appeared in the winner's column more than fifty times. It was a sweet combination, but then the state of Pennsylvania has richly nourished Hogan's career. Of the four U.S. Opens he won, he captured two in Pennsylvania in 1950 and 1953, and had the trophy shipped to his home in Texas—a golfing state. It was in Fort Worth, Dallas, Houston, and El Paso that many of the game's great players were spawned, where three great courses blossomed—Colonial, Preston Trail, and Champions. North Texas State College dominated collegiate golf in the 1950s; the University of Houston in the 1960s. Yet, it was not until 1973 that Texas had a first-class golfing resort—Horseshoe Bay—out in what is called LBJ country, properly named Texas Hill Country, just outside Austin.

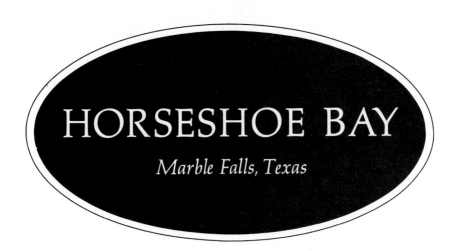

HORSESHOE BAY

Marble Falls, Texas

When Texans speak fondly about a special stretch of Texas land, there usually is oil or a natural-gas field beneath its crusty surface or rising from it, a department store named Neiman-Marcus, a giant oval football stadium where Texas University annually beats Texas A & M or, spreading over 200 acres, a golf course, its green fairways lined with pecan and oak trees, where the competitive course record still is held by either Ben Hogan or Byron Nelson. Perhaps because Texas lacks the dramatic coastline of northern California or the majestic Rockies of Colorado, Texans rarely talk beauty, except in the one area known as Texas Hill Country. To non-Texans it is best known as the birthplace of Lyndon Baines Johnson.

The Hill Country begins 20 miles west of Austin, where Highway 71 begins to dip and rise with the land. Road signs read "Beware of Washes." Limestone bluffs jut out above the Pedernales River and Flat Rock Creek. In the distance you can see huge outcroppings of granite—Packsaddle Mountain, site of the last Indian fight in

Texas, in 1873, thrusts upward to an altitude of 1,620 feet. From the tops of the hills you can see the mighty Colorado River, tamed and flowing slowly, its banks revealing the reddish clay soil of the Hill Country.

Texas Hill Country's most prominent citizen, President Lyndon Baines Johnson, rounding up a Hereford.

(*Left*) The fine bunkering on the 1st hole of the Horseshoe Bay Country Club, a 389-yard par 4.

The Colorado is dammed seven times over 150 miles, forming seven lakes that vary in length from 6 to 65 miles. Lake LBJ is of average size, 20 miles long and 2 miles wide. It is the only lake of the seven that has a constant water level. It is also the lake with the tallest inland lighthouse in Texas.

The lighthouse is now a symbol of Texas's latest contribution to the game of golf: Horseshoe Bay, a luxury-resort/residential development nourished by Texas oil and ingenuity and planned with a typically Texan affinity for bigness. Within half a decade, Horseshoe Bay is to have the largest complete Robert Trent Jones, Inc. golfing complex in the United States—63 holes. Now it has one first-class Bob Jones, Jr. course —its fairways seemingly gashed through the granite and limestone—the venue of the revived Texas State Open.

The resort also has a 6,000-foot-long airstrip capable of handling a DC-9 jet, a marina capable of handling medium-size yachts, a lodge capable of handling 250 guests (who actually are housed in a colony of low, spreading condominiums), a swimming pool, a dozen tennis courts, and a kitchen that serves that Texas specialty, chicken-fried steak. But even more impressive is the lofty ambition of the resort's founders, who confidently predict that Horseshoe Bay is going to be the Sea Pines Plantation, without the sea, of the Southwest. Sound pretentious? Maybe. But not in a state where professional baseball is played in an air-conditioned stadium and the only way a first-time guest to Preston Trail Golf Club in Dallas can find the clubhouse is to remember that it is smaller than the houses surrounding it.

Even so, the idea that Horseshoe Bay will be the Sea Pines of the Southwest is all the more remarkable because its cofounder,

Norman Hurd (cousin Wayne Hurd is the other), did not know until 1971 that Sea Pines existed, never had met Charles Fraser, and never before had planned a large resort/residential community. Norman Hurd does not use terms like "visual pollution." When he speaks, it is almost in a whisper, with a voice barbed with prairie twang. His face is deeply lined and ruddy, and his hands are callused and scarred. He gives the impression that he would be just as happy out there by an oil rig, in the dust storms and the blue northers in Eastland and Ranger, Texas, where in fact he spent some of his oil-business years.

He came to the Hill Country to buy two acres of lake-front property, but finding none for sale, he settled into a Texas-size deal and purchased three ranches totaling 5,500 acres. The land has 13 miles of shoreline, from which his resort recedes into the hills, blending beautifully with the landscape. "We hope," Hurd said in 1971, "this resort looks like it comes out of this beautiful ground and goes back into it."

He was true to his word, using the native granite and limestone for the foundations of clubhouses and homes, siding them with bleached cedar, and incorporating strict zoning and building codes. (The maximum height of any building is 25 feet above the natural elevation.) Vast animal preserves where no hunting is allowed were established, though nearby ranches provide some of the best deer hunting in Texas. The Horseshoe Bay airstrip is a wealth of airplanes on any given weekend during the hunting season (November 1 to the first Sunday in January), lined with at least ten million dollars' worth of Lear jets.

Though the airstrip is particularly enticing to hunters, flying golfers, and potential home buyers, it is a Texas luxury feature, since Horseshoe Bay is within 200

Tom Kite, Horseshoe Bay's resident and touring pro, hits a long-iron shot over a lake on the 190-yard par-3 8th during the final round of the revived Texas State Open in 1975, played at Horseshoe Bay.

miles of eighty percent of the population of the state. And in Texas 200 miles is not a long way, as any Texan will tell you. He will also tell you many other things about the state that a non-Texan might find staggering. First, there are more private airstrips in Texas than in any other state. Second, if you drove from Houston to Los Angeles, by the time you left Texas you would be halfway there. Third, you could put the total square miles of the United States's original thirteen colonies into Texas.

Thus it was not unusual that the first lots sold at Horseshoe Bay were next to the airstrip, where home owners could simply taxi their Pipers or Cessnas down the road and onto the runway. The roads winding through the resort are therefore wide. The road running a quarter of a mile straight to the main lodge is 80 feet wide, a boulevard in fact, with the median lined with tall pampas grass.

Accommodations vary in price according to size. There are two-room suites and large rooms with two double beds, all furnished with color television and large bay windows that do not open. Since they are in Texas, all rooms are air-conditioned. The colony of condominiums is a short walk from the main lodge, a low building made of granite and cedar, with large windows that command views of Lake LBJ and the lighthouse, which chimes every hour. All meals are served there. The dining rooms are small and quaint. The menu varies little, mainly offering good beef, especially a variety of cuts of steak, which if ordered rare are cooked very, very rare. Dinner is informal and usually a festive gathering. Men and women dress according to their moods —which means anything from Levis to mink. After dinner on weekends, a small combo plays until the main bar closes at 2:00 A.M.

For those who have enjoyed more than their quota of bourbon and still insist upon driving, a word of caution is needed. Horseshoe Bay's head of private security is a former Texas Ranger (of the law-enforcement agency, not the baseball team) who picks up not only drunken drivers but also an occasional marijuana smuggler.

The golfer can get his highs on the golf course, for Jones's layout, a stern but fair test, offers the average golfer ample opportunities for pars and birdies. There are at least five holes that are easy, even if your drive slices or hooks. One of the easiest is the 1st hole. From a raised tee, the golfer cannot see the green, which lies at the bottom of a slope 389 yards from the championship tee (365 regular and 335 ladies'). The hole doglegs slightly to the right. The fairway dips and then rises slightly from the tee. Down either side of the fairway stand tall pampas grass and half a dozen live oak trees. At the elbow of the dogleg is a bunker. Bordering the sides of the fairway are the 9th fairway on the right and the 10th fairway on the left. The ideal drive is just to the left of the fairway bunker, leaving the ball on the crest of the hill and providing the golfer with a clear view of the green and the hope that he does not pull or hook his second shot. Three deep bunkers line the left of the fairway all the way to the green, which is further protected by a bunker in the right front and rear. It is not the hardest shot the golfer will face

on the course, but it does test him just enough to remind him to keep his head still and his backswing slow. Even if he does neither on his first two shots and ends up short of the green, he can pitch on for a possible par or a cinch bogey. So the 1st hole will not ruin a golfer's score. The 2nd will.

It is a medium-length par 3 (three of the four par 3s play over water), which can be disastrous if the golfer misses the green. The tee sits adjacent to a large outcropping of granite. In front and to the right of the golfer is a large pond. The hole measures 162 yards from the championship tee (140 yards regular and 130 yards ladies'). The green is large and bunkered on either side and rises steeply from front to rear. A shot hit to the front edge with bite will roll back into the water, and a shot hit over the green leaves a delicate pitch shot over a mound to the downward-sloping green.

The first two holes set the character of the course, at once liberally redeeming and strictly punitive. The course measures 6,839 yards from the championship tees (6,358 yards regular and 5,893 ladies'), and there are 71 bunkers (only 20 fairway bunkers), but water comes into play on eleven holes, and while the fairways are amply wide, the course favors neither the golfer who draws nor the golfer who fades the ball. The average golfer can slice and hook all day and not find trouble, provided he slices and hooks on the proper holes (any but the par 3s), though such luck is as rare as finding Penncross bent-grass greens in Texas. Well,

Ben Crenshaw on his way to scorching Horseshoe Bay's bent-grass green with a final round of 64 in the 1975 Texas State Open. Here he explodes from the greenside bunker where he put his second shot on the 530-yard par-5 12th.

The green of the most spectacular hole on the course, the 219-yard par-3 17th. There is no alternative route to the green. On your first, second or third shot you must clear sixty yards of Slick Rock Creek.

Horseshoe Bay has them—slick, true, and undulating. They are also large and elevated, and four are placed diagonally to the fairway, making shots to them all carry.

The hardest hole on the course is the 16th, the number-two handicap hole on the incoming nine. It is a long par 4, measuring 419 yards from the championship tee (405 regular and 380 ladies'), but it plays longer because it plays uphill, all the way. The hole doglegs slightly right, with a bunker to the right, 256 yards from the tee. Out-of-bounds and thick woods of live oak, cedar, and mesquite line the fairway down the right side from the tee to the green. The

ideal drive is just left of the fairway bunker; even then the green looks far away. It is, leaving the golfer with not only a long iron shot or fairway wood shot to an elevated, well-guarded green, but a whimpering wish for some of the power of a Ben Crenshaw. In the 1975 Texas State Open, played at Horseshoe Bay, Crenshaw won at 20 under par (the course was not set up for tournament play), scorching the bent-grass greens with a 64 the final round. Helping his four sub-par rounds were four 4s at the 16th. For the field, the hole played to a degree of difficulty of 4.7 strokes.

If the 16th is the hardest, the 17th is the

most spectacular. It too is one of those rare holes in golf in which the imitation is better than the original. For Horseshoe's 17th is a copy of the 17th hole at Chicago's Medinah Country Club, site of the 1949 and 1975 U.S. Opens. Both are par 3s, demanding a long iron or wood shot over water—all carry; there is no alternate route to the green. From the championship tee at Horseshoe's 17th, the golfer looks down to four terraces of tees, from which the hole plays between 219 and 150 yards. The golfer also sees three live oak trees on the left side of the fairway and then the 60-yard-wide Slick Rock Creek, with its high banks of limestone. Fifteen yards from the creek is the green, guarded by long shallow bunkers on either side and by one protecting the entire back of the green. Whereas the 17th green at Medinah rises steeply from front to rear, making it all but impossible to get down in two putts from the back edge if the pin is in the front, Horseshoe's 17th green is less severe. It rises gently from front to center and then levels off, making the hole a fairer one without sacrificing its dramatic appeal or playing value.

The 17th incorporates what is best about the course, which is routed over interesting terrain, with large outcroppings of granite, small rushing waterfalls, steep limestone banks siding creeks that meander throughout the course, giving it its exciting playing value. Like most of Jones's courses, it is a strong test from the championship tees and a fair test from the regular tees. But from neither is it as severe as Doral's Blue Course or Dick Wilson's other flat inland masterpiece course, at La Costa Country Club—the course the pros struggle around during the Tournament of Champions.

LA COSTA
COUNTRY CLUB
Carlsbad, California

In the spring of 1975 Deane Beman, commissioner of the Tournament Players' Division of the PGA, announced the cancellation of the Tournament of Champions, the reason being that it somewhat resembled the revamped World Series of Golf both in format and in competitors. It was a surprising announcement that produced an equally surprising undercurrent of protest from the tournament players, who usually protest only about roughs being too long or greens too slick. When the Tournament Policy Board met a month later, they rescheduled the tournament. The T of C, as it is called, would stay. The protest was not only a strong vote that the T of C should remain an essential part of the professional tour, but an indication that the pros basically liked where it was played—La Costa.

The T of C is a 72-hole medal-play event, but comprises an elite field of pros who

within the year have won either a PGA tournament or one of the major professional championships. First prize is $40,000. However, there is no 36-hole cut, and a pro who plays like a six handicapper, as

The Tournament of Champions's champion, five-time winner Jack Nicklaus, in the process of winning the 1977 T of C. As usual, he is all concentration.

(*Left*) Johnny Miller drives to his first Tournament of Champions victory in 1974. It was a year in which he won seven tournaments and broke the yearly money-earning record with winnings of $353,021. Note that at nearly the halfway point on his downswing, Miller has his head well behind the ball, his right elbow close to his side, and his knees and hips perfectly synchronized, as he pushes against a firm left side.

Bruce Crampton did in 1971, struggling around for four days 29 over par, still earns $2,500—the amount guaranteed to every player. Such lack of pressure gives the tournament a low-key, relaxing air, in which the pros enjoy being feted with lavish buffets and cocktail parties, while for those occupational hazards such as tired muscles, aching ligaments, sun-parched skin, and seared nerves, they are pampered with saunas, rubdowns, mineral-pool baths, Swiss and Scotch showers, with all expenses for player and family generously picked up by La Costa. No wonder there was a protest.

La Costa is located 90 miles south of Los Angeles, 30 miles north of San Diego and 20 miles south of a town called San Clemente. Yet, in its relationship to reality, it is closest to Disneyland, 50 miles north. As a resort, it resembles the Land of Oz—all 7,000 acres of it—where people come to shape up their golf or tennis games, tone up their muscles, dry out their bodies, and slim down their waists—anything to look forever youthful. Here, the Wicked Witch of the West is middle age.

Whereas many other resorts were built and dominated by one man, La Costa was built by a syndicate out of Las Vegas with a gambling-casino background. La Costa received its first of many blemishes when, a few months after it opened in 1965, it was reported that the $100 million the place cost to build had come from the scandal-ridden Teamsters pension fund. It is no secret that various members of the Mafia hang out there. And it was there, just 20 miles south of San Clemente, where John Dean, John Ehrlichman, and others planned to deal with the Watergate cover-up.

Even so, La Costa has taken on a very definite West Coast chic—actors and actresses often come from Los Angeles or off

location to relax. Dean Martin, Phil Harris, Carol Burnett, Jack Lemmon, Diana Ross, Barbra Streisand, Bette Davis, and Ava Gardner sprinkle the grounds with Hollywood stardust. However, the most frequently seen celebrity is Burt Bacharach, who lives just down the road in Del Mar and comes there to play tennis two or three times a week with pro Pancho Segura. The employees' favorite celebrity is Carol Burnett, who spends most of her days there dressed very un–La Costa-like in blue jeans, a T-shirt, and sneakers. As one employee said, "We have to put up with so much bad-mannered money around here that it is an absolute delight to get someone down to earth like Carol Burnett, who acts like she doesn't have a dime and couldn't care less."

One of the employees' favorite stories regarding bad-mannered guests has to do with an occurrence in the women's spa. A rather portly woman curtly asked a masseuse to stop the massage she was giving another guest, and to give her a Scotch-mist shower. The masseuse told the woman very politely she would have to wait her turn. The woman became more insistent that her needs be attended to, and the masseuse became equally adamant that they would be—when it was her turn. Finally the woman said to the masseuse, "Well, kiss my ass." Sizing up the situation and the woman, the masseuse said, "You'll have to mark the spot, lady, because you look all ass to me."

Yet when one guest was asked whether she did not think La Costa was just a bit nouveau riche, she replied, "Oh, gosh no, it's right outside of La Jolla." Most guests do not care whether there is new money, old money, or even tainted money around. They go for the luxury, excellent facilities, and celebrity watching. In actual fact, La Costa is several resorts very poshly rolled

The sandy problems you must negotiate as you approach the green on the 551-yard par-5 9th. To make matters worse, the hole usually plays into the wind.

into one. Its spa facilities for men and women cost $6 million, twice as much as the golf course. It is a tennis resort with 25 courts and pro Pancho Segura, who is Jimmy Connors's teacher. It is a golfing resort with former touring pro Tommy Jacobs and a pro shop that looks like an annex of Joseph Magnin.

Uniquely, it offers two completely different resort lifestyles. You can stay in one of the 279 hotel rooms near the clubhouse. Each room is large, with two double beds, color television, a dressing room, and a large bathroom. The carpeting is thick—wall to wall. From each room, it is but a short walk to the main clubhouse, a big two-level beige shingled building that is the hub of activity. It houses several cocktail lounges, five restaurants—one for dieters only, one specializing in French cuisine, one Italian, a steak-and-chops restaurant, and one for seafood. All in all, the cuisine is good and plentiful, while the service varies from excellent to poor. Dinner is a dressy occasion, not formal, but very fashionable—West Coast casual chic. Neckties are required for men only in the main dining room and in the Pisces Room, but expensive Italian loafers are almost standard attire.

While the nightlife at most resorts consists of either old PG-rated movies or a few rubbers of bridge, at La Costa's the nightlife begins later and gets louder. There are newly released movies, bridge, backgammon lessons, and even a palmist, all to be enjoyed before venturing to the Tournament of Champions Lounge. The resort

173

bounces with live entertainment and dancing until the small hours, serving up more than a whirling atmosphere.

For those following a different lifestyle or desiring more privacy, La Costa offers a variety of villas for rent, where a guest or guests can have a swimming pool almost to themselves and bask in a secluded existence.

La Costa likes to refer to itself as Paradise Found, and for the golfer whose wife or companion does not play golf, it is indeed something of a paradise. The man can play golf while the woman spends her days in the spa, exercising, getting massages, going to the beauty salon, getting facials, or taking a bus to nearby La Jolla for shopping. Needless to say, it is less expensive if she plays golf, even if not well. A new nine called the Orange Nine, which is geared for the less aggressive player, has been added (more are on the drawing boards). For women, it measures 2,638 yards, for men 2,986 yards. The tree-lined fairways are wide, with only a few fairway bunkers. Greens are small and well bunkered, though. There is no rough. The Orange Nine was designed to reduce play on the regular course used for the T of C, the Green and Gold nines.

They were designed by Dick Wilson in 1965, and, as he usually did, he planned and built a course to fit the existing terrain, a river basin in a valley. He dressed the 230 acres in $1.6 million worth of springy turf, with 112 bunkers and seven lakes, which make up the 11 water holes. He laid out his nines in a wide V shape, with each nine beginning and ending by the clubhouse. Unlike Stanley Thompson, Wilson did not believe that playing only nine holes was a cardinal sin. From the fairways, forming the perimeter of the course, rise gentle hills scraped smooth by bulldozers,

on which stand that favorite California commodity—condominiums. The other fairways are lined with cypress, sycamore, and Monterey pine trees.

From the beginning, the course was built for tournament play—a bold move precipitated by, of all people, Howard Hughes. One of the developers of La Costa, Allard Roen, sold his Desert Inn in Las Vegas, where the T of C had originated, to Hughes, but the deal did not include the rights to the T of C. It was not that Hughes did not like golf; on the contrary, in his youth he had been an ardent, low-handicap golfer. One day he asked his pro whether he would ever be as good as Bobby Jones, and when the pro said no, Hughes stopped playing. The reason Hughes did not want the T of C around the Desert Inn is that he did not like all those people gazing up at his suite.

So in 1969 the T of C moved to La Costa with the blessings of Hughes and the PGA, who dislike having legalized gambling associated with their tournaments. When 29 pros arrived at La Costa in the third week of April that year, most no doubt wished they were back in Vegas, where they had a better chance of rolling snake-eyes than of getting up and down from the greenside rough in two. The tournament officials had turned Wilson's difficult but fair course into a pretrial U.S. Open test. They narrowed the fairways to 30 yards, let the rye-grass rough grow to almost six inches bordering the fairways and around the greens, then sat back and listened to the game's finest players complain about the rough. "You get tired just walking through it to get to the fairways," said Billy Casper. "I only played nine holes, then I had to stop and sharpen my wedge," quipped George Archer. In four days only two men broke par; winner Gary Player was four under at 284, and Lee Trevino was two under. Of the 128 rounds, there were only 10 sub 70s, seven by former U.S. Open winners. There were four scores of 80 or higher, one recorded by Jack Nicklaus, who ended up 8 over par.

Two years later, with the rough still high and thick, Nicklaus's score, but not many others, came down. Jack won nine under par. But there were 27 rounds of 77 or higher, and only six players broke 290.

For regular play, the rough is cut down to one inch. However, the rest of the course is maintained in tournament condition. In fact, year-round it is in such good condition that "winter rules" were enforced only once between 1973 and 1976. The lush fairways are both a plus and a minus. The ball sits up very well, but the turf yields little roll —a minus for the short hitters, but also a plus, for a drive drawing or fading too much will not roll into the thick rough.

It is thus best to play the course from the regular tees at 6,446 yards (6,855 championship; 5,638 ladies'). The course plays to every lush yard of its length, and more. Most of the greens are guarded by three or four bunkers and are elevated—making every shot to them all carry. The greens are of average modern size, thus putting the premium on accurate driving and second shots, not putting.

The front nine is not distinctive, except for a waterfall on the 7th hole, a par 3 of 181 yards (158 yards regular and 126 ladies'), and the long 449-yard (425-yard regular; 327-yard ladies') 5th, a straight hole usually played into a quartering right-to-left wind. During one round of the 1971 T of C, it did not yield one birdie to the 34 contestants.

On courses designed for tournaments, the 18th hole usually is a strong par 4 or 5, one that will be a thump in the gut to the player under pressure and one that will

Gary Player rolls in a thirty-foot birdie putt on the 4th green to win the first T of C played at La Costa, in 1969. That year the rough was so severe that only two players broke par for seventy-two holes. Player was four under and Lee Trevino two under.

Frustration and triumph on the 540-yard par-5 17th. (*Above*) In the 1970 T of C, Gardner Dickinson emotes utter exasperation over a putt that failed to drop for a birdie. (*Right*) In 1975 Tom Watson grins with immense satisfaction after sinking a birdie putt.

keep the gallery on edge, with great expectations. Not only does La Costa have a strong finishing hole, a 428-yard (403 regular and 293 ladies') par 4, slightly uphill to an elevated green surrounded by three bunkers, but in a sense its last three holes are 18ths. They are called the Last Mile. The 16th is a long 409-yard (390-yard regular and 272-yard ladies') par 4 doglegging slightly to the right. A good drive will leave a long iron or fairway wood shot to a fairly large contoured green guarded on either side and in back by yawning bunkers. It is a good hole to put the golfer in the proper aggressive frame of mind he needs to play the 17th, the best hole on the course, a 560-yard par 5 (540 yards regular and 402 yards ladies').

The long tee lies in an opening in front of which stretches 100 yards of rough. Down the left side of the fairway are clusters of cypress and sycamore trees and four bunkers, two to catch badly hooked drives and two farther down, creeping into the fairway. On the right of the fairway, 300 yards from the tee, begins a kidney-shaped lake that pushes to the edge of the green. A good drive should be down the right center of the fairway. But it is the second shot that the golfer must play with the greatest care, ideally with a slight fade to the edge of the pond in order to leave an open shot into the green. Along the left side of the green stretches a yawning bunker.

In case the length of the last three holes does not make the golfer wish for some of Jack Nicklaus's power, there is the fact that they usually play into a stiff west wind coming off the Pacific, only three miles away. In 1975, when Gary Player lost the T of C to Al Geiberger, he hit the 16th green with a screaming one-iron shot, while on the 10th hole, which at 435 yards plays only seven yards shorter—but downwind —he reached the green with a short iron.

At La Costa, Player has won the T of C once and has never finished worse than second. Yet despite the severity of the course, he praises it. "This is golf," he once said of it. "If a man is to be penalized for missing a one-foot putt, he should be equally penalized for missing a drive."

Such remarks could make Pinehurst's Donald Ross roll over in his grave in the Sandhills of North Carolina, where the soil was once considered too poor for a corpse to be buried in properly.

PINEHURST

Pinehurst, North Carolina

Any golfer who has ever boasted about great golf in the United States has boasted about Pinehurst—its six courses, its sandy-soil fairways, so easy to walk on, and its warm, dry air, so easy to breathe. And those golfers who especially relish the artistry of a well-hit chip shot and watching the ball roll up a mound, slide down the side of another, and cross a crowned green warm to the name of Pinehurst. It is where their fathers and even their grandfathers golfed. In 1962, when the U.S. Amateur finally was played over Pinehurst No. 2, one sportswriter proclaimed, "This is as appropriate a gesture to history as it would be to play the World Series at Baseball's Hall of Fame in Cooperstown, N.Y."

But the essence of golf at Pinehurst may be best understood by recalling the amorous adventures of a young unmarried couple who were invited as guests to a black-tie dinner dance at the Pinehurst Country Club in the late 1950s. During the evening they became more and more romantically involved, and at ten o'clock they decided to abandon the dance floor to seek a place where they could be alone. As they walked down the first fairway of Pinehurst No. 2

America's most ingenious golf course architect, Donald Ross. He has designed over six hundred courses, on which forty-five national championships have been played.

(*Left*) One of North Carolina's best and most popular golfers, Billy Joe Patton, picks the ball off a fairway bunker to capture his third Men's North and South Amateur in 1963. The tournament, which began in 1901, has been played the same number of times as the U.S. Amateur.

Course, they accidentally stumbled into the left-side fairway bunker. Sensing it was a quiet place where they would not be disturbed, they wasted little time before engaging in their passionate pursuits. The man undid his black tie and unbuttoned his suspenders; the woman began to ease out of her gown. A guard who roamed the grounds at night heard the commotion, walked to the bunker, shone his flashlight on the couple, and asked, "Are you members?"

The embarrassed man, hoping the guard would leave, lied, "Yes, we are."

But the officious guard stood there and motioned with his flashlight for the couple to leave. After quickly redressing, the couple started to go. "Wait!" shouted the guard. "You can't be members. No member of Pinehurst would leave a bunker unraked."

Any self-respecting Pinehurst member would sooner say that Pinehurst was not the golfing capital of the United States than under any circumstances leave a bunker unraked. The odds on either happening are as low as the odds on consecutively birdieing the par-4 5th hole on Pinehurst No. 2, a feat accomplished only once. So deeply embedded are the rules and etiquette of golf in the minds of the members and residents of Pinehurst that they have become a way of life among those who understand that golf, more than any other game, reflects the realities of life. In golf, as in life, you follow through and play the course as you find it. When Pinehurst's golfing autocrat, Richard Tufts, was asked once about players who move the ball around while playing "winter rules," he answered, "We are becoming a nation of nudgers." Just the reverse has been the ideal of Pinehurst since it was founded by James Walker Tufts in 1895.

It was not his intention to turn his resort into a golfing capital, but that is what it now is. Other resorts' claims to being golfing capitals are accurate only to the extent that they are to Pinehurst what state capitals are to Washington, D.C. True, the game is not governed from Pinehurst, but for years its number-one resident, Richard Tufts, helped to guide and shape golf in the United States with such care that none other than Joe Dey called him "Mr. Golf." No other man has been chairman of more committees of the USGA than Richard Tufts, who was also its president from 1956 to 1957. A few of his contributions include standardizing a course's condition for USGA national competitions, helping to start junior and senior USGA championships, and serving as a leading architect of the USGA's handicap system.

The fact that every great player since Harry Vardon—who helped popularize Pinehurst—has walked its fairways adds to the resort's stature, but even more important is that more national tournaments have been held at Pinehurst than anywhere else in the Americas. In 1929 its list of tournaments numbered sixteen. Its Men's North and South Amateur, originally called the United North and South, started in 1901 and has been played every year since—as many times as the U.S. Amateur. The Women's North and South Amateur has been played consecutively since 1903. The North and South Open started the same year and lasted until 1951. In fact, Pinehurst was the first resort to welcome the golfing professionals by holding a tournament for them and also putting them up free of charge.

Now there is the Colgate Hall of Fame Classic, annually played at Pinehurst in August, and a World Golf Hall of Fame. But both are new and reflect a definite change at the resort, where for three-quarters of a century, until 1970, when the Tufts family relinquished control of Pinehurst, the prevailing idea of major change had been changing a stretch of golf holes from one course to another. Some forty holes have changed courses in this manner. When No. 5 Course was opened in 1961, Pinehurst was the first resort to advertise that it had five courses. However, at the turn of the century it took only one course there to provide Americans with one of the worst excuses for playing golf—that it was good for their health.

It was the healthful climate of North Carolina's Sandhill area—the warm, dry air and the mild winters—that so attracted James Tufts that he made several visits there before he decided to build a resort in 1895. A quite proper Bostonian, James was a cousin of Charles Tufts, who donated the land on which Tufts University now stands. As Charles Tufts was acquiring a modest fortune as a brick maker and real-estate developer, James was amassing a larger fortune as one of the first men to successfully develop a commercially feasible method of silver-plating. In 1891 he consolidated his firm with the American Soda Fountain Company, and four years later he retired. He was fifty-six at the time and not in robust health. He felt the rejuvenating climate of the Sandhills would be ideal for him and other people of some means who wanted to get away from harsh northeastern winters.

Tufts initially bought 5,000 acres of cut-over timberland for one dollar an acre. The Page family, who sold Tufts the land, thought they had put over one of the best business deals in North Carolina history. The soil was considered so poor that it was said a corpse had to be buried in commercial fertilizer if it was expected to rise on Judgment Day.

A member of the Page family wrote a friend in New York City about the deal: "I

The quite proper Bostonian and founder of Pinehurst, James Walker Tufts. When he bought more than five thousand acres of seemingly worthless sand for one dollar an acre in 1895, the sellers thought they had put over one of the best business deals in North Carolina history.

have had an amusing experience," began Walter Hines Page. "There is an old chap up in Boston who I fear has more money than good common sense, and he had a wild scheme in the back of his head that he can make a resort up here in these barren sand wastes. We have just finished extracting the turpentine from a large number of pines on a big acreage and then cut them up for lumber. There are about ten thousand acres in all. I asked him to make an offer and he suggested it might be worth $1.00 an acre, but I closed the deal by selling it to him for $7,500. He gave me his check for $500 to bind the bargain, but I am afraid that I will never see him once he gets home and thinks it over."

With that unrelenting Yankee pride and determination, Tufts returned and brought with him plans drawn by America's first—and now generally regarded as its greatest—landscape architect, Frederick Law Olmsted. Olmsted's plan called for a village common with a town hall at one end and a church at the other. The streets would wind around a village green; and the shops and other businesses would be clustered around the common. He ordered 200,000 trees and shrubs, and designed a series of 60-foot-wide lanes. He lined the lanes with longleaf pine, holly, dogwood, and magnolia trees, behind which small cottages were built. So circuitous were the lanes that even long-time residents often got lost in the maze of greenery. It had all the charm of a quaint New England town.

When the Holly Inn was completed in 1898 Tufts sent out notices to northern doctors that "consumptives are welcome." But at that time tuberculosis was thought to be a contagious rather than hereditary disease. The next year Tufts sent notices to doctors saying "consumptives excluded." Until 1970 the deeds to houses sold to future Pinehurst residents specified that no one with tuberculosis could buy a house. Pinehurst thus has been one of the few resorts in the world where discrimination was practiced on the basis of health.

In 1898 Tufts noticed a few people hitting golf balls over a few makeshift golf holes in the pastureland. He ordered a nine-hole course built to accommodate such whims of his guests. It was completed in February and measured 2,561 yards. A year later nine more holes were added to it, bringing its length to 5,176 yards. It was Course No. 1, and every new course should be as blessed. In March 1900 England's greatest golfer, Harry Vardon, on a golfing tour in the United States, gave a four-round

exhibition at Pinehurst. His best round was a 71, but more impressive was his steadiness. He averaged 1.8 strokes on what were then sand greens. On fifteen holes the difference between his best and worst scores was only one stroke, and on the other three only two strokes. As Vardon golfed his way around the United States, completing his visit by capturing the U.S. Open, he praised Pinehurst's marvelous climate and particularly its terrain. The sandy soil that had seemed so useless for growing anything, let alone for burying a corpse, was in fact ideal for a golf course. Though the Sandhill area could not be more landlocked, its courses have the character of Great Britain's links courses. They are, in fact, inland links.

Tufts, another nongolfing resort developer, finally realized what he had in 1902, when he brought Donald Ross down from Massachusetts to be the resort's golf pro. Ross, who had learned the game under old Tom Morris at St. Andrews and had been a pro and greenskeeper at Royal Dornoch Links in Scotland, took one look at the terrain and told his boss, "Sand and golf go together." In the next two decades Pinehurst became the United States's golfing capital. In 1901 The Carolina Hotel (now the Pinehurst Hotel), a four-story yellow clapboard structure, opened. In 1907 No. 2 Course opened, in 1910 No. 3, and in 1919 No. 4. With four courses designed by Ross, Pinehurst truly was a golfer's mecca. The Tuftses kept putting on more and more tournaments and Donald Ross kept obliging Pinehurst's patrons, who, after playing

Barbara McIntire digs up some North Carolina dirt as she pitches to a green to win her first Women's North and South Amateur in 1957. She would win the tournament five times.

his courses, wanted him to design courses in their home towns. So sought after was Ross that often he was designing half a dozen courses at once. In all, he designed 600 courses, on which 45 national championships have been played, 30 USGA national championships, including, on six different Ross courses, the U.S. Opens. In 1951 the Ryder Cup Matches were played over Pinehurst No. 2, and in 1962 the U.S. Amateur was played there.

Before the mid-1930s No. 2 was considered to be a very good but not a great course. It was always long. When it opened, it measured 5,750 yards—long for 1907. But as golf-equipment manufacturers kept introducing livelier golf balls, which flew farther, Ross was forced either to push his raised tees back farther or to design a new sand green that would look as though it had always been there. In fact, he changed the course four times. His last change was in 1934, when he convinced Richard Tufts that if he wanted a true championship course he would have to have grass greens. Tufts agreed, and Ross took the occasion to remodel most of his greens. It was the best thing that ever happened to No. 2.

By 1935 Ross had become the supreme architectural strategist. "Look at his courses," architect Pete Dye once remarked, "and you see a lot of shots not found on modern courses. He is one of the very few designers who were or are able to put real purpose into each shot on every hole." For where Ross was a genius was around the greens. He believed that golf should be a pleasure and not a penance, and that the tee shot, being the longest shot, must be allowed the most room for error; thus his deceptively wide fairways compensated for his small greens. "A tee shot may be penalized either by narrowing the area in which the longer player is hitting," Ross

once wrote, "or by giving him an advantage for the second shot according to the placing of the tee shot." The good golfer who has played a Ross course understands this principle only too well. After a pushed drive, the golfer may find his ball sitting up nicely in the fairway, but it is only a momentary reprieve for his error. He then faces the almost impossible task of trying to negotiate the ball to a small green fortified by bunkers and puffy muffin-shaped mounds. A high shot that lands softly will do, but it must be the proper club and the proper shot, for Ross felt that an expert golfer should not only be able to hit every club well, but also to hit a variety of shots with every club.

In designing a hole, he would first carefully select the green site, a practice Pete Dye later would adopt, because Ross believed that the most important feature of any hole was the shot to the green. He then would mold the green area with mounds and swells and usually shape the green like an inverted saucer, further reducing the target area and making it even more difficult for the highly skilled golfer, but seemingly easier for the less skilled player to get his bogey.

The first hole on Pinehurst No. 2 introduces the golfer quickly to Ross's technique. It is a medium-long par 4, a little over 400 yards and lined on either side by longleaf pine. The fairway curves slightly right to left to a green guarded in the back by pines. A bunker protects the left side of the green, forcing the player to shoot away from it, to the right of the green, where there is no bunker. But here the subtle strategy of Ross comes into play. For it is better to be in the bunker than on the right in a deep hollow filled with undulations that, for the golfer to run the ball up the bank at just the right speed and have it roll near the pin, demand

Ben Hogan drives off the tee of the 433-yard par-4 18th on No. 2 Course on the way to winning his first professional tournament, the 1940 North and South Open. First prize was $1,000.

a chip shot hit with all the deftness it would take to hit a ball off a greased cookie sheet.

When Ross put his final touches on No. 2, he declared it his masterpiece. And to see if it would hold up under championship conditions, it was selected as the site of the 1936 PGA Championship. The 36-hole qualifying rounds were proof enough that Pinehurst No. 2 was unequivocally a championship course. Walter Hagen failed to qualify for the PGA Championship for the first time in his career. After the first round of match play William Richardson of the *New York Times* wrote, "If the PGA Championship lives to be a thousand years old, it may never produce as many upsets as it did today at Pinehurst." Three former champions were defeated. An unknown pro named Jack Patroni defeated Gene Sarazen by taking only eleven putts on the outgoing nine.

In the 36-hole finals it was Denny Shute versus long-hitting Jimmy Thomson, who all day was outdriving Shute, often by as much as 100 yards. But it was Shute's great artistry around the greens that enabled him to defeat Thomson three and two. Especially relishing Shute's masterwork was Donald Ross, who had the rare architect's delight of refereeing the first 18 holes.

Four years later, in the second round of the North and South Open, a pro took only one chip and 31 putts and hit all but two greens in regulation figures, to post a 67, which followed a first-round 66. The pro was a 28-year-old by the name of Ben Hogan. His 67 was aided considerably by his

(*Overleaf*) Hogan, in his peak years, explodes from a bunker on the 487-yard par-5 8th as he goes undefeated in his matches in the 1951 Ryder Cup Match at Pinehurst.

185

brilliant play over the last four holes, which he played in only 12 strokes (four 3s), scoring a par, an eagle, a par, and a birdie. It enabled him to win his first tournament. First prize was $1,000.

As spectacularly as Hogan played the last four holes, his feat was outdone in the finals of the 1951 Men's North and South Amateur. Billy Joe Patton stood two up on the 14th tee, wondering where to display the trophy in his home in Morganton, North Carolina. He played the last five holes neatly in one under par, only to lose one down on the 18th green when his opponent, Hobart Manley, rolled in a 30-foot putt for his fifth consecutive 3.

However, the 72-hole record over Pinehurst No. 2 is 271, with which the game's finest shotmaker, Ben Hogan, won the 1942 North and South Open. Yet once when Hogan was asked whether the course had any truly great holes, he said, "The trouble with Pinehurst is that when you try to think of one great hole, you can't. Nothing jumps into your mind." Pinehurst members would challenge even Hogan. After all, they somewhat intimidated former President Dwight Eisenhower when he was there to watch the finals of the 1962 U.S. Amateur. "I can't talk golf today," Ike said. "This town is filled with experts."

Pinehurst's experts know that the 5th hole on No. 2 Course is the best hole of the course, of the 108 holes, and some even go so far as to say that it is the best 5th hole in the United States. The hole measures 438 yards from the championship tee (431 regular and 402 ladies') but plays like a hole measuring 460 yards. The tee is set in a chute of long-leaf pine. In back of the tee,

through a sparsely wooded area, you can see the present World Golf Hall of Fame, where golf's greatest players are enshrined. If one is tempted to take a longing look at the building before teeing off, while trying to remember all those instruction tips which the greats have given the golfing world, it is not a bad idea. "When hitting off of pine needles, take a firm stance and don't pick the ball off," Jack Nicklaus once wrote. And "No one ever swung the golf club too slowly," Bobby Jones once said. Each is a good tip to remember before hitting your drive. It is a blind shot. The fairway dips, then rises slightly. Down the right side are longleaf pine, dogwood, holly, oak, and out-of-bounds. The left side is lined with more pine and pine needles. But the major hazard is a huge dip on the left side of the fairway, 170 yards from the tee, that runs down to the bordering 4th hole. The fairway swings gently right to left. The fairway is tipped in the same direction, leaving a second shot usually with a sidehill, hook lie: yet another of Ross's strategies. The green lies in a natural amphitheater and is best approached from the right side of the fairway. Seventy yards in front of the left side of the green is a long bunker; another one guards the left side of the green. On the right of the green, justly placed several paces from the right edge, are two more bunkers. Mounds right and left further protect the crowned green, which slopes from right to left. The ideal drive is a slight fade. The second shot can be anything from a three wood to a long iron. There are not many par 4s where Nicklaus must use a long iron to reach a green—not even the 2nd hole at Scioto Country Club, also a Ross course, which measures 436 yards and which Nicklaus plays with a driver and a six iron. But during the 1975 World Open he was hitting a driver and a three iron on the 5th, and

A more mellow Hogan, even smiling at photographers as he is inducted into Golf's Hall of Fame.

not all that well. In four rounds, he bogied the hole three times and parred it only once.

In 1949 the hole was shortened and converted from an easy par 5 to a par 4 that now ranks as the most difficult on the course. But it was not so hard in the finals of the 1975 Men's North and South Amateur for Curtis Strange, who had the audacity to birdie the hole twice in one day, a feat that produced more controversy in Pinehurst than when former New York governor and presidential hopeful Thomas Dewey visited Pinehurst for a few days to play golf in the early 1950s. Word got around that he was staying at The Carolina, but word also spread that in his first round over No. 2 he shot a 108, which even in the Republican stronghold of Pinehurst would not have won him many votes.

One reason Dewey and other public figures liked to frequent Pinehurst was that the Tuftses owned the town, and outside press and photographers never were allowed in. More than one photographer vowed he would go to the local police—to which the Tuftses would say, "Go right ahead." The police were employed by the Tuftses. Since 1928 they have kept a card file on all guests who stayed in their hotels and ranked them from A (good) to D-U (undesirable). One journalist stated that Pinehurst had a better filing system than Hitler's.

In early 1952 the touring pros were classified as personae non gratae at Pinehurst, because of neither their faith nor their creed, but their greed. After the 1951 Ryder Cup Matches, all but two of the American Ryder Cup players deserted Pinehurst's North and South Open. They felt that the purse was not big enough. Sam Snead stayed to defend his title, but after two rounds put him out of contention, he too

departed, leaving only Ryder Cupper Henry Ransom. It was a bitter disappointment to Richard Tufts, who believed that the pros always had regarded Pinehurst's North and South Open as more than just another stop on the tour. After all, Pinehurst was the golfing capital of the United States. He replaced the tournament with a North and South seniors for men and women.

It was one of the few accepted changes in Pinehurst, where many residents still mourned the demise of the stymie. It was an era when blacks were not allowed to walk on the streets of Pinehurst at night. But as one resident blithely asked, "Why would anyone, black or white, want to walk there anyway? There's no place to go, nothing to see, nothing to do." Before the 1962 Amateur, it was realized that to get the first-day field of 72 matches through the course before dusk it would be necessary to start the earliest twosome at 6:30 A.M. "I'll be darned if I'll make anyone play golf at that hour," said Joe Dey, who evidently had never played on a public city course. "Let's institute Pinehurst daylight saving time." It was hardly a startling remark to the many who believed that Pinehurst had been on its own time zone since 1895.

For it was not until 1962 that the Holly Inn became fully air-conditioned and a swimming pool was put in. A debate over whether The Carolina should have a swimming pool lasted for almost a decade. One finally was installed in 1972. At both the Holly and The Carolina, black tie was mandatory attire for men on Thursday and Saturday evenings, even into the late 1950s. Thursday night finally went, and then Saturday. Nonetheless, the Pinehurst spirit of "the preservation of the land and the right of the privileged to live quietly without intrusion by alien people and customs" remained, as did the number-one topic of conversation: how could Pinehurst be run better?

The answer came in late 1970 when the Tuftses decided to sell their golfing mecca to Diamondhead Corporation, whose managers referred to their firm as the General Motors of land development. They paid a Cadillac-size $9.6 million for Pinehurst, immediately spent $6 million redecorating The Carolina, and changed its name to the Pinehurst Hotel. They also changed many of the old policies of the hotel, including the rules about attire. Tie and jacket at first were still required for men at dinner, then only jackets, and finally jackets were not suggested. At that, the manager, who had been there two decades, put up an outraged argument. He was fired. The old ways had gone with the renovating. The lobby's wing and wicker chairs were gone, making it look more like a modern motel lobby.

The only old way that seems to stay at Pinehurst is North Carolina's liquor law that forbids buying liquor by the drink. The state is known as a "brown bag" state. Diamondhead did its best to have the law changed, and not even the minister of the local Community Presbyterian Church objected to that change. He did object when Diamondhead built several tennis courts and a road through the town park. "The vandals have come," he preached on Sunday.

Condominiums had sprung up on courses No. 3 and No. 5. So close were the condominiums to the fairways on No. 5 that in the spring before the first World Open was to be played at Pinehurst in November 1973, Joe Dey, who was then commissioner of the PGA tour, made an inspection trip and declared that the condominiums were too close to the fairways and destroyed the

Pinehurst's autocrat until 1970, Richard S. Tufts. He helped to guide and shape the game of golf in the United States with such care that none other than Joseph C. Dey called him "Mr. Golf."

character of No. 5. In order not to repeat their mistake, the management hired Robert Trent Jones to remodel No. 4. It is now the most difficult course after No. 2. Courses No. 1 and No. 3 are the easiest, and next are No. 5 and No. 6.

But not all the changes have been for the worse. No. 2 Course is maintained in better condition than a decade ago, and the golfer who does not have a medical certificate now must walk No. 2—a giant step forward into the past. The lobby of the Pinehurst Hotel has been redecorated in a more traditional style, while its best rooms on the second and third floors are large double rooms with two double beds—parlor suites which sport a contemporary decor.

Although traditionally the cuisine in Pinehurst was American, and the best place in town to dine in the late 1960s and early 1970s was the Pine Crest Inn, once owned by Donald Ross, where Jack Nicklaus stayed when he won the 1959 Men's North and South Amateur, the Pinehurst Hotel is now the best. It features American and Continental cuisine prepared by a first-class Swedish chef whose specialty is Veal Medallion, a dish that was a favorite of Sweden's King Oscar. All the soups at the hotel now are homemade, even the consommés. Jackets are now required for men at dinner. It is a policy that pleases many of the old-time residents of Pinehurst, who had all but boycotted the hotel since 1970 and now are beginning to feel that the managers of Diamondhead are coming to their senses.

However, in the spring of 1976, when a spa unimaginatively named the Evergreen opened at the Pinehurst Country Club, one old-time resident who lived in a section of town known as Millionaire Hill saw Richard Tufts on the street and said in a voice sounding as if his sinuses were stuffed with pâté, "Dick, have you seen that new goddam spa? Why, with that and all those tennis courts, the town is beginning to look like something out of Palm Springs."

"They're sure wasting enough money trying," Tufts said.

The inviting green of the par-3 4th hole of The Homestead's Cascades Course, cast against typical Virginia
autumn colors.

Inside and out, The Homestead evokes a timeless sense of order and tradition. (*Clockwise from left*) The main lobby at afternoon tea; the par-5 17th and the par-3 18th; the par-4 13th, where Swift Run Stream flows devilishly to the green.

Where golfers wish golf balls still floated. One of the most controversial holes in golf, the par-4 17th of The Concord's Championship Course. It is such golf holes that caused golfers to name the course "The Monster."

From whatever tee the golfer uses on the par-3 17th at
Horseshoe Bay Country Club, Slick Rock Creek has to
be crossed. There's no easier route to the green.

Pinehurst: America's first great golfing resort. (*Left*) The renowned statue on the practice putting green. (*Above*) A typical small, crowned green designed by Donald Ross. This is on the notorious par-4 5th hole of Pinehurst's No. 2 Course.

The diverse and ingenious work of architect Dick Wilson. The par-3 9th hole of the Blue Course at the Doral Country Club . . .

. . . and his greenside bunkering at the par-4 6th hole
at La Costa Country Club.

DESERT RESORTS

LA QUINTA
HOTEL
Palm Springs, California

What is becoming a rather shopworn story among the touring golf professionals concerns the man who traveled the farthest to hit a golf ball, astronaut Alan Shepard. It seems that as Admiral Shepard stood on the moon ready to hit the first lunar golf shot, he gazed down an imaginary fairway to an imaginary green far away and, seeing all those bunkerlike craters, said, "My God, Robert Trent Jones has been here."

The golfer who has traveled to some of the world's more remote corners and discovered that Robert Trent Jones not only has been there before him, but has routed a course over what once was swampland or lava, and dotted the fairways with bunkers, should not be surprised. Jones has designed or remodeled 400-plus courses in 42 states and 19 countries.

Yet the golfer has only to travel 110 miles due east of Los Angeles into the Colorado Desert to another of America's great golfing capitals, Palm Springs, to discover that there in another of California's lotus lands

The host of the Bob Hope Desert Classic realizes again that golf was not meant to be a funny game.

(*Left*) The green of the 396-yard par-4 18th at La Quinta Country Club. It typifies one of the problems the golfer faces: narrow entrances to deep two- and three-tiered greens. There is also the depth-perception problem common to all golf courses in Palm Springs—the mountains in the background create the illusion that the green is closer than it actually is.

195

is not one bunker, green, or tee marker that bears the Jones touch, which may be reason enough why Jones, in one of his more salty remarks, refers to the whole place as a vast wasteland. Such remarks make him about as popular there as Jack Nicklaus in Latrobe, Pennsylvania. For the residents of Palm Springs are a proud and zealous lot, highly civic-minded, and always ready to lend their time, talent, and money—all plentiful—to worthy causes for the betterment of Palm Springs and the Coachella Valley. Some years ago there was talk of opening a dog track and even a poker parlor. The news reached one of the ladies of the Palm Springs Historical Society, and soon more phones were ringing than if it had been rumored that Zsa Zsa Gabor had just run off with a penniless golf pro. The men were hounded out of town.

In 1970 the Regional Air Pollution Authority was organized to fight against the building of an oil refinery nearby in San Gorgonio Pass. The RAPA won its battle; then, armed with $50,000 in local donations, which in Palm Springs is about as easy to raise for such causes as a fourth for $5 Nassau, began further ecological studies in water, air, noise, and visual pollution.

All matters are close to the eyes, ears, and hearts of Palm Springers, who like to keep their town, at least outwardly, as non-commercial as possible. There are building ordinances. No building may exceed a height of 65 feet. No neon signs are allowed —nor are billboards or any rotating signs. There is even a shadow ordinance, which prohibits the construction of a building that would cast a shadow on public thoroughfares or on a neighbor's property. Sunshine is to Palm Springs as oil is to Texas. The word "motel" is prohibited; instead "motor hotels" appear.

While the town keeps a low profile commercially, this is a mirage. The town, in fact, the entire Coachella Valley, with its "cove communities" nestled beneath the mountains, is provided not only with some of the best things money can buy, but with some of the best and worst ways wealth can be displayed. Take the swimming pool. Palm Springs has more swimming pools per capita than any other city, town, or village in the world—5,200, or one for every five people. The running joke is that when it rains in Palm Springs, which is seldom— its average rainfall is only seven inches— it rains chlorine. Not only is the number of pools staggering, but also the variety of shapes. There are kidney-shaped pools, heart-shaped pools, pools shaped after the erotic areas of the female anatomy. There are monogram pools which match the owner's initials. One home owner built a pool that occupied one-half his total floor area, curving through his front hall and into part of the living room. When he gave his housewarming party, two entering guests accidentally took a step backward and fell into the pool. The genial host, not wanting his guests to appear foolish, promptly jumped into the pool fully clothed.

Whenever an important visitor is to arrive in Palm Springs at night, all pool owners are asked to switch on their underwater lights. In 1964 when President Lyndon Johnson arrived for a visit during the daytime, the mayor was baffled as to how to impress the President. He declared, "We've

(*Left*) Charlie Farrell, often called "Mr. Palm Springs." In 1931 he bought 200 acres at $30 each and founded The Racquet Club, and with it brought tennis and movie stars to Palm Springs. (*Right*) One of Farrell's many friends, Spencer Tracy.

got to get some kind of gimmick to welcome guys like this—something that will be symbolic of Palm Springs. You know the way Honolulu greets folks with hula dancers? Is there anything we could do with a bunch of golfers in golf carts?"

Depending on which innkeeper or other member of the chamber of commerce you talk to, he will say that the golf car was either invented or developed in Palm Springs. The fact that a golf car of sorts had been around since 1912 makes little difference. The fair assumption is that the golf car developed into part of the game of golf in Palm Springs. A golfer would as soon start his round without his putter as to play without a golf car. Of course, playing golf at all in the hot, clear desert air over terrain that as of 1949 was no more than a sandy wasteland filled with cacti, bushes, and rattlesnakes is one of the miracles the desert produces. And the fact that golf, not tennis, is sport number one in Palm Springs is even more surprising.

In 1931 Palm Springs had one paved street, two hotels with a few tennis courts, a few dude ranches, and private homes. It also had sunshine. That was what actor Charlie Farrell wanted. "I was worn out from pictures," said the star of *Seventh Heaven*. "I just wanted to sit in the sun and maybe play a little tennis." He and his friend and fellow tennis buff, Ralph Bellamy, bought 200 acres for $30 an acre and founded the Racquet Club as a place where they and their friends could play tennis. Such friends included Hollywood's Marlene Dietrich, Douglas Fairbanks, Sr., Jack Warner, Clark Gable, Spencer Tracy, Ginger Rogers, Carole Lombard, Mary Pickford, and Janet Gaynor.

From a complex of two courts which were, in Farrell's words, "the two best money could buy," the club slowly expanded to

fourteen courts, a swimming pool, dining room, bar, and, more recently, cottages. To pay for the early expansion, Farrell and Bellamy sold off some of their land for $500 an acre. Today an acre adjacent to the club sells for $60,000.

Half an acre in the cove communities in Indian Wells or La Quinta, to name only two of many, sells for around $40,000. One man responsible for such real-estate values is Johnny Dawson, an amateur golfer of the 1930s and 1940s whom Bobby Jones then called probably the greatest amateur golfer in the world. Unfortunately, during Dawson's peak years, he served as a salesman and a promotion man for A. G. Spalding Company and was declared a "non-amateur" by the USGA and was therefore not eligible to compete in the U.S. Amateur. He did compete in other amateur tournaments and built up an impressive record. In 1942 he completed a California grand slam by winning the state's open and amateur and the Southern California Amateur. In 1946 he regained his full amateur status, and in the first three U.S. amateurs he played in, he proved he could play the kind of golf that might have brought him further national recognition. In each event, he lost to the eventual winner. In the 1947 U.S. Amateur he was a finalist, losing two and one to Skee Riegel at Pebble Beach.

His loss was Palm Springs's gain. During the early postwar years, he was selling real estate in Los Angeles and making frequent trips to Palm Springs. Like Pebble Beach's Samuel Morse, who grasped the potential marketing value of golf on the Monterey peninsula, Dawson realized golf would flourish in the desert, provided six factors always were considered—water, soil, sun, view, wind, and washes.

He first discovered two tables of water beneath the desert floor. Samplings of the soil revealed that it was saturated with sodium clays, which are detrimental to growing grass, but that with large quantities of sulfur the problem could be solved. Taking several flights over the desert, he noticed deep paths in the sand, caused by the desert winds. These revealed areas which would be unsuitable for growing grass. Then, with watch in hand, he discovered that as he went farther eastward, away from the San Jacinto Mountain range, he could gain ninety minutes more of sunlight in the winter.

This brought him to Thunderbird Dude Ranch, 182 acres in Palm Desert, ten miles east of Palm Springs. It had an excellent view of the mountains and a well that would produce 2,000 gallons of water a minute. It would be an oasis with vistas of green fairways lined with huge date palms, eucalyptus, and second homes. But potential investors, seeing the land of sand and brush and the ranch house with no glass windows, only canvas hanging from the porch frames, thought Dawson's brain had been addled by too much sun. Ben Hogan took one look at the place and said, "You'll never build a golf course out here."

However, Hogan, the great practitioner, the man who carefully engineered what is considered the finest modern golf swing, was never known as a great speculator. Oilmen are. And one invested $100,000 in Dawson's project. Soon Bing Crosby, Bob Hope, Phil Harris, and Ralph Kiner followed. In September 1950 Dawson, with architect Lawrence Hughes, Donald Ross's former construction engineer, started molding the fairways. "Building the course was just a question of pushing sand around," Dawson later recalled. The course opened three months later, and within a year and a half, all 87 building lots had been sold. The Palm Springs golf boom was on. Two

A 1950s photo of Johnny Dawson, the man responsible for making Palm Springs another of America's golfing capitals. Dawson realized that if golf was to flourish in the desert, six factors always had to be considered: water, soil, sun, view, wind, and washes.

years later, Tamarisk Country Club opened, then Indian Wells, and in 1956 Eldorado.

In 1959 La Quinta Country Club opened with much pomp. Cutting the ribbon and then hitting a 200-yard drive with a slight fade was President Eisenhower, who for the remainder of his presidency was given a winter home at La Quinta. However, he played the course infrequently, preferring shorter Eldorado and Seven Lakes.

La Quinta resort and its community make up the oldest of the cove communities, founded in 1926 by Walter Morgan, owner of a fish-and-oyster business in San Francisco. Preferring the hot, dry climate to San Francisco's fog, Morgan bought 1,000 acres at one dollar each from the

Southern Pacific Railroad, then built a hacienda and bungalows for his visiting friends. La Quinta is now shaded by date palms and orange and eucalyptus trees, and gardens of bougainvillaea and 500 rose bushes have been embroidered on the desert floor. The hacienda and bungalows have been replaced by Spanish Mediterranean-style buildings, but the resort is homey and quaint and old-fashioned for Palm Springs —to such a degree that tie and jacket are required attire for men at dinner.

It is the smallest of America's greatest resorts. There are only 76 rooms in 30 secluded bungalows. A full house is only 150 people. The resort sprawls over 30 acres, not including the golf course. The 22 suites, with bedroom, living room, and two baths, are the best accommodations, but all rooms are comfortable. Several years ago, the management was urged by its clientele to increase the number of rooms. Would not 100 more rooms be better? But the management refused, saying, "La Quinta should be maintained just as it is—a quiet place appealing to nice people."

One couple returning for a vacation after several years' absence were greeted in the lobby by the head bellman, who addressed them by their Christian names, inquired about their home town, children, and said, "Why, it's nice to see you again, it has been several years." The time between visits had been seven years. When the couple checked out, the man happened to see a card kept on him, which included dates of his previous vacations at the resort, the names of his children, his business, title, and former employment.

That personal service is part of the hotel's employment practice. Most of the help have been there at least a decade, and the bellboys, in keeping with tradition, are Filipino. The bell captain has been there forty years. A virtual United Nations of help serves up the cuisine. The chef is Scandinavian, the maitre d' is German, and the waiters are either European or Mexican. Meals are served in the main dining room or the patio, both decorated in Spanish style. Occasionally there are Mexican-fiesta evenings, when a variety of Mexican dishes are served up, and once a week a steak fry is held in the desert. Dishes not to be missed are Pheasant La Tivoli and an old-time favorite, peanut-butter pie. Nightly entertainment is limited to dancing, except on Monday evenings. Strangely, the resort shows no movies, not even *Grand Hotel*, starring Greta Garbo, who was once a highly visible guest at La Quinta, or *The Godfather*, whose director, Francis Ford Coppola, is a member of La Quinta Country Club.

In 1972 the members bought the club from the hotel; guests can still play the course, but only after 11:30 A.M. However, guests of La Quinta who are members of USGA clubs can play the 26 courses in Palm Springs and the Coachella Valley, except Thunderbird and Eldorado. All clubs but these two extend reciprocal playing privileges to members of USGA clubs.

The La Quinta golf course wanders over 130 acres. It was designed by Lawrence Hughes and closely supervised by Johnny Dawson, whose major contribution was the 18th hole, a longish par 4 that doglegs around a pond. In the distance the golfer sees the impressive Santa Rosa Mountains —their nodular sides cast from dawn to dusk in shades of purple and pink. It is an

Arnold Palmer shows his army how to play La Quinta by punching iron shots to the front of the greens and letting the ball roll to the pin. Such shotmaking has made him the tournament's only five-time winner.

President Dwight Eisenhower, for years Palm Springs's most distinguished winter resident, watching the game he loved so much.

unforgettable view, one Dawson particularly likes. "The finishing hole on any resort course," he stated after the course was just completed, "should be impressive enough to draw the golfer back."

When the pros play La Quinta—one of four courses they play in the 90-hole, five-day Bob Hope Desert Classic—they leave less impressed. In 1971, when Arnold Palmer won his fourth Classic, he played La Quinta the first day in five under par 67 and then announced, "I'm glad that one is behind me. Bermuda Dunes and Tamarisk are tough, solid courses, but La Quinta can kill you off quick."

The reason the pros are not particularly fond of the course is that it is a long and narrow 6,904 yards from the championship tees (6,555 regular and 6,074 ladies'). One

or the other does not bother the pros, but the combination—long and narrow—where the pros cannot get on the green on the par 5s in two, and on half the par 4s are not hitting wedges to the green—raises tempers and scores. In 1976, of the 220 rounds played over La Quinta, there were only two sub-70 rounds. Since 1964 the average score on the course by the pros has been 74.6.

There is out-of-bounds on sixteen holes, but only on the 2nd and 4th is there out-of-bounds right and left. Of the four par 5s, there is out-of-bounds right on the 5th and left on the 6th, 11th, and 13th. But the big problem the pros face trying to get home in two is the narrow entrances to the greens, which are easy to hit from 80 yards out with a pitching wedge, but exceptionally difficult to hit from 240 yards out with a three wood. Bunkers and mounds have been shoved close to the greens. The mounds were Dawson's idea. He believed that a pitch shot over a mound to a green required more skill than a bunker shot.

Getting the ball close to the pin at La Quinta requires skillful shotmaking. The greens are deep, elevated, and two and three tiered, with the last tier always shallow. The backs of the greens drop off four or five feet. Thus when the pins are placed in the last tier, the approach shot must be made with great care. In 1974 Lee Trevino hit his second shot to the 9th green, six feet from the pin; but the pin was back, and the ball took one skip and bounded down the hill, leaving Trevino with the nearly impossible task of getting the ball down in two. He did not, and took a bogey. Five-time Classic winner Arnold Palmer has solved the problem by hitting punch shots to the front of the greens and letting the ball roll back.

It was no surprise to Dawson in 1970 when he followed a well-known pro around La Quinta and counted the number of times he was short of the pin: fourteen times. Besides the fear of having the ball roll down the back edge of the green, there is a depth-perception problem—common to all golf courses in Palm Springs—where the mountains are a backdrop. This creates the illusion that the green is closer than it actually is; 150 yards looks like 130 yards.

Fortunately, the problem does not exist on the 2nd hole, the hardest on the course and the most controversial. It measures 433 yards from the championship tee (416 regular and 401 ladies'). There is out-of-bounds left and right, and the fairway is thickly lined with tamarisk and eucalyptus trees. The hole plays slightly uphill to a long, rolling green, guarded on either side by a bunker. The problem is the tee shot. Pushing toward the center of the fairway, pinching it to only 20 yards wide in the landing area, are two bunkers. The left-side bunker is 220 yards from the tee and 15 yards long; the right-side bunker is 250 yards from the tee. The pros complain that the only way to play safe is to play short of the bunkers, using either a three or four wood or a long iron. That leaves them with a fairway wood or a long iron to the green. The pros do gamble and try to fly the left-side bunker. Palmer did it in 1975, and though it cleared the bunker, the ball caught a eucalyptus tree. He had to punch the ball

out, and ended up taking a bogey. In 1976, in contention to win his sixth Classic, Palmer tried to play safe off the tee, using a three wood; he pushed the ball out-of-bounds right, and ended up taking a triple-bogey seven.

The 2nd was equally unkind to Nicklaus in the same Classic. Having played the incoming nine first, in two under, he bogeyed the 2nd, and on the next four holes went from two under par to three over par. He completed his round as only Nicklaus can—by holing a wedge shot in on the 8th for an eagle and birdieing the 9th.

The same day, Johnny Miller played the 2nd as he usually does—by driving with a three wood short of the bunkers, knocking a long iron onto the green, and two-putting for a par. Even so, he ended his round with a one over par 73—his only over-par round in the Classic since 1974. He won by three shots and became the Classic's first repeat winner and, in doing so, became one of the most formidable of desert golfers. Of nine professional men's tournaments played in the California and Arizona deserts in the winters of 1974 through 1976, Miller won seven: two Bob Hope Desert Classics, three Tucson opens and two Phoenix opens, one year scorching the Bermuda grass off the old Phoenix Country Club with 24 under par.

THE WIGWAM
Phoenix, Arizona

Phoenix is a large city with a long and distinct golfing tradition. The Phoenix Country Club opened in 1900, twelve years before Arizona achieved statehood. The Phoenix Open, one of the oldest tour tournaments still in existence, began in 1935. It is just one year younger than the Masters.

When the pros leave Phoenix in their wake, par is a badly battered figure drowned by a wave of birdies and eagles. In 1975 Johnny Miller's winning score was 24 under par. In the Valley of the Sun, or what the Phoenix Chamber of Commerce calls Metropolitan Phoenix, which now encompasses 247.7 square miles, there are 53 public or semiprivate courses and 14 private clubs. However, it was sixty-six years before the city could boast that it had one of the very best newer courses in the southwest—a championship course to equal the best of Palm Springs.

The Gold Course of the Goodyear Golf and Country Club, part and parcel of The

Wigwam, opened in 1966 and gave Phoenix what every major city needs: a championship course to entice golfing tourists. The local press quickly labeled the course The Monster. The management of The Wig-

Johnny Miller putts out after four rounds as hot as a Phoenix sun in August, winning the 1975 Phoenix Open at twenty-four under par.

One of Phoenix's most prominent personages, Barry Goldwater, a five-handicap golfer before he entered politics. Goldwater, a third-generation Arizonan, relaxes in the desert near Scottsdale. The buckboard, Stetson hat and Levis mark him as a true man of the Southwest.

wam, however, refers to it in such terms as "the sleeping giant," not because it met the fondest nightmares of its creator, Robert Trent Jones, but because its four-round tournament playing value still is untested by the touring pros. It has, though, been the site of two Arizona Men's State Amateurs, two Arizona Women's State Amateurs, the U.S. National Seniors, two American Airlines Astrojet tournaments—in which a professional football player and a professional baseball player are teamed in a net better ball competition—and three times has been a sectional qualifying site for the U.S. Open. But in all this play, the best scores from the championship tees, from which the course measures 7,220 yards and carries a course rating of 74.2, have been four 69s.

That it took sixty-six years for Phoenix to get a course equal in class to the Goldwater Department Store—one that can be as unsoothing to the male ego as Main Chance is soothing to that of the female—is as much an embarrassment to the local chamber of commerce as are the scores in the Phoenix Open. That Phoenix's number-one course should be at The Wigwam is almost equally puzzling, because until 1964 it had not been the most golfing-conscious of resorts.

Since it opened in 1929 The Wigwam has been operated on a financially prudent scale by the Goodyear Tire and Rubber Company, which likes to promote the resort as a conservative get-away-from-it-all-place for the decision-weary executive desiring a climate ideal for sinusitis, arthritis or rheumatism—and not wanting a golf course where getting its full playing value would be inflationary to his score.

Initially, The Wigwam was a small guest ranch with only twenty-four rooms. When a guest registered, he was assigned, along with a room, a horse. Cookouts and horse-back rides through the desert were the main activities. There was only one tennis court (now there are eight with Plexipave surfaces and six lighted for night play) and a nine-hole golf course. In 1939 the course was expanded to 18 holes, and in 1961 was revamped and supplied with an irrigation system.

In 1964 the Goodyear executives in Akron, Ohio, felt it was just fine that they had the blimp hovering high above football stadiums and golf courses to bring spectacular aerial photos to the television viewer, and it was also fine that they dominated the tire industry in the golf-car market. But for Goodyear, 1964 was a bad year. The executives could gaze westward to Palm Springs, with all those golf courses and second-home developments springing up, and realize where much of The Wigwam's old clientele was now going. Even worse, the executives only had to look across town to Goodyear's chief competitor, the Firestone Tire and Rubber Company, to see the miles of free publicity Firestone was getting after it converted its mediocre corporate course into one of the country's best tournament courses.

To compete with Firestone and Palm Springs was indeed a blimp-size problem. The first step was to give The Wigwam a Palm Springs image: vistas of green fairways and a luxurious second home–condominium project. One hundred new rooms were added to the resort, bringing the total to 220, set in low, spreading adobelike buildings. In keeping with the resort's style, the colony of buildings is connected to the

The green on the 2nd hole, a 393-yard par 4, on The Wigwam's Gold Course. Guarding the green is one of two ponds which collectively claim forty balls daily.

main lodge by a network of palm-lined paths.

To go with the new image, the Goodyear executives hired Robert Trent Jones. Instead of telling him they wanted a championship course, but one easy enough for the average player, they wisely asked for two different courses. Jones had all but two holes of the old course (now holes one and two of the Blue Course) plowed under, and then he set to work designing the Blue Course to play to a comfortable 6,107 yards from the men's tees (5,117 ladies'). He installed 27 bunkers, put in 6 ponds, and left the fairways wide. A howling slice or a snapped duck hook would not be severely penalized. Besides being geared for the average player, the Blue Course serves as an ideal warm-up course for the golfer who has spent the winter in a cold climate.

From the beginning, the Gold Course was designed to be not just a championship course, but one for competitive play—it is to be hoped, the future home for the Phoenix Open, where the scores would be at par and so would Goodyear's publicity program. Jones, who hardly needs encouragement when designing or remodeling a course for tournaments, began plotting his course over what had been cotton and alfalfa fields. Along the flat desert land, he created hillocks, raised the tees, flattened the greens and planted them with seaside bent grass. He lined the fairways with eucalyptus, salt cedars, cypresses, mesquites, black olives, orange trees, and date palms. Eight ponds were put in and ringed with weeping willows, and a tributary curled menacingly around three greens. Then came the bunkers—100 to be exact—half being fairway bunkers, some of which jut so far into the fairways that they pinch the width of the landing areas to a mere 25 yards. At the elbows of the doglegs, of which there

are eight, Jones placed a cluster of bunkers strategically, to catch a tee shot not hit long enough by the greedy golfer. And Jones knows there is hardly a golfer who never gets greedy. He also knows most golfers would rather be on the green, even 75 feet from the pin, than off the green, with a 20-foot chip shot to the pin. Thus his penchant for large greens. On the Gold Course they average 11,000 square feet, are tiered and filled with swells, but without the subtle breaks that one finds on the East and West courses at The Broadmoor.

Another Jones trademark is long tees. The members and returning guests who play the Gold Course have a standard bet for a first-time player—that he cannot hit an eight iron from the back to the front of the 13th tee. It is a bet to be declined. The tee is 150 yards long. The total yardage of the tees is 1,616 yards. From the front of the tees, at the ladies' tees, the course measures 5,604 yards; from the regular tees 6,469 yards. Even at that length, three of the par 5s are over 500 yards; however, only one par 4 is over 400 yards. At any length, the best holes are the 2nd and the 8th, both par 4s.

The tee on the 2nd is slightly raised. On the right side is a tall salt cedar and on the left a large date palm. The fairway is narrow, with a line of salt cedars down the left side and with clusters of them down the right. At first glance, the conservative player might want to drive with a three wood, making sure he keeps the ball in the fairway, but the hole measures 396 yards from the championship tee (393 yards regular and 311 ladies'), and distance is needed off the tee. The golfer does not want a long iron or fairway wood shot into the green. It is generously large but bordered by two ponds that claim an average of forty golf balls daily.

Powers of the Southwest at the 1950 Phoenix Open: (*left to right*) Jimmy Demaret, Robert W. Goldwater, Sr., Ben Hogan—at the only tournament ever named after him—and Del E. Webb.

The second shot on the 8th is even harder. The hole is longer, measuring 443 yards from the championship tee (397 regular and 310 ladies'), and is open, as is much of the fairway, exposed to an occasional north wind that comes whining down through the valley. On the left side of the fairway are mesquites and three bunkers. Down the right side of the fairway are cypress trees and more mesquites, which grow along a tributary that first cuts in front of the tee, runs the entire length of the fairway, and finally winds fiendishly in front of the green and along its left side. The green itself is hourglass-shaped, elevated, and positioned diagonally to the fairway. The ideal drive for the golfer who draws the ball is down the right center of the fairway, as the green is long, running from right to left, but extremely shallow. A half

209

club less and the golfer is in the tributary; a half club more and the ball hits the rear of the green and rolls off. The green rises from front to center, then slopes downhill toward the tributary and a bunker at the right rear of the green. The great characteristic of the hole is that there is no way for the golfer to play safe.

If the golfer has played boldly for sixteen holes on some of America's greatest desert golf holes like the 2nd, 3rd, 8th, and 10th, and has been justly rewarded, then steps on the 17th tee, knowing that two comparatively easy, shortish par 4s remain, and begins to relax, he has fallen into one of Jones's carefully raked psychological bunkers. One golfer who did was Donny Powers, a student at Arizona State University, who was playing the course to qualify for a local collegiate tournament. All he had to do was par the last two holes to be the first man to break 70. He drove well off the 17th tee, then, letting up on his second shot, he pulled it badly into the tributary left of the green. On his fourth shot he had to pitch over a bunker—certainly not a difficult shot for a man playing under-par golf, except that across the green is one of two ponds, which also guards the 2nd green. As one error often breeds another, he caught his pitch shot fat, put it in the bunker, then hit his bunker shot thin and sailed the ball over the green into the pond. Out in six, on the green in seven, he two-putted for a horrendous nine. Thus on one hole he went from three under par to two over.

For the man who tires of trying to bring a monster to its knees and who finds that

Temperamental Tommy Bolt, unchanged at age fifty-seven, angrily throws a wedge after missing a shot during the 1975 U.S. National Seniors, played over the Gold Course.

the Blue Course is just too short, there is the new West Course, which from the men's tees stretches between 6,314 and 6,861 yards. Date palms, small black olives and eucalyptus line the fairways, but the trees are young. Although they are little protection from the wind, at least they do not obscure the westward views of White Tank Mountain. The terrain is rolling, and the large Bermuda-grass greens sweep into the fairways. Some are tucked in swells, producing several blind second shots. There are five lakes, a winding stream, and three dozen bunkers, but all are placed so as to catch only the most errantly hit shot.

The West Course is situated 500 yards across Litchfield Road from the main clubhouse—the hub of daytime activities. With the swimming pool (there is another by the lodge), tennis courts, and golf, it is indeed a sporting place, with a bar and lounge which serves lunch.

Though the resort spreads over 14,000 acres, including the village of Litchfield Park, the longest walk from the main lodge to a first tee, tennis court, or shopping center is just over a quarter of a mile. Accommodation rates vary according to size and location. Rooms adjacent to the lodge pool are the choicest. In the matter of room size, they range from larger to largest. There are twin-bedded rooms, private bungalows, two-bedroom suites, and fairway casas, each with four bedrooms and a parlor. All rooms have color television and are furnished well, some with fireplaces and high-beamed ceilings.

The first meal at The Wigwam was Thanksgiving dinner in 1929, served to exactly twenty-four people. Today the Terrace Dining Room, which is actually two rooms, now seats over 450 guests. They are large rooms, usually brightly decorated with orange tablecloths and lighted with a soft yellow light. The menu changes every night, and the cuisine almost matches the variety of dishes. If there is a specialty of the house, it is the fruit and vegetables. They are fresh. In season, from December to April, fresh produce means picked that day. It is.

Most guests are there for one or two weeks, making it a friendly, relaxed resort. It is not dressy or formal, except that men must wear coat and necktie after 6:00 P.M. in the lodge, and women must be "appropriately" attired. Pants suits now are accepted in the Terrace Dining Room, but shorts are not—on either men or women.

It is a strong policy, and it was sternly challenged, not by a woman but by a man, who arrived for dinner one evening wearing Bermuda shorts. The maitre d' told him he would have to change if he wished to be seated. The man replied that he was a personal friend of Goodyear's chairman of the board, E. J. Thomas. If it is true that the world is filled with maitre d's who turn the other cheek with an outstretched palm, they are not at The Wigwam. Policy was policy to this maitre d'. The man retired to the bar and after a few drinks again challenged the policy and threatened to call E. J. Thomas if he was not allowed to be seated, even though it was after midnight. "Go ahead," said the maitre d'. The man did, woke Goodyear's chairman of the board out of a sound sleep, was told that the maitre d' was absolutely correct, and in no uncertain terms was informed that if he continued to behave in such unexecutive fashion, he would never be welcome at The Wigwam.

A man who is always welcome is Robert Trent Jones, who to this day shudders with disbelief at one of his visits. For an incident occurred to him that should happen to every golfer who has ever cursed and moaned about that seemingly diabolic mind

of Jones's. Shortly after the Gold Course opened, Jones returned to see how his desert masterpiece was maturing, and went to play a round with the then resident pro, V. O. "Red" Allen. When they reached the 3rd hole, a 233-yard par 3, with an elevated green sloping diagonally from left to right and a large half-crescent-shaped bunker guarding the left side of the green, Jones claimed it was the hardest of the four par 3s—the pros certainly would not score many birdies here. With that announced, Jones, who is a good golfer when he gets a chance to play, hit his tee shot just short of the green. Then Allen hit and knocked the ball four feet from the pin. The ball took one bounce and jumped into the cup— a hole-in-one, the ultimate put-down. To this day Allen loves to recall what it is like to score a hole-in-one in the presence of the course's architect. "Well," says Allen, "Jones just said, 'That was one helluva shot,' and stood there shaking his head."

The most famous of modern golf course architects, Robert Trent Jones, negotiating hazards of his own making over the Gold Course. For every golfer who has cursed that seemingly diabolical mind of Jones's, he received the ultimate put-down of his course from an opponent who left the architect cursing and shaking his head in utter disbelief.

Guide to Resorts

A Note on Rates

To bring resort rates up to date, one would have to publish with the speed of light, and not even Bobbs-Merrill can do that. Resorts resolve the problem of the continuing seasonal and yearly rate fluctuation simply by stating in their rate sheets: "Rates subject to change without notification." The easiest way to obtain current rates is to write or call the resort; many have toll-free numbers. The coding of rates used here is to serve only as a general guideline; it is not meant to be either specific or timely. Keep in mind that while almost nothing ever goes down in price, almost everything goes up.

When tabulating the cost of a vacation, remember that a state tax will be added to your bill. The taxes range from 3 to 6 percent. Many resorts have instituted an automatic-gratuity policy of 10 to 15 percent per person per day. After establishing the total cost of your vacation, a good rule of thumb is to add a minimum of 15 percent to the total cost for miscellaneous expenses.

Resort green fees change more frequently than daily rates. There are not only in-season and off-season rates but also daily and weekend rates. Again, for specific green fees, contact the resort. The average daily in-season green fee to play the courses in this book is $10. There are notable exceptions. Doral Country Club has no green fees—they are incorporated into the daily room rate. To play Pebble Beach, guests of Del Monte lodge pay $15 and up. The average fee for a golf car for two is $12; caddie fee, single, is $8.

Just as the three-hour round of golf is vanishing, you can no longer just stroll to the first tee and expect to tee off. Reserved starting times have become mandatory at resorts and should be made a minimum of 24 hours ahead.

Most of the resorts included in this book now offer golf package plans. They are the most economical way to take a golfing vacation—with a saving of approximately 20 percent of the daily room rate, over a given period of time. All include the green fee and, usually, breakfast and dinner in the rate. Golf cars or caddies usually are extra. Most package plans are available year-round except in season.

Included with the coded general rate range are the resorts' daily meal plans. They are AP, American Plan, three meals daily; MAP, Modified American Plan, two meals daily; E, European Plan, no meals included in the daily rate.

GENERAL RATE CODE

A	$100 to $135 daily	D	$45 to $80 daily
B	$85 to $110 daily	E	$30 to $60 daily
C	$60 to $95 daily	F	$20 to $30 daily

214

THE CLOISTER

Sea Island, Georgia 31561
Tel: 800–841–3223
In season: February 1–May 31

ACCOMMODATIONS

The Cloister Hotel, its Hamilton House, Retreat House, River House, guest houses and cottages

RATES

	daily rate	plan
IN SEASON		
double occupancy	B	AP
single occupancy	D	AP
OFF SEASON		
double occupancy	C	AP
single occupancy	D	AP

Automatic 15-percent gratuity per person per day
Package plans available

GOLF
36 holes

Sea Island Golf Club
caddies and golf cars

Seaside Nine
Lengths and pars

men's championship tees	3,371 yds
regular tees	3,244 yds
par	36
ladies' championship tees	2,989 yds
regular tees	2,647 yds
par	39

Retreat Nine
Lengths and pars

men's championship tees	3,506 yds
regular tees	3,267 yds
par	36
ladies' championship tees	3,002 yds
regular tees	2,905 yds
par	38

Plantation Nine
Lengths and pars

men's championship tees	3,343 yds
regular tees	3,166 yds
par	36
ladies' championship tees	2,783 yds
regular tees	2,650 yds
par	36

Marshside Nine
Lengths and pars

men's championship tees	3,248 yds
regular tees	3,045 yds
par	36
ladies' championship tees	2,790 yds
regular tees	2,582 yds
par	37

Course rating: any combination of nines

men's championship tees	72.1
regular tees	70.3
ladies' championship tees	72.7
regular tees	70.2

OTHER FACILITIES
tennis: 14 courts
swimming: ocean and fresh-water pool
skeet and trap shooting
fishing: inshore saltwater
boating

LOCATION
Sea Island is halfway between Savannah, Georgia, and Jacksonville, Florida.

HOW TO GET THERE

From Atlanta
By car: Interstate 75 south to Perry, Ga., and pick up U.S. Highway 341 east to Brunswick. Take causeway toll bridge across the Intracoastal Waterway to Demere Road. Go two blocks and turn left on Sea Island Road. Follow to North First Road, which runs direct to The Cloister.

By plane: Atlanta's Hartsfield International Airport. Air South direct to McKinnon Airport, Saint Simons Island. Limousine service available from airport to The Cloister upon request.

From Palm Beach
By car: Interstate 95 north to Brunswick. See "How to Get There from Atlanta."

By plane: Palm Beach International Airport. Delta or National Airlines direct to Jacksonville International Airport. Limousine service available from Jacksonville Airport to The Cloister upon request.

From Washington, D.C.
By car: Interstate 95 south. Where I-95 is incomplete, pick up U.S. Highway 17 south to Brunswick. See "How to Get There from Atlanta."

By plane: Washington National Airport. Eastern or National Airlines non-stop to Jacksonville International.

CREDIT CARDS
The Cloister honors no credit cards, but does accept personal checks.

COSTASUR'S
CASA de CAMPO

La Romana, Dominican Republic
Tel: 800–223–6620 (except in New York State, Tel: 212–333–4100)
In season: December 15–April 30

ACCOMMODATIONS
Casa de Campo and Hotel Romana

RATES	daily rate	plan
Casa de Campo		
IN SEASON		
double occupancy	A	MAP
single occupancy	B	MAP
OFF SEASON		
double occupancy	C	MAP
single occupancy	C	MAP
Hotel Romana		
IN SEASON		
double occupancy	C	MAP
single occupancy	D	MAP
OFF SEASON		
double occupancy	C	MAP
single occupancy	D	MAP

Automatic 10-percent gratuity per person per day
Package plans available

GOLF
36 holes

Campo de Golf Cajuiles
caddies and golf cars

Cajuiles No. 1
Lengths and pars

men's championship tees	6,843 yds
regular tees	6,255 yds
par	72
ladies' tees	5,697 yds
par	73

Course rating

championship tees	72.5
regular tees	70.5
ladies' tees	72

Cajuiles No. 2
Lengths and pars

men's championship tees	6,198 yds
regular tees	5,392 yds
par	71
ladies' tees	4,521 yds
par	71

Course rating

championship tees	70
regular tees	68
ladies' tees	68

OTHER FACILITIES
tennis: 45 courts
swimming: 2 beaches, 3 fresh-water swimming pools
horseback riding
polo
trap and skeet shooting
boating
fishing: river and deep-sea
snorkeling

LOCATION
Costasur, Hotel Romana, and Casa de Campo are located in La Romana along the southeastern shore of the Dominican Republic, 65 miles east of Santo Domingo.

HOW TO GET THERE
By plane only

From Chicago
O'Hare International Airport. United Airlines to New York City's Kennedy International Airport, connecting with either American or Air Dominicana Airlines direct to Las Americas Airport, Santo Domingo. Via Miami's International Airport, Eastern or Delta Airlines, connecting with either Pan Am or Air Dominicana Airlines direct to Las Americas Airport. Limousine service available from Santo Domingo to La Romana.

From Miami
Miami International Airport. Pan Am or Air Dominicana Airlines non-stop to Las Americas Airport, Santo Domingo.

From New York City
Kennedy International Airport. American or Air Dominicana Airlines non-stop to Las Americas Airport, Santo Domingo.

CREDIT CARDS
Costasur honors American Express, BankAmericard, Diners Club, and Master Charge. Personal checks are also accepted.

DEL MONTE
LODGE

Pebble Beach, California 93953
Tel: 408–624–3811
In season: February 1–November 30

ACCOMMODATIONS
Del Monte Lodge

RATES	daily rate	plan
IN SEASON		
double occupancy	A	MAP
single occupancy	B	MAP
OFF SEASON		
double occupancy	B	MAP
single occupancy	C	MAP

GOLF
54 holes
caddies and golf cars

Pebble Beach Golf Links
Lengths and pars

men's championship tees	6,815 yds
regular tees	6,343 yds
par	72
ladies' tees	5,273 yds
par	72

Course rating

championship tees	75
regular tees	72
ladies' tees	73

Spyglass Hill Golf Course
Lengths and pars

men's championship tees	6,810 yds
regular tees	6,277 yds
par	72
ladies' tees	5,556 yds
par	72

Course rating

championship tees	76.1
regular tees	74.1
ladies' tees	72.3

Cypress Point Club (does not have reciprocal playing privileges with members of other USGA clubs)
Lengths and pars

men's championship tees	6,464 yds
regular tees	6,265 yds
par	72
ladies' tees	5,722 yds
par	75

Course rating

championship tees	72
regular tees	71
ladies' tees	72.8

OTHER FACILITIES
tennis: 8 courts
swimming: fresh-water pool
horseback riding
trap and skeet shooting
hunting
fishing

LOCATION
Pebble Beach is located 125 miles south of San Francisco and 350 miles north of Los Angeles.

HOW TO GET THERE

From Chicago
By car: Interstate 80 west to San Francisco. Pick up Highway 101 to Salinas. Turn west on Monterey Peninsula Highway and drive to Monterey. Turn left again in Monterey onto Fremont. Continue to Highway 1 (Munras). Turn left again. Continue to Pebble Beach gate.

By plane: O'Hare International Airport. United Airlines direct to Monterey Airport. United Airlines, connecting either at Los Angeles International Airport with United or Hughes Air West, or at San Francisco International Airport with United, to Monterey Airport. Limousine service from Monterey Airport to Del Monte Lodge available upon request.

From Los Angeles
By car: Highway 101 north to Salinas. From Salinas see "How to Get There from Chicago."

By plane: Los Angeles International Airport. United or Hughes Air West direct to Monterey Airport.

From San Francisco
By car: See "How to Get There from Chicago."

By plane: San Francisco International Airport. United Airlines direct to Monterey Airport.

CREDIT CARDS
Del Monte Lodge honors American Express, BankAmericard, and Master Charge. They also accept personal checks.

DORADO BEACH
HOTEL

Dorado Beach, Puerto Rico 00646
Tel: 809–796–1600
In season: December 20–Easter

ACCOMMODATIONS
Dorado Beach Hotel

RATES

	daily rate	plan
IN SEASON		
double occupancy	A	MAP
single occupancy	A	MAP
OFF SEASON		
double occupancy	B	MAP
single occupancy	C	MAP

Package plans available

GOLF
36 holes

Dorado Beach Golf Club
Golf cars only

West Course
Lengths and pars

men's championship tees	6,913 yds
regular tees	6,396 yds
par	72
ladies' tees	5,834 yds
par	74

Course rating

championship tees	72.6
regular tees	70
ladies' tees	72

East Course
Lengths and pars

men's championship tees	7,005 yds
regular tees	6,430 yds
par	72
ladies' tees	5,805 yds
par	74

Course rating

championship tees	72.3
regular tees	70.2
ladies' tees	72.3

OTHER FACILITIES
tennis: 7 courts
swimming: 2 saltwater pools, beach
deep-sea fishing
snorkeling
water-skiing
sailing
gambling

LOCATION
Dorado Beach, on the northern coast, 20 miles west of San Juan.

HOW TO GET THERE
By plane only

From Atlanta
Atlanta's Hartsfield International Airport. Eastern Airlines non-stop to San Juan International Airport, Dorado Wings Airline to Dorado Beach. Car-shuttle service available from Dorado Beach Airport to the resort.

From New York City
Kennedy International Airport. Eastern or American Airlines non-stop to San Juan International.

From Washington, D.C.
Baltimore/Washington Airport. Eastern Airlines non-stop to San Juan International. Dulles International Airport. American Airlines non-stop to San Juan International.

CREDIT CARDS
Dorado Beach honors American Express, BankAmericard, Diners Club, and Master Charge. They also accept personal checks.

MAUNA KEA BEACH
HOTEL

Kamuela, Hawaii 96743
Tel: 808–882–7222
In season: Year-round

ACCOMMODATIONS
Mauna Kea Beach Hotel

RATES

	daily rate	plan
YEAR-ROUND		
double occupancy	A	MAP
single occupancy	A	MAP

Package plans available

GOLF
18 holes

Mauna Kea Beach Golf Course

Golf cars and pull carts

Lengths and pars

men's championship tees	7,016 yds
regular tees	6,488 yds
par	72
ladies' tees	5,831 yds
par	72

Course rating	
championship tees	74
regular tees	71
ladies' tees	73

OTHER FACILITIES
tennis: 9 courts
swimming: ocean and fresh-water pool
snorkeling
scuba diving
sailing
fishing
horseback riding
hunting

LOCATION
Mauna Kea is on the northwestern coast of the Island of Hawaii, approximately 150 air miles southeast of Honolulu.

HOW TO GET THERE
By plane only

From Los Angeles or San Francisco
Los Angeles or San Francisco International Airport. Northwest, Pan Am, Western, or United Airlines non-stop to Honolulu International Airport, then Aloha or Hawaiian Airlines direct to Kona Airport. Bus shuttle or taxicab available from airport to Mauna Kea Beach Hotel.

From Chicago
O'Hare International Airport. Continental or United Airlines direct to Honolulu International Airport, then Aloha or Hawaiian Airlines direct to Kona Airport.

From Dallas
Dallas/Fort Worth International Airport. Braniff International non-stop to Honolulu International Airport, then Aloha or Hawaiian Airlines direct to Kona Airport.

CREDIT CARDS
Mauna Kea honors no credit cards, but does accept personal checks.

PRINCEVILLE
AT HANALEI

Hanalei, Hawaii 96714
Tel: 800–525–6541
In season: Year-round

ACCOMMODATIONS
Pali Ke Kua and Princeville Sealodge, Alii Kai condominium rentals and golf cottages

RATES
Vary according to number of rooms and location

	daily rate	plan
Pali Ke Kua and Princeville Sealodge	D	E
Alii Kai condominiums and golf cottages	D	E

Weekly and monthly rates available
Package plans available

GOLF
27 holes
Princeville Makai Golf Club
golf cars and pull carts

Ocean Nine
Lengths and pars

men's championship tees	3,460 yds
regular tees	3,060 yds
par	36
ladies' tees	2,755 yds
par	36

Woods Nine
Lengths and pars

men's championship tees	3,436 yds
regular tees	3,116 yds
par	36
ladies' tees	2,788 yds
par	37

Lake Nine
Lengths and pars

men's championship tees	3,488 yds
regular tees	3,148 yds
par	36
ladies' tees	2,671 yds
par	36

Course rating: any combination of nines

men's championship tees	73
regular tees	70
ladies' tees	71

OTHER FACILITIES
tennis: 18 courts
swimming: ocean and 5 fresh-water pools
fishing
sailing
snorkeling

LOCATION
Princeville is on the northern coast of the Island of Kauai, 100 air miles northwest of Honolulu.

HOW TO GET THERE
By plane only

From Denver
Stapleton International Airport. United, Western, or Continental Airlines direct to Honolulu International Airport, Hawaiian or Aloha Airlines to Lihue Airport on Kauai. Rental cars available at airport. Limousine service available from airport to Princeville upon request.

From New York City
Kennedy International Airport. United Airlines direct to Honolulu International Airport.

From Seattle
Seattle/Tacoma International Airport. Continental, Northwestern, Pan American, or Western Airlines non-stop to Honolulu International.

CREDIT CARDS
Princeville honors American Express and Master Charge. Personal checks are also accepted.

SEA PINES
PLANTATION

Hilton Head Island, South Carolina 29928
Tel: 803–785–3333
In season: March 1–October 31

ACCOMMODATIONS
Hilton Head Inn, condominiums, villas, and homes

RATES	daily rate	plan
Hilton Head Inn		
IN SEASON		
double occupancy	D	E
single occupancy	D	E
OFF SEASON		
double occupancy	E	E
single occupancy	E	E

Condominiums, villas, and homes vary in rate according to the number of rooms and location.

IN SEASON	B	E
OFF SEASON	C	E

Weekly and monthly rates available
Package plans available

GOLF
54 holes
golf cars only

Harbour Town Golf Links

Lengths and pars	
men's championship tees	6,655 yds
regular tees	5,784 yds
par	71
ladies' tees	4,880 yds
par	71

Course rating	
championship tees	75
regular tees	70
ladies' tees	70

	Ocean Course	Sea Marsh Course
Lengths and pars		
men's championship tees	6,622 yds	6,443 yds
regular tees	6,234 yds	6,196 yds
par	72	72
ladies' tees	5,408 yds	5,654 yds
par	72	72
Course rating		
championship tees	71	70
regular tees	69	69
ladies' tees	70	70

OTHER FACILITIES
tennis: 53 courts
swimming: ocean and 4 fresh-water pools
deep-sea fishing
inshore saltwater fishing
sailing
boating
water-skiing
horseback riding
bird-watching

LOCATION
Sea Pines Plantation is located on the southern tip of Hilton Head Island, 60 miles north of Savannah.

HOW TO GET THERE

From Atlanta
By car: Interstate 75 south to Macon, at which point the highway becomes Interstate 16. Follow to end and pick up U.S. Highway 221 north to U.S. Highway 80 east to Savannah. Take U.S. Highway 17 north to U.S. Highway 278 east to Hilton Head Island.

By plane: Atlanta's Hartsfield Airport. Florida Airlines direct to Hilton Head Municipal Airport. Limousine service to Sea Pines available. Or Delta Airlines to Savannah's Travis Field Airport. Limousine service to Sea Pines available upon request.

From Memphis
By car: Interstate 40 east to Asheville. Pick up Interstate 26 south to U.S. Highway 15. Go south and pick up Alt. U.S. Highway 17. At Ridgeland pick up U.S. Highway 278 to Hilton Head.

By plane: Memphis International Airport. Delta or Eastern Airlines, connecting via Atlanta's Hartsfield with Delta to Savannah's Travis Field Airport.

From New York City
By car: New Jersey Turnpike to the end. Cross Delaware Memorial Bridge. Pick up U.S. Highway 301 south, bypassing Washington, D.C. Just past Bowling Green, Va., take Interstate 95 south to Santee, S.C. Connect with U.S. Highway 15 south to Alt. U.S. Highway 17. At Ridgeland pick up U.S. Highway 278 to Hilton Head.

By plane: LaGuardia, Kennedy International, or Newark Airport. Delta, Eastern, Piedmont, or United Airlines via Atlanta's Hartsfield, connecting with Delta Airlines to Savannah's Travis Field Airport. Direct flights on National Airlines to Savannah's Travis Field Airport, from Kennedy International and Newark airports only.

CREDIT CARDS
Sea Pines honors American Express, BankAmericard, C&S, Diners Club and Master Charge. Personal checks are also accepted.

BANFF SPRINGS
HOTEL

Banff, Alberta, Canada TOL-OEO
Tel: 403–762–2211
In season: May 15–October 15

ACCOMMODATIONS
Banff Springs Hotel

RATES

	daily rate	plan
IN SEASON		
double occupancy	D	E
single occupancy	E	E
OFF SEASON		
double occupancy	F	E
single occupancy	F	E

GOLF
18 holes
Banff Springs Golf Course
golf cars and pull carts

Lengths and pars

men's championship tees	6,643 yds
regular tees	6,282 yds
par	71
ladies' tees	5,977 yds
par	74

Course ratings

men's championship tees	71
regular tees	71
ladies' tees	74

OTHER FACILITIES
tennis: 5 courts
swimming: 2 pools, indoor and outdoor
hiking
fishing
horseback riding

LOCATION
Banff Springs is located in Banff National Park, 555 miles northeast of Vancouver and 80 miles west of Calgary.

HOW TO GET THERE

From Montreal

By car: Trans-Canada Highway west through Calgary direct to Banff.

By plane: Dorval or Mirabel International Airport. Air Canada, CP Air non-stop to Calgary International Airport. Brewster Transport shuttle bus to Banff. Rental cars also available.

From Los Angeles

By car: Interstate 15 north to Coutts, Canada. Pick up Highway 4 to Lethbridge, at which point the highway becomes Highway 2. Follow to Calgary. Pick up Trans-Canada Highway to Banff.

By plane: Los Angeles International Airport. Hughes Air West or Western Airlines direct to Calgary.

Other U.S. cities with direct flights to Calgary are Chicago, Denver and San Francisco.

From Vancouver

By car: Trans-Canada Highway east direct to Banff.

By plane: Vancouver International Airport. Air Canada or CP Air non-stop to Calgary International.

CREDIT CARDS
Banff Springs Hotel honors American Express, Carte Blanche, Chargex & Associates (BankAmericard), Canadian Pacific, and Air Canada-CN. Personal checks are also accepted.

THE BROADMOOR

Colorado Springs, Colorado 80901
Tel: 303–634–7711
In season: May 1–November 1

ACCOMMODATIONS

The Broadmoor Hotel, Broadmoor South, and Broadmoor West

RATES	daily rate	plan
IN SEASON		
double or single occupancy	C	E
OFF SEASON		
double or single occupancy	E	E

GOLF
54 holes

The Broadmoor Golf Club
caddies, golf cars and pull carts

East Course

Lengths and pars

men's championship tees	7,154 yds
regular tees	6,550 yds
par	72
ladies' tees	6,081 yds
par	73

Course ratings

championship tees	72
regular tees	69.2
ladies' tees	74.9

West Course

Lengths and pars

men's championship tees	7,036 yds
regular tees	6,309 yds
par	72
ladies' tees	5,662 yds
par	73

Course ratings

championship tees	71.9
regular tees	68.8
ladies' tees	73

South Course

Lengths and pars

men's championship tees	6,935 yds
regular tees	6,277 yds
par	72
ladies' championship tees	5,371 yds
ladies' regular tees	4,790 yds
par	72

Course ratings

men's championship tees	70.5
men's regular tees	67.4
ladies' championship tees	66.8
ladies' regular tees	64.8

OTHER FACILITIES
tennis: 16 courts
swimming: 3 pools
boating
ice-skating (year-round)
boating
horseback riding
hiking
skeet and trap shooting
squash
hunting

LOCATION
The Broadmoor is located on the outskirts of Colorado Springs, 75 miles south of Denver.

HOW TO GET THERE

From Chicago
By car: Interstate 80 west to Merino, Colorado, at which point the highway becomes Interstate 76. Follow to Denver. Pick up U.S. Highway 87 south to Colorado Springs. Turn west on Highway I-25 to The Broadmoor exit.

By plane: O'Hare International Airport. Continental Airlines direct to Colorado Springs's Peterson Field Airport. United Airlines or TWA direct to Denver's Stapleton International Airport. Connect with Continental Airlines to Peterson Field. Limousine or taxi service available from airport to The Broadmoor.

From Dallas
By car: Highway 114 west to U.S. Highway 287 to Amarillo. Pick up U.S. Highway 87 to Raton, N.M. Then take Interstate 25 north to Colorado Springs. Take Highway I-25 to The Broadmoor exit.

By plane: Dallas/Fort Worth International Airport. Braniff or Continental Airlines direct to Colorado Springs.

From Los Angeles
By car: State Highway 91 north to Interstate 15 north to Cove Fort, Utah. Pick up Highway 4 east to U.S. Highway 89 north to Salina, Utah. Pick up Highway 4 again east connecting with Interstate 70 east to Grand Junction, Colo. Take U.S. Highway 50 south to Montrose. Continue east on U.S. Highway 50 to Penrose. Then pick up Highway 115 north to Colorado Springs. Pick up Highway I-25 east to The Broadmoor exit.

By plane: Los Angeles International Airport. Continental Airlines direct to Colorado Springs's Peterson Field. United Airlines direct to Denver's Stapleton Field, connecting with Continental Airlines to Colorado Springs.

CREDIT CARDS
The Broadmoor honors no credit cards, but does accept personal checks.

THE CONCORD

Kiamesha Lake, New York 12751
Tel: 914–794–4000
In season: June 20–September 15

ACCOMMODATIONS
The Concord Hotel and Golf Clubhouse

RATES	daily rate	plan
The Concord Hotel		
IN SEASON		
double occupancy	A	AP
single occupancy	E	AP
OFF SEASON		
double occupancy	B	AP
single occupancy	E	AP
Golf Clubhouse		
IN SEASON		
double occupancy	A	AP
single occupancy	B	AP
OFF SEASON		
double occupancy	A	AP
single occupancy	C	AP

Package plans available

GOLF
45 holes

The Concord Golf Courses
caddies and golf cars; pull carts only on the International and Challenger courses

The Concord Championship Course
Lengths and pars

men's back championship tees	7,780 yds
regular championship tees	7,205 yds
regular tees	6,793 yds
par	72

no ladies' tees or par

Course rating

men's back championship tees	76
regular championship tees	75
regular tees	73.5

The International Course
Lengths and pars

men's championship tees	6,600 yds
men's and ladies' regular tees	6,250 yds
men's par	71
ladies' par	76

Course rating

championship tees	69.9
men's and ladies' regular tees	68

The Challenger Course (nine holes)
Length and par

men's and ladies' tees	2,200 yds
par	32

No course rating

OTHER FACILITIES
tennis: 26 courts (16 indoor)
swimming: 3 pools (1 indoor)
boating
fishing
ice-skating (year-round)
skeet shooting
horseback riding
handball
basketball
baseball

LOCATION
The Concord is 90 miles northwest of New York City.

HOW TO GET THERE
By car only. The nearest commercial airport is the Albany County Airport.

From Boston
Interstate 90 west to Interstate 91. Go south to Hartford, Conn. Pick up Interstate 84 west to Highway 17 Quickway west to exit 105B. Follow signs to The Concord.

From New York City
New Jersey Palisades Parkway to Interstate 87 north. Proceed to exit 16 and go north on Route 14 Quickway to exit 105B. Follow signs to The Concord.

From Toronto
Take F. Gardiner Expressway south to Queen Elizabeth Way west to Ontario Route 405 east to U.S. Interstate 190 south across Lewiston–Queenston Bridge to Interstate 290 south to Interstate 90 east to Syracuse, N.Y. Pick up Interstate 81 south to Binghamton, N.Y. Take Route 17 Quickway east to exit 105B. On Route 42 follow signs to The Concord.

CREDIT CARDS
The Concord honors American Express, BankAmericard, Carte Blanche, Diners Club, and Master Charge. Personal checks are accepted upon proper identification.

THE HOMESTEAD

Hot Springs, Virginia 24445
Tel: 703–839–5500
In season: April 1–November 7

ACCOMMODATIONS
The Homestead and The Cascades Inn

RATES	daily rate	plan
The Homestead		
IN SEASON		
double occupancy	A	AP
single occupancy	D	AP
OFF SEASON		
double occupancy	B	AP
single occupancy	D	AP
The Cascades Inn		
IN SEASON ONLY		
double occupancy	C	MAP
single occupancy	E	MAP

Automatic 15-percent gratuity per person per day
Package plans available

GOLF
54 holes

The Homestead Golf and Tennis Club
caddies, golf cars, and pull carts

The Cascades Course
Lengths and pars

men's championship tees	6,568 yds
regular tees	6,234 yds
par	71
ladies' tees	5,586 yds
par	72

Course rating

championship tees	71.2
regular tees	69.5
ladies' tees	71.1

The Lower Cascades Course
Lengths and pars

men's championship tees	6,726 yds
regular tees	6,381 yds
par	72
ladies' tees	5,943 yds
par	72

Course rating

championship tees	71.9
regular tees	70.2
ladies' tees	73.1

The Homestead Course
Lengths and pars

men's regular tees	5,922 yds
par	71
ladies' tees	5,212 yds
par	72

Course rating

regular tees	67.9
ladies' tees	69.1

OTHER FACILITIES
tennis: 15 courts
swimming: 3 pools (1 indoor pool)
horseback riding
trout fishing
skeet and trap shooting
lawn bowling
carriage rides
spa facilities

LOCATION
The Homestead is located 170 miles southwest of Washington, D.C.

HOW TO GET THERE
From Cleveland
By car: Interstate 77 south to Charleston, W.V. Take U.S. Highway 60 east, just past Rainelle, W.V. Pick up Interstate 64 east to Covington. Take U.S. Highway 220 north to Hot Springs.

By air: Hopkins Field. Eastern Airlines direct to Woodrum Field in Roanoke, Va. Connect with Piedmont Airlines direct to Ingalls Field in Hot Springs. Limousine service available from Ingalls Field to The Homestead upon request.

From Richmond
By car: U.S. Highway 60 west to Clifton Forge, Va. Pick up Interstate 64 west to Covington. Take U.S. Highway 220 north to Hot Springs.

By air: Richard E. Byrd Airport. Piedmont Airlines direct to Washington National Airport, connecting with Piedmont to Ingalls Field, Hot Springs.

From Washington, D.C.
By car: U.S. Highway 211 west to New Market, Va. Pick up Interstate 81 south to Staunton. Take Route 254 west, connecting with Route 42 southwest to Warm Springs. Pick up U.S. Highway 220 south to Hot Springs.

By plane: Washington National Airport. Piedmont Airlines direct to Ingalls Field, Hot Springs.

CREDIT CARDS
The Homestead honors no credit cards, but does accept personal checks.

THE OTESAGA
HOTEL

Cooperstown, New York 13326
Tel: 607–547–9931
In season: June 15–September 15

ACCOMMODATIONS
The Otesaga Hotel

RATES

RATES	daily rate	plan
IN SEASON		
double occupancy	C	MAP
single occupancy	D	MAP
OFF SEASON		
double occupancy	D	MAP
single occupancy	E	MAP

Automatic 15-percent gratuity per person per day
Package plans available

GOLF
18 holes

The Leatherstocking Golf Course
caddies, golf cars, and pull carts

Lengths and pars

men's regular tees only	6,554 yds
par	72
ladies' tees	5,857 yds
par	75
Course rating	
men's regular tees	71
ladies' tees	72

OTHER FACILITIES
tennis: 2 courts
swimming: pool and lake
sailing
boating
water-skiing
fishing
hiking

LOCATION
Cooperstown is 70 miles west of Albany.

HOW TO GET THERE
By car only. The nearest airport to Cooperstown is Utica's Oneida County Airport.

From Boston
Highway 9 west to Interstate 90. Go north and west to Fort Plain, N.Y. Pick up Highway 80 south straight to Cooperstown.

From New York City
New Jersey Palisades Parkway north to Spring Valley. Connect with Interstate 87 north to Albany. Pick up Interstate 90 west to Fort Plain. Take Highway 80 south direct to Cooperstown.

From Montreal
Highway 15 south to the border. Pick up U.S. Interstate 87 south to Saratoga Springs, N.Y. Take Highway 50 south to Scotia. Connect with Interstate 90 west to Fort Plain. Take Highway 80 south to Cooperstown.

CREDIT CARDS
The Otesaga Hotel honors American Express, Bank-Americard, and Master Charge. Personal checks are also accepted.

BAY HILL
CLUB AND LODGE

Orlando, Florida 32811
Tel: 305–876–2429
In season: December 15–April 30

ACCOMMODATIONS
Bay Hill Lodge and condominiums

RATES	daily rate	plan
Bay Hill Lodge		
IN SEASON		
double occupancy	D	E
single occupancy	E	E
OFF SEASON		
double occupancy	E	E
single occupancy	F	E
Condominiums		
YEAR-ROUND RATE ONLY	C	E

Weekly and monthly rates available

Automatic 15-percent gratuity per person per day
Package plans available

GOLF
27 holes

Bay Hill Club
caddies on request only; golf cars

Challenger and **Champion** nines comprise the main course.

Lengths and pars

men's championship tees	7,055 yds
regular tees	6,583 yds
seniors' tees	6,103 yds
par	72
ladies' tees	5,318 yds
par	73

Course rating

championship tees	73.7
regular tees	70.4
seniors' tees	69.5
ladies' tees	70

Charger Nine
Lengths and pars

men's championship tees	3,090 yds
regular tees	2,957 yds
seniors' tees	2,787 yds
par	36
ladies' tees	2,476 yds
par	36

No course rating

OTHER FACILITIES
tennis: 6 courts
swimming: pool
water-skiing
fishing

LOCATION
Bay Hill is 12 miles southwest of Orlando.

HOW TO GET THERE

From Cleveland
By car: Interstate 80 south, bypassing Youngstown, Ohio, at which point the highway becomes Interstate 76; it later changes to Interstate 70. Drive to Frederick, Md., pick up Interstate 270 south, bypass Washington, D.C. via Interstate 495 south. At Alexandria, Va., pick up Interstate 95 south. Where 95 is not completed follow local highways connecting with Interstate 95. Drive to Daytona Beach, Fla. Then take Interstate 4 west to Orlando. From downtown Orlando, take I-4 west to Sand Lake Road (SR 528-A). Turn right on Sand Lake Road. Drive to Apopka-Vineland and turn right again. Bay Hill will be approximately 1 mile down on the left.

By plane: Hopkins International Airport. Eastern Airlines non-stop to Orlando's Jetport Airport. Limousine service available to Bay Hill upon request. Taxi service also available.

From New York City
By car: New Jersey Turnpike to the end. Cross Delaware Memorial Bridge. Pick up U.S. Highway 301 south, bypassing Washington, D.C. Just past Bowling Green, Va., take Interstate 95 south. For further directions see "How to Get There from Cleveland."

By plane: LaGuardia, Kennedy International or Newark Airport. Eastern or National Airlines non-stop to Orlando's Jetport Airport.

From Toronto
By car: Highway 5 south to Queen Elizabeth Way. Bypass Niagara Falls, N.Y., via U.S. Interstate 190 to Interstate 90 east. Continue on to Syracuse, and then pick up Interstate 81 south to Harrisburg, Pa. Take Interstate 83 south to Baltimore, Md., bypassing it via Interstate 695 south, connecting with Interstate 95 to Washington, D.C. For further information see "How to Get There from Cleveland."

By plane: Toronto International Airport. Eastern Airlines connecting via Atlanta's Hartsfield International Airport with Eastern Airlines to Orlando's Jetport Airport. Air Canada to New York City's Kennedy International Airport, connecting with Eastern Airlines non-stop to Orlando's Jetport.

CREDIT CARDS
Bay Hill honors American Express, BankAmericard, and Master Charge. Personal checks are also accepted.

DORAL
COUNTRY CLUB

Miami, Florida 33166
Tel: 800–327–6334
In season: December 15–Easter

ACCOMMODATIONS
Doral Country Club

RATES

		daily rate	plan
IN SEASON			
double occupancy		A	MAP
single occupancy		B	MAP
OFF SEASON			
double occupancy		C	MAP
single occupancy		D	MAP

Package plans available

GOLF
81 holes

Doral Country Club
caddies on request only; golf cars

	Blue Course	Gold Course
Lengths and pars		
men's championship tees	7,065 yds	7,258 yds
regular tees	6,627 yds	6,655 yds
par	72	71
ladies' tees	6,189 yds	No ladies' tees
par	72	or par
Course rating		
championship tees	73	74
regular tees	70.1	71
ladies' tees	75	

	White Course	Red Course
Lengths and pars		
men's championship tees	6,726 yds	6,480 yds
regular tees	6,121 yds	6,057 yds
par	72	71
ladies' tees	5,527 yds	5,157 yds
par	72	72
Course rating		
championship tees	71	70
regular tees	69	69
ladies' tees	69	68.2

Green Course (nine-hole par 3)	
Length and par	
regular men's and ladies' tees	1,034 yds
par	27
No course rating	

OTHER FACILITIES

tennis: 20 courts	water-skiing
swimming: pool	fishing
sailing	baseball
boating	basketball

LOCATION
Doral Country Club is 15 miles west of downtown Miami.

HOW TO GET THERE

From Chicago
By car: Interstate 65 south to Louisville, Ky. Pick up Interstate 64 west to Lexington, Ky. Take Interstate 75 south, bypassing Atlanta via Interstate 285 south, then pick up Interstate 75 south to Leesburg, Fla., connecting with the Florida Turnpike south to North Miami. Take Interstate 95 south to Interama Interchange. Take the Palmetto Expressway south to 36th Street exit. Go west on 36th Street one block and turn right. Go one block and turn left into Doral Country Club.

By plane: O'Hare International Airport. Eastern, Delta, or Northwest Airlines, direct to Miami International Airport. Taxi service available for the 10-minute drive to Doral Country Club.

From New York City
By car: New Jersey Turnpike to the end. Cross Delaware Memorial Bridge. Pick up U.S. Highway 301 south, bypassing Washington, D.C. Just past Bowling Green, Va., take Interstate 95 south, taking local highway where Interstate 95 is incomplete. Take Interstate 95 to Miami. From Miami to Doral see "How to Get There from Chicago."

By plane: LaGuardia, Kennedy International, or Newark Airport. Eastern, Delta, or National Airlines direct to Miami International Airport.

From Montreal
By car: Take Highway 15 south to the border. Pick up U.S. Interstate 87 south to Suffern, N.Y., connecting with the Garden State Parkway. Pick up Interstate 295 (N.J. Turnpike) at Perth Amboy, N.J. From there see "How to Get There from New York City and Chicago."

By plane: Dorval International Airport. Eastern, Delta, or Air Canada direct to Miami International Airport.

CREDIT CARDS
Doral Country Club honors American Express, Bank-Americard, Carte Blanche, Diners Club, Doral credit card, and Master Charge. Personal checks are also accepted.

HOTEL HERSHEY

Hershey, Pennsylvania 17033
Tel: 717–533–2171
In season: April 1–November 1

ACCOMMODATIONS
Hotel Hershey and Hershey Country Club

RATES	daily rate	plan
Hotel Hershey		
IN SEASON		
double occupancy	C	MAP
single occupancy	D	MAP
OFF SEASON		
double occupancy	C	MAP
single occupancy	E	MAP
Hershey Country Club		
IN SEASON		
double occupancy	E	E
single occupancy	E	E
OFF SEASON		
double occupancy	F	E
single occupancy	F	E

Automatic 15-percent gratuity per person per day
Package plans available

GOLF
45 holes

Hershey Country Club
 caddies (Hershey Country Club only); golf cars and pull carts (at hotel course only)

West Course
 Lengths and pars

men's championship tees	6,928 yds
regular tees	6,696 yds
par	73
ladies' tees	6,244 yds
par	77

 Course rating

championship tees	73
regular tees	71.7
ladies' tees	74.7

East Course
 Lengths and pars

men's championship tees	7,240 yds
regular tees	6,515 yds
par	71
ladies' tees	5,680 yds
par	71

 Course rating

championship tees	74.4
regular tees	71
ladies' tees	71.6

Hotel Hershey Golf Course (9 holes)

Length and par	
men's regular and ladies' tees	2,680 yds
par	34

 No course rating

OTHER FACILITIES
tennis: 7 courts (4 at country club and 3 at hotel)
swimming: 3 pools (1 indoor)
horseback riding
hiking
lawn bowling

LOCATION
Hershey is 15 miles east of Harrisburg.

HOW TO GET THERE

From Columbus

By car: Interstate 70 east. In Pennsylvania it is Interstate 76. Drive to High Spire, Pa. Take Interstate 283 north to Harrisburg. Pick up U.S. Highway 422 east to Hershey. At first interchange in Hershey turn left on Route 39 north. Go 3 blocks, then turn left again on Hotel Road. Leads directly to the hotel.

By plane: Port Columbus Airport. Allegheny Airlines via Pittsburgh's Greater Pittsburgh Airport connecting with Allegheny direct to Harrisburg International Airport. Limousine service to Hotel Hershey available upon request.

From New York City

By car: New Jersey Turnpike south to exit 10. Pick up Interstate 287 west to Interstate 78, which changes to Interstate 81. Twenty miles before Harrisburg take Route 743 to Hershey. Turn right on Airport Road. Go 3 blocks to Hotel Road, and turn right to the hotel.

By plane: Kennedy International Airport. Allegheny Airlines non-stop to Harrisburg International Airport.

From Philadelphia

By car: Interstate 76 west. Turn right onto U.S. Highway 322 direct to Hershey. Continue through town to interchange. Pick up Route 39 north. Go 2 blocks and turn left onto Hotel Road, which goes directly to the hotel.

By plane: Philadelphia International Airport. Altair Airlines direct to Harrisburg International Airport.

CREDIT CARDS
The Hotel Hershey honors American Express, Bank-Americard, Diners Club, and Master Charge. Personal checks are also accepted.

HORSESHOE BAY

Marble Falls, Texas 78654
Box 7766
Tel: 512–598–2511
In season: May 1–September 15

ACCOMMODATIONS
Condominiums

RATES

	daily rate	plan
Vary according to number of rooms		
IN SEASON	C	E
OFF SEASON	D	E

Weekly and monthly rates available
Package plans available

GOLF
18 holes

Horseshoe Bay Country Club
golf cars only

Lengths and pars

men's championship tees	6,839 yds
regular tees	6,358 yds
par	72
ladies' tees	5,893 yds
par	72

Course rating

championship tees	73
regular tees	71.4
ladies' tees	74.2

OTHER FACILITIES
tennis: 12 courts
swimming: pool and lake
water-skiing
sailing
boating
fishing
horseback riding
hunting

LOCATION
Horseshoe Bay is located 60 miles northwest of Austin.

HOW TO GET THERE

From Dallas

By car only: Interstate 35 south to Georgetown. Take Highway 29 west to Burnet. Pick up U.S. Highway 281 south to Marble Falls. Follow Highway 71 west direct to Horseshoe Bay.

From Denver

By car: Take U.S. Highway 87 south to Colorado Springs. Pick up Interstate 25 south to Raton, N.M. Then take U.S. Highway 87 south to Amarillo, Tex. Proceed on U.S. Highway 287 south to Fort Worth. Bypass Fort Worth via Interstate West 35, connecting with Interstate 35 south to Georgetown. Take Highway 29 west to Burnet and then take U.S. Highway 281 south to Marble Falls. Pick up Highway 71 west to Horseshoe Bay.

By plane: Stapleton International Airport. Braniff or Texas International Airlines direct to Austin's Robert Mueller Municipal Airport. Rental cars available at airport.

From Houston

By car only: Interstate 10 west to Columbus and then pick up Highway 71 direct to Horseshoe Bay.

CREDIT CARDS
Horseshoe Bay honors American Express, BankAmericard, Diners Club, and Master Charge. Personal checks are also accepted.

LA COSTA
COUNTRY CLUB

Carlsbad, California 92008
Tel: 714–438–9111
In season: July 1–September 16

ACCOMMODATIONS
La Costa Country Club and villas

RATES	daily rate	plan
La Costa Country Club		
IN SEASON		
double or single occupancy	D	E
OFF SEASON		
double or single occupancy	D	E
Villas		
Rates vary according to number of rooms		
IN SEASON	A	E
OFF SEASON	B	E

Package plans available

GOLF
27 holes

La Costa Country Club
caddies and golf cars

Green and **Gold** nines comprise main course used for the Tournament of Champions.

Lengths and pars	
men's championship tees	6,855 yds
regular tees	6,446 yds
par	72
ladies' tees	5,638 yds
par	73

Course rating	
championship tees	73.5
regular tees	71
ladies' tees	71.4

Orange Nine

Lengths and pars	
men's championship tees	2,986 yds
regular tees	2,846 yds
par	36
ladies' tees	2,638 yds
par	35

No nine-hole course rating

OTHER FACILITIES
tennis: 25 courts
swimming: ocean and 4 fresh-water pools
horseback riding
deep-sea fishing
boating
spa facilities

LOCATION
La Costa is 30 miles north of San Diego.

HOW TO GET THERE
From Chicago
By car: U.S. Highway 66 south to Springfield, Mo. Take Interstate 44 west to Oklahoma City, Okla., where Interstate 44 changes to Interstate 40. Continue west to Barstow, Calif. Take Interstate 15 south to Highway 91 southwest, connecting with Interstate 5. Go south direct to Carlsbad and follow signs to La Costa.

By plane: O'Hare International Airport. American or United Airlines non-stop to San Diego Air Terminal. Limousine service from airport to La Costa available upon request.

From Los Angeles
By car only: Take Interstate 5 south direct to Carlsbad. Follow signs to La Costa.

From San Diego
By car only: Take Interstate 5 north direct to Carlsbad. Follow signs to La Costa.

CREDIT CARDS
La Costa honors American Express, BankAmericard, and Master Charge. Personal checks are also accepted.

231

PINEHURST

Pinehurst, North Carolina 28374
Box 4000
Tel: 800–334–9560 (in North Carolina only, call
919–295–3131)
In season: March 15–May 15

ACCOMMODATIONS
Pinehurst Hotel and villas

RATES

	daily rate	plan
Pinehurst Hotel		
IN SEASON		
double occupancy	B	MAP
single occupancy	C	MAP
OFF SEASON		
double occupancy	C	MAP
single occupancy	D	MAP

Villas

Rates vary according to number of rooms

IN SEASON	C	E
OFF SEASON	D	E

Automatic 15-percent gratuity per person per day
Package plans available

GOLF
108 holes

Pinehurst Country Club
caddies and golf cars

	No. 1	No. 2
Lengths and pars		
men's championship tees	6,129 yds	7,051 yds
regular tees	5,853 yds	6,618 yds
par	70	72
ladies' tees	5,389 yds	5,850 yds
par	73	74
Course rating		
championship tees	68	73
regular tees	67.5	71
ladies' tees	71	74

	No. 3	No. 4
Lengths and pars		
men's championship tees	6,013 yds	6,905 yds
regular tees	5,760 yds	6,492 yds
par	71	72
ladies' tees	5,317 yds	5,932 yds
par	72	73
Course rating		
championship tees	68	72.8
regular tees	67	71
ladies' tees	71	73

	No. 5	No. 6
Lengths and pars		
men's championship tees	6,946 yds	6,745 yds
regular tees	6,369 yds	6,375 yds
par	72	72
ladies' tees	5,838 yds	5,740
par	74	74
Course rating		
championship tees	73	73
regular	71	71.5
ladies' tees	73	74.4

OTHER FACILITIES

tennis: 12 courts	sailing
swimming: 2 pools	boating
horseback riding	archery
skeet and trap shooting	spa facilities

LOCATION
Pinehurst is 65 miles southwest of Raleigh, N.C.

HOW TO GET THERE

From Atlanta

By car: Interstate 85 north to Concord, N.C. Pick up
Highway 73 east to Bisco. Take U.S. Highway 220 south
to Route 221 east to Pinehurst.

By plane: Hartsfield International Airport. Eastern or
United Airlines non-stop to Raleigh-Durham Airport.
Limousine service from airport to Pinehurst available
upon request.

From Philadelphia

By car: New Jersey Turnpike to the end. Cross Delaware
Memorial Bridge. Take U.S. Highway 40 south, connect-
ing with U.S. Highway 301 south. Continue to Bowling
Green, Va. Then take Interstate 95 south to Petersburg,
connecting with Interstate 85 south to Henderson, N.C.
Pick up bypass 185 to U.S. Highway 15 south. Just past
Sanford, take U.S. Highway 1 to Southern Pines. At in-
terchange take route 211 west to Pinehurst.

By plane: Philadelphia International Airport. Eastern
Airlines direct to Raleigh/Durham Airport. Allegheny
or Piedmont Airlines, connecting at either Washington
National Airport or Baltimore's Friendship Airport with
Eastern, Allegheny, or Piedmont Airlines to Raleigh/
Durham Airport.

From Richmond

By car: Interstate 95 south to Petersburg. From that point
see "How to Get There from Philadelphia."

By plane: Richard E. Byrd Airport. Eastern Airlines non-
stop to Raleigh/Durham Airport.

CREDIT CARDS
Pinehurst honors American Express, BankAmericard,
Diners Club, and Master Charge. Personal checks are
also accepted.

LA QUINTA
HOTEL

La Quinta, California 92253
Tel: 714–564–4111
In season: January 20–Easter (La Quinta Hotel opens in mid-October and closes in mid-May)

ACCOMMODATIONS
La Quinta Hotel

RATES

	daily rate	plan
IN SEASON		
double occupancy	A	AP
single occupancy	B	AP
OFF SEASON		
double occupancy	B	AP
single occupancy	C	AP

Automatic 15-percent gratuity per person per day

GOLF
18 holes

La Quinta Country Club
golf cars only

Lengths and pars

men's championship tees	6,904 yds
regular tees	6,555 yds
par	72
ladies' tees	6,074 yds
par	74

Course rating	
championship tees	72.8
regular tees	71.7
ladies' tees	73.8

OTHER FACILITIES
tennis: 6 courts
swimming: 1 pool
fishing
horseback riding

LOCATION
La Quinta is located 120 miles east of Los Angeles and 20 miles west of downtown Palm Springs.

HOW TO GET THERE
From Dallas
By car: Highway 77 north to Interstate 35, north to Oklahoma City, Okla. Take Interstate 40 west to Flagstaff, Ariz. Then take Interstate 17 south to downtown Phoenix. Turn right, or west, on Buckeye Road (U.S. Highway 80). Follow to Buckeye and then go north to Wintersburg. Just past Wintersburg pick up Interstate 10 west. Drive through Indio, Calif., and go 8 miles west to Washington Blvd. Turn left. Cross Highway 111 and continue 2 miles to Eisenhower Drive. Turn right and drive directly to hotel.

By plane: Dallas/Fort Worth International Airport. American or Hughes Air West direct to Palm Springs's Municipal Airport. Limousine service from airport to La Quinta available upon request.

From Los Angeles
By car: Interstate 10 east direct to Palm Springs. From Palm Canyon Drive South, drive to East Palm Canyon Drive and turn left. Drive to Rancho Mirage and turn left again onto Country Club Road. Turn left on Washington Blvd., cross Highway 111, and continue for 2 miles to Eisenhower Drive. Turn right and drive directly to hotel.

By plane: Los Angeles International Airport. American, Hughes Air West, or Western Airlines non-stop to Palm Springs.

From San Francisco
By car: Interstate 580 east, connecting with Interstate 5 south to Los Angeles. Just beyond Pasadena Freeway turn left, or east, onto Interstate 10 east direct to Palm Springs. From Palm Springs's center to La Quinta see "How to Get There from Los Angeles."

By plane: Hughes Air West or Western Airlines non-stop to Palm Springs Municipal Airport.

CREDIT CARDS
La Quinta Hotel honors no credit cards, but does accept personal checks.

THE WIGWAM

Litchfield Park, Arizona 85340
Tel: 602–935–3811
In season: February 1—Easter (The Wigwam opens the first week in October and closes the last week in May)

ACCOMMODATIONS
The Wigwam and villas

RATES	daily rate	plan
The Wigwam		
IN SEASON		
double occupancy	B	AP
single occupancy	C	AP
OFF SEASON		
double occupancy	C	AP
single occupancy	D	AP

Villas
Rates vary according to number of persons.

IN SEASON	C	AP
OFF SEASON	D	AP

GOLF
54 holes

Goodyear Golf and Country Club
golf cars and pull carts

	Gold Course	Blue Course
Lengths and pars		
men's championship tees	7,220 yds	
regular tees	6,469 yds	6,107 yds
par	72	70
ladies' tees	5,604 yds	5,117 yds
par	72	70
Course rating		
championship tees	74.2	
regular tees	71.3	66.5
ladies' tees	72	69

	West Course
Lengths and pars	
men's championship tees	6,861 yds
regular tees	6,314 yds
par	72
ladies' tees	5,859 yds
par	72
Course rating	
championship tees	69
regular tees	68
No rating from ladies' tees	

OTHER FACILITIES
tennis: 8 courts
swimming: 2 pools
horseback riding
skeet and trap shooting

LOCATION
The Wigwam is located in Litchfield Park, 15 miles west of downtown Phoenix.

HOW TO GET THERE
From Chicago
By car: U.S. Highway 66 south to St. Louis, Mo. Pick up Interstate 44 west to Oklahoma City, Okla., where the highway becomes Interstate 40. Continue on it to Flagstaff, Ariz., and take Interstate 17 south into Phoenix. Drive 11 miles on Interstate 17, through Phoenix, to Indian School Road and turn right, or west. Drive for 15 miles to Litchfield Road and turn right. Drive 3 miles to Litchfield Park.

By plane: O'Hare International Airport. American Airlines or TWA non-stop to Phoenix's Sky Harbor Airport. Limousine service from airport to The Wigwam available upon request.

From Denver
By car: Interstate 25 south to Albuquerque, N.M. Take Interstate 40 west to Flagstaff, Ariz., and then take Interstate 17 south to Phoenix. From downtown Phoenix, see "How to Get There from Chicago."

By plane: Stapleton International Airport. Frontier or Western Airlines non-stop to Phoenix's Sky Harbor Airport.

From Vancouver
By car: Highway 99 south to U.S. border. Pick up U.S. Interstate 5 south to Sacramento, Calif. Take Temporary Interstate 5 beyond Sacramento, connecting with Highway 99 south to Bakersfield, and then take Highway 58 east to Barstow. Pick up Interstate 40 east just past Hualapal Peak, Ariz., and take U.S. Highway 93 south to Wickenburg, and pick up U.S. Highway 60, connecting with U.S. Highway 89 into Phoenix, where it becomes Grand Avenue. Drive 8 miles to Indian School Road and turn right, or east. Go 15 miles on Indian School Road to Litchfield Road and turn right again. Drive 3 miles to Litchfield Park.

By plane: Vancouver International Airport. Western Airlines direct to Phoenix's Sky Harbor Airport.

CREDIT CARDS
The Wigwam honors no credit cards, but does accept personal checks.

Bibliography

BOOKS

Amory, Cleveland. *The Last Resorts*. New York: Harper & Brothers, 1958.
————. *Who Killed Society?* New York: Harper & Brothers, 1960.
Barkow, Al. *Golf's Golden Grind*. New York: Harcourt Brace Jovanovich, 1974.
Baron, Harry. *Golf Resorts of the U.S.A.* New York: New American Library, 1967.
Birmingham, Stephen. *The Right People*. Boston: Little, Brown, 1968.
————. *The Right Places*. Boston: Little, Brown and Co., 1973.
Corcoran, Fred, and Harvey, Bud. *Unplayable Lies*. New York: Meredith Press, 1965.
Didion, Joan. *Slouching Towards Bethlehem*. New York: Farrar, Straus & Giroux, 1968.
Dobereiner, Peter. *The Game with the Hole in It*. London: Faber and Faber Ltd., 1970.
Gibson, Nevin. *The Encyclopedia of Golf*. New York: A. S. Barnes and Co., 1958.
Golf Digest editors. *Great Golf Courses of the World*. New York: Golf Digest, 1974.
Golf Magazine editors. *America's Golf Book*. New York: Charles Scribner's Sons, 1970.
Grimsley, Will. *Golf: Its History, People & Events*. New Jersey: Prentice-Hall, Inc., 1966.
Hepburn, Andrew. *Great Resorts of North America*. New York: Doubleday and Co., 1965.
Ingalls, Fay. *The Valley Road*. Cleveland: World Publishing Co., 1949.
Jenkins, Dan. *The Dogged Victims of Inexorable Fate*. Boston: Little, Brown, 1970.
————. *Sports Illustrated's The Best 18 Golf Holes in America*. New York: Time, Inc., 1966.
Keller, O. B. *The Bobby Jones Story*. Atlanta: Tubber & Love, 1953.
Kelly, Kitty. *The Glamour Spas*. New York: Pocket Books, 1975.
McCormack, Mark. *Arnie*. New York: Simon and Schuster, 1967.
Nicklaus, Jack. *Take a Tip from Me*. New York: Simon and Schuster, 1968.
————, and Wind, Herbert Warren. *The Greatest Game of All*. New York: Simon and Schuster, 1969.
Plimpton, George. *The Bogey Man*. New York: Harper & Row, 1968.
Price, Charles. *The World of Golf*. New York: Random House, 1962.
Scharff, Robert, and editors of *Golf Magazine*. *Encyclopedia of Golf*. New York: Harper & Row, 1970.
————. *Golf Magazine's Great Golf Courses You Can Play*. New York: Charles Scribner's Sons, 1973.
Snead, Sam, and Stump, Al. *The Education of a Golfer*. New York: Simon and Schuster, 1962.
Tufts, Richard. *The Scottish Invasion*. Pinehurst, N.C.: Pinehurst Publishers, 1962.
Vanstory, Burnette. *Georgia's Land of the Golden Isles*. Athens, Ga.: University of Georgia Press, 1970.
Wind, Herbert Warren. *Herbert Warren Wind's Golf Book*. New York: Simon and Schuster, 1971.
————. *The Story of American Golf*. New York: Alfred A. Knopf, 1975.

PERIODICALS AND NEWSPAPERS

American Golfer
American Heritage
Antiques
Architectural Forum
Architectural Record
Business Week
Collier's
Esquire
Fortune
Golf Digest
Golf Magazine
Golf World
Harper's
House Beautiful
House & Garden
Life
Literary Digest
Look
The New Yorker
New York Herald Tribune
New York Times
New York Sun
Newsweek
Richmond Times-Dispatch
Saturday Evening Post
Saturday Review
Smithsonian
Sports Illustrated
Time
Town & Country
USGA Golf Journal
Vogue

Photo Credits

Photos on the following pages were reproduced by permission of these persons and organizations:

15 Courtesy Del Monte Properties
16 Courtesy The Cloister
17 Wide World Photos
19 Courtesy The Cloister
20 United States Golf Association
21 Wide World Photos
22 Courtesy The Cloister
23 Courtesy The Cloister
26 Paul Barton
27 Paul Barton
29 Paul Barton
30 Ruffin Beckwith, *Golf World*
31 Paul Barton
32 Paul Barton
34 Courtesy Del Monte Properties
35 United States Golf Association
36 United States Golf Association
37 *Clockwise:* United States Golf Association, United Press International, United States Golf Association.
38 United States Golf Association
42 and 43 United Press International
45 Courtesy Del Monte Properties
46 Courtesy Del Monte Properties
48 Courtesy Rockeresorts, Inc.
49 Wide World Photos
52 Wide World Photos
53 Courtesy Rockeresorts, Inc.
54 Leonard Kamsler, *Golf Magazine*
56 Courtesy International Management Group
57 Courtesy Rockeresorts, Inc.
59 Courtesy Rockeresorts, Inc.
62 *Top:* Courtesy International Management Group; *bottom:* Courtesy Rockeresorts, Inc.
64 Walter Looss, Jr.
65 Courtesy Princeville Corp.
67 Walter Looss, Jr.
68 Museum of Modern Art
70 Courtesy Princeville Corp.
72 Leonard Kamsler, *Golf Magazine*
73 Ruffin Beckwith, *Golf World*
75 *Top:* Ned Brown; *bottom:* Ruffin Beckwith, *Golf World*
76 Bill Doggrell
78 and 79 William E. Cornelia

83 New York State Historical Association
84 Courtesy Canadian Pacific Railroad
85 Courtesy Canadian Pacific Railroad
86 Courtesy Canadian Pacific Railroad
87 Museum of Modern Art
91 Hugh Power
92 United States Golf Association
93 United Press International
95 Bob McIntyre
98 and 99 United States Golf Association
100 Courtesy The Broadmoor
102 Leonard Kamsler, *Golf Magazine*
103 Courtesy The Concord
105 Bill Mark
106 and 107 Bill Mark
110 United Press International
112 Leonard Kamsler, *Golf Magazine*
113 Leonard Kamsler, *Golf Magazine*
114 Courtesy The Homestead
115 Courtesy The Greenbrier
118 United States Golf Association
119 Wide World Photos
120 Courtesy The Homestead
122 New York State Historical Association
123 New York State Historical Association
124 New York State Historical Association
126 Courtesy National Baseball Hall of Fame and Museum, Inc.
127 United States Golf Association
128 and 129 New York State Historical Association
130 United States Golf Association
133 Courtesy Doral Country Club
134 Courtesy Bay Hill Club & Lodge
135 Courtesy Bay Hill Club & Lodge
137 United States Golf Association
139 Courtesy Bay Hill Club & Lodge
140 Paul Barton
142 Bert Neale
143 Courtesy Doral Country Club

145 United Press International
148 and 149 *Clockwise:* United Press International, Courtesy Doral Country Club, United Press International.
152 Courtesy Hotel Hershey
153 Courtesy Hotel Hershey
154 United States Golf Association
158 United Press International
159 United Press International
160 Courtesy Hershey Country Club
162 Courtesy Horseshoe Bay
163 Lyndon Baines Johnson Memorial Library
165 Courtesy Horseshoe Bay
167 Courtesy Horseshoe Bay
168 Courtesy Horseshoe Bay
170 Leonard Kamsler, *Golf Magazine*
171 Wide World Photos
173 Courtesy La Costa Country Club
175 United Press International
176 United Press International
178 Wide World Photos
179 United States Golf Association
181 United States Golf Association
183 Wide World Photos
185 *New York Times*
186 and 187 Wide World Photos
188 Leonard Kamsler, *Golf Magazine*
191 United States Golf Association
193 Courtesy Palm Springs Chamber of Commerce
194 Sidney H. Noles, *Palm Springs Life*
195 Leonard Kamsler, *Golf Magazine*
197 Courtesy The Racquet Club
199 Bernard Anderson
201 United Press International
202 Leonard Kamsler, *Golf Magazine*
204 Slim Aarons
205 Wide World Photos
207 Courtesy The Wigwam
209 Courtesy The Phoenix Country Club
210 Wide World Photos
212 and 213 Courtesy The Wigwam

Color photos were reproduced by permission of the following persons and organizations:

Sea Island Golf Club: Fred Baldwin
Pebble Beach Golf Links: Dick Rowan
Casa de Campo's Cajuiles: Paul Barton
Na Pali Coast, Hawaii: Walter Looss, Jr.
Sea Pines Plantation: Courtesy Sea Pines Plantation

Casa de Campo: Paul Barton
The Homestead: *(first photo)* Courtesy The Homestead, *(others)* Leonard Kamsler, *Golf Magazine*
The Concord: Courtesy The Concord
Horseshoe Bay: Courtesy Horseshoe Bay

Pinehurst: *(left)* Leonard Kamsler, *(right)* Ruffin Beckwith
Doral Country Club: Courtesy Doral Country Club
La Costa Country Club: Courtesy La Costa Country Club

236

Index